Beverly Buchanan, Athens, GA, 8 July 1995

Beverly Buchanan, Athens, GA, 8 July 1995

a video by Judith McWillie

edited by Mo Costello and Katz Tepper

Soberscove Press | Chicago

Soberscove Press
Chicago, Illinois
soberscove.com

Beverly Buchanan, Athens, GA, 8 July 1995: A Video by Judith McWillie

Unless noted otherwise, all video stills in this book are from the following videos (listed below) in the Judith McWillie Videotapes 20455, Southern Folklife Collection, Wilson Special Collections Library, University of North Carolina at Chapel Hill. Used with permission of the artist.

pp. 35-218: Judith McWillie, *Videotape 67: Beverly Buchanan, Athens, Ga., 8 July 1995: Part 1*, 1995. Digitized VHS tape, sound, color, 121 min.

pp. 243–67: Judith McWillie, *Videotape 43: Son Thomas Set Up Shots/Delta, Hawkins Bolden, Mary Lou Furcron, 20 December 1986*, 1987. Digitized VHS tape, sound, color, 121 min.

The Judith McWillie Collection, 1970s-2010s, includes 150 videos and can be accessed via the following URL: https://finding-aids.lib.unc.edu/catalog/20455

pp. 226, 228–30: Artworks by Beverly Buchanan © Estate of Beverly Buchanan

Every effort has been taken to locate and obtain the permissions of rights holders. The publisher apologizes for any errors or omissions in the credits herein and will incorporate any corrections into future reprints and editions.

Publisher's Cataloging-in-Publication Data

Names: Costello, Mo, editor. | Tepper, Katz, editor.
Title: Beverly Buchanan , Athens , GA , 8 July 1995 : a video by Judith McWillie /
edited by Mo Costello and Katz Tepper.
Description: Includes bibliographical references. | Chicago, IL: Soberscove Press, 2026.
Identifiers: LCCN 2026935614 | ISBN 9781940190372 trade paperback
Subjects: LCSH Buchanan, Beverly, 1940-2015. | McWillie, Judith, 1946 -. | Furcron, Mary Lou.
| African American artists. | African American artists--Southern States. | African American art--Southern States. | African American women artists--United States. | Outsider art--Southern States. | BISAC ART / African American & Black | ART / American | ART / Sculpture & Installation | ART / Women Artists
Classification: LCC N6537.B828 B82 2026 | DDC 709.2--dc23

Copyediting and proofreading: Rachel Walther
Design: Jake Brower
First printed in 2026
Printed in Lithuania

Distributed by
ARTBOOK | D.A.P.
75 Broad Street, Suite 630
New York, NY 10004
artbook.com

Cover: Judith McWillie, Stills from *Videotape 67: Beverly Buchanan, Athens, Ga., 8 July 1995: Part 1*, 1995. Digitized VHS tape, sound, color, 121 min.

For Beverly Buchanan, Judith McWillie, and Mary Lou Furcron, in honor of your shared forcefield.

We live on the mercy of each other.

Mary Lou Furcron

Contents

Preface

This book takes its name, *Beverly Buchanan, Athens, GA, 8 July 1995*, from an unedited two-hour video that Judith McWillie recorded with Beverly Buchanan in her home studio and garden in 1995. Thirty years after that documentary was filmed, we began shaping this hybridized tribute. The book you hold emerges from dwelling in the company of its namesake source material, with care and duration.

At the center of this undertaking is a deeply relational record between Buchanan and McWillie, one that ultimately privileges their dialogic exchange over an individuated subject. We were drawn to the video's polyphonic nature and endeavored to listen closely to its currents. We watched it over and over again—sometimes viewing it without sound, sometimes listening to it without visuals—studying it frame by frame, syllable by syllable. This prolonged attention became a form of communing, and our collaboration echoed and amplified the notes we picked up on. We were two artists listening to two artists speaking about a third artist, Mary Lou Furcron.

Guided by the work of artists using disability frameworks to multiply form, we approached the movement from video to printed book as an experiment in expanding access. We studied artworks that employ captioning, visual description, and related access tools to interrupt a single mode of entry and illuminate different textures within a work. Shifting this primary document across media similarly stretches the possibilities of experience and opens new pathways of engagement. Each medium carries time, pacing, and attention distinctly, privileging different forms of emphasis and posing particular demands.

We structured this book into several sections. At the heart is our text and image-based translation of the titular video, composed of transcription, description, and video stills. A section of annotations—"People," "Places," and "Endnotes"—thickens the context surrounding the recording.

The essay "Your Eye Did What My Eye Would Like to Do: Reverence and Remembrance in the Work of Beverly Buchanan, Judith McWillie, and Mary Lou Furcron" situates the practices of the three artists represented here, articulating what's at stake in their experimental modes of commemoration. We also brought together a selection of companion materials from Buchanan's and McWillie's archives, which underscore the centrality of Furcron's impact on both artists. Finally, we invited McWillie to rewatch the titular video she recorded with Buchanan thirty years earlier and share her "Present Day Reflections."

Our adaptation of *Beverly Buchanan, Athens, GA, 8 July 1995* is offered as a gesture of devotion. It is an effort toward carrying Buchanan and McWillie's conversation—and Furcron's spirit therein—into the present, where it remains enduringly relevant.

—Mo Costello and Katz Tepper

Your Eye Did What My Eye Would Like to Do

Reverence and Remembrance in the Work of Beverly Buchanan, Judith McWillie, and Mary Lou Furcron

Katz Tepper

Early in the two-hour documentary video *Beverly Buchanan, Athens, GA, 8 July 1995*, shortly after Buchanan has invited Judith McWillie inside her home, Buchanan remarks, "I enjoyed your video *so much*. It was the best I'd ever seen, because *your eye did what my eye would like to do*—focus on *exactly* what you focused on."[1] As the afternoon continues to unfold in the unedited recording, Buchanan repeats, "The video is so wonderful Judy. . . . Your eye is just perfect. You focused on exactly what I would have. You went to the rocks . . ."[2] She continues, "Your video is so poetic and so wonderful."[3]

Buchanan's affectionate sentiments refer to the video *Mary Lou Furcron, Vesta GA.*, recorded by McWillie on May 9, 1987.[4] The video is an unedited documentary interview with the eponymous seventy-six-year-old architect, gardener, and maker Mary Lou Furcron, though it notably exceeds the bounds of the tradition.[5] Of the seventy-nine minutes of footage, approximately forty shift away from Ms. Furcron entirely, instead framing the land she cultivated and the structures and furniture she crafted in her homemaking.[6]

---

1. See "Beverly Buchanan, Athens, GA, 8 July 1995" in this volume, p. 73.
2. "Beverly Buchanan, Athens, GA, 8 July 1995," 200.
3. "Beverly Buchanan, Athens, GA, 8 July 1995," 208.
4. The title is taken from the video's opening image, which features digital text created in-camera at the start of the recording (see p. 243). McWillie also produced a sixty-minute edit from this footage, titled *Mary Lou Furcron: I Stay on My Ground*, drawn from a quotation by Furcron within the recording.
5. Mary Lou Furcron was born in 1912.
6. The use of the honorific title "Ms." borrows from Buchanan's text "Sculpture for Ms. Mary Lou Furcron," c.1990–94, reproduced on pp. 224–25. Beverly Buchanan Papers, 1912–2017, Archives of American Art, Smithsonian Institution, Washington, DC.

As the recorded conversation with Furcron moves in and out of audibility, *Mary Lou Furcron, Vesta, GA.* follows McWillie's "eye" through her handheld camera as she lingers with a tender attention on the surrounding landscape, moving from the trees, verdant green plums hanging from their branches, to the swept yard, garden flora, and rocks. With the same reverential observance, she records Furcron's indirect presence in the hand-built details of her architectures and objects, pausing on the asymmetrical posts of a bench, lovingly tracing its roughly nailed joints. In the conversation with Buchanan eight years later, McWillie refers to this haptic information as "the fervent touch."[7]

In *Mary Lou Furcron, Vesta, GA.*, these sensuously recorded images and sounds come together to constitute a multifocal portrait, blending direct representation with a holistic rendering of landscape and built environment. As the utilitarian titles of McWillie's videos suggest, the person and the place, and the stuff the person made from the place, are rendered inseparable. In one sequence, McWillie slowly zooms in on the ladder Furcron pieced together out of trees from the land, leaning against a tree on the land.

Furcron was already in her seventies when McWillie and Buchanan each separately befriended her—McWillie in 1983, and Buchanan around 1989. Both had been encouraged by colleagues and acquaintances familiar with their respective documentary projects to travel to the rural unincorporated community of Vesta, Georgia, and introduce themselves to Furcron. McWillie, a white Southern woman originally from Tennessee, and Buchanan, a Black Southern woman originally from North Carolina, had both developed experimental approaches to documenting and historicizing the underrecognized aesthetic canon of Black Southern vernacular architectures and yards. In McWillie's efforts to preserve these threatened practices, her primary archival tools were video, writing, and curating, while Buchanan's interdisciplinary approach spanned documentary photography and sculpture, text, artist books, and drawing-based

7. "Beverly Buchanan, Athens, GA, 8 July 1995," 179.

"tributes."[8] When McWillie first learned that Buchanan had also been regularly making the forty-five minute drive east from Athens to visit with Furcron, she gifted Buchanan a copy of her 1987 VHS tape.

Buchanan and McWillie's shared reverence for Furcron, and their mutual appreciation for each other's experimental methods, form the triangulated ground from which the recording on July 8, 1995 emerges. Rooted in the specificities of lived experience and place, and textured by the recording technology itself, this profoundly relational primary document arises from the reciprocal interplay between its participants. Converging motivations and curiosities—and Furcron's enduring impact—animate their spoken conversation, while McWillie's sensitive eye attunes to the quiet frequencies of Buchanan's material environment, enacting a form of nonverbal dialogue. The documentary's oral, visual, sonic, and compositional rhythms trace a cocreated moment in time, producing a nonlinear and embodied record. Punctuated by sudden spatial shifts, in-camera jump cuts, out of focus and backlit visuals, and speech that is meandering and occasionally delirious, the video documents a situated, fragmentary poetics of relation.[9] In doing so, it offers an alternative form of history, illuminating the work of Buchanan, McWillie, and Furcron through the social, affective space of remembrance.

* * * * *

At the time of the 1995 recording, Buchanan had been living in the college town of Athens for eight years. After first renting a house in the wooded suburban Forest Heights neighborhood, in 1991 she purchased the centrally located, sprawling Victorian house on Boulevard Avenue, where she lived for the remainder of the decade. This live-work house constituted her studio during a pivotal and prolific period of her career.

---

8. Buchanan often titled her works "Tributes," each dedicated to a specific individual. For example, she created two sculptures called *Tribute to Mary Lou Furcron*, in 1989 and 2009, documented on pp. 222–23 and 236–39. McWillie similarly invoked the term in her 1984 video *A Tribute to Dilmus Hall—Experimental Tape 1, 1984*, echoing Buchanan's 1990 drawing *In Honor of Dilmus Hall. From Athens, GA*.
9. The use of this term loosely draws from Édouard Glissant's *Poetics of Relation*, "in which each and every identity is extended through a relationship with the Other," and which "senses, assumes, opens, gathers, scatters, continues, and transforms." Édouard Glissant, *Poetics of Relation*, trans. Betsy Wing (University of Michigan Press, 1997), 11, 94–95.

The year before McWillie's recording, Buchanan was recognized with a National Endowment for the Arts Fellowship and a Pollock-Krasner Foundation Award, while her sixteen-year mid-career survey exhibition, *ShackWorks*, debuted at the Montclair Art Museum in New Jersey, going on to travel for two years across nine states.

Buchanan's path to building a career as a Southern artist was marked by nonlinear pivots and returns. Born in 1940 in Fuquay, North Carolina, she was raised in Orangeburg, South Carolina, a county along the north fork of the Edisto River bearing the scars of its former cotton plantation economy. After the abolition of slavery, the region's powers attempted to reconstitute that economy through sharecropping, binding much of the majority Black population to continued exploitative labor and land arrangements.[10] This charged landscape proved formative for Buchanan, who grew up on the campus of the state's only public HBCU, South Carolina State University, which was founded as a land-grant agricultural institution nine years after emancipation. Her father, Walter Buchanan, served there as dean of the School of Agriculture.[11]

As a child, Buchanan often accompanied her father on "trips to rural farm families," witnessing his fieldwork which combined aspects of agricultural science, education, and social work.[12] It was on these trips that Buchanan first spent time inside the distinctive, hand-built dwellings she called "shacks," which would become her primary subject matter

10. Cedric J. Robinson describes, "Each shift in the apparatus of repression had been associated with the changing forms of exploitation as Blacks moved from being slaves to being sharecroppers." Cedric J. Robinson, *Black Marxism: The Making of the Black Radical Tradition*, 3rd ed. (University of North Carolina Press, 2021), 204.

11. In Buchanan's 2005 handwritten notes for a speech in the women's studies department at the University of Michigan, she notated the major chronology of her life and work, beginning with growing up on campus in Orangeburg, followed by "Background of Walter Buchanan." Buchanan Papers, Archives of American Art.

12. In an untitled, undated typed text, Buchanan narrates her memories of childhood, writing "Visits: trips to rural farm families with my father. That's what they were. Visits, in my household was another word for 'teaching somebody something' whether it was how to can peaches from my mother or rotating crops by my father. . . . We were saying hello offering assistance (advice) if asked, responding to new crops or mourning unsuccessful dead crops or sick animals. Farm children usually followed their parents' lead and attitudes and everybody seemed to like daddy and I learned from him without realizing." Buchanan Papers, Archives of American Art.

later in life.[13] Through an experimental practice that merged research, documentary, and studio work, Buchanan drew on these early experiences as an adult, reanimating her memories of rural Black life as a continued source of study. In Athens, she procured a copy of her late father's 1929 thesis, "Economic and Social Conditions of Negroes as Tenants and Farm Laborers in South Carolina," and reproduced a series of photographs depicting sharecroppers and their environments from his negatives.[14]

At the encouragement of her mother, Marion Buchanan, Buchanan initially pursued the academic path her father had charted. After earning her BS from Bennett College in North Carolina in in 1962, Buchanan moved to New York not for art but for science and medicine, completing an MS in 1968 and an MPH in 1969 at Columbia University with a focus on parasitology. Following her studies, she worked full time in medicine as a medical technologist for the Veterans Administration in the Bronx and as a health educator for the East Orange Department of Health in New Jersey.

In 1971, in the spare hours between her day job shifts, she began taking classes at the Art Students League in New York, studying with Harlem Renaissance painter Norman Lewis. Two years later, Buchanan started exhibiting her work at Cinque Gallery, the artist-run nonprofit founded by Lewis, Romare Bearden, and Ernest Crichlow to champion under-recognized artists of color. Buchanan's paintings and concrete sculptures from this period took the form of proto-Minimalist abstractions, but her subject matter drew from the surrounding built environment and explored the inherently raced and classed conditions of urban space. With *Torn Walls* and *Black Walls*, series whose titles directly invoke architecture, Buchanan distilled the urban surfaces of New York and New Jersey into textured color field paintings. Continuing to draw from the landscape of the city, she expanded into sculpture in the late 1970s, when she began casting cement in cardboard box molds to create simplified, three-dimensional

13. Buchanan's notes for her speech at the University of Michigan continue: "He talked with [the farmers] while I played with the children." Followed by "IV. saw lots of shacks."

14. Buchanan maintained a photocopy of Walter Buchanan's thesis paper for his master's of science at Ohio State University. In 1990, Buchanan's housemate, Patricia Phagan, requested a circulating copy through interlibrary loan on Buchanan's behalf, but the library was unable to locate it.

forms that resembled "discards" from buildings "in a state of demolition."[15] By then, Buchanan was regularly exhibiting her work, and she left her career in medicine to pursue art full-time.[16]

Spurred by economic hardship and a desire to situate her work in a Southern context, Buchanan made the unlikely decision in 1977 to leave the tri-state area and move to the postindustrial city of Macon in central Georgia.[17] As she elaborates in McWillie's 1995 video, "It was that I had to find my own relationship to what I was, what I thought I wanted to do. And it wasn't working. And it didn't work until I came South. Well, it began a little bit in New Jersey. I just didn't–couldn't call it something. But I could call it something once I got back home."[18] Home, for Buchanan, applied to the general region. In Macon, Buchanan developed a practice of driving through the city and surrounding counties commemoratively installing the fragmentary cement sculptures she called "frustula" in the unmarked burial grounds of enslaved people. During this period, Buchanan completed multiple large-scale, site-specific cement sculptures, including *Ruins and Rituals* (1979) and *Unity Stones* (1983), both in Macon. A National Endowment for the Arts grant in 1981 supported Buchanan's major work *Marsh Ruins*: three large tabby-coated cement mounds,[19] notably built and installed directly in the marsh vegetation and waters between the coastal city of Brunswick, Georgia, and the barrier island St. Simon's, a site charged by its centrality in the Transatlantic slave trade.[20]

---

15. In Buchanan's 1978 artist statement, "WALL FRAGMENTS—Series Cast in Cement," she writes: "They are inspired by urban ruins but are created, 'in my own image.'" Buchanan Papers, Archives of American Art.
16. This biographical narrative draws from Park McArthur and Jennifer Burris Staton's recent scholarship on Buchanan's life and work in *Beverly Buchanan 1978–1981* (Athénée Press, 2015).
17. In the circa 1983 manuscript for an article spotlighting Buchanan's work, she is quoted describing her move to Macon: "Something had to give. I needed to live where it was warmer and less expensive. I got tired of having to compete for everything." Buchanan Papers, Archives of American Art.
18. "Beverly Buchanan, Athens, GA, 8 July 1995," 103.
19. Describing *Marsh Ruins*, Patricia Ekpo notes, "Tabby concrete is a labor-intensive mixture of oyster shell particles and quicklime, sand, ash, and water produced by slaves and utilized largely in plantation architecture in the antebellum Southeast." Patricia Ekpo, "A Little Shortness of Breath: The Open Black Body as Southern Landscape," *The Georgia Review* 79, no. 4 (Winter 2025): 933.
20. This narrative draws from recent scholarship on Buchanan's Macon period by Amelia Groom in *Beverly Buchanan: Marsh Ruins* (Afterall Books, 2020) as well as Andy Campbell's "'We're Going to See Blood on Them Next': Beverly Buchanan's Georgia Ruins and Black Negativity," Rhizomes: Cultural Studies in Emerging Knowledge, no. 29 (2016), https://rhizomes.net/ issue29/campbell/ index.html.

While Buchanan's work maintains a resistance to chronological narration, her studio practice underwent a significant shift around 1984, following the completion of these physically demanding bodies of work and concurrent with worsening symptoms of chronic illness. Maintaining her thematic attunement to land and space, Buchanan began creating smaller scale "shack sculptures"—mimetic miniatures that paid tribute to Black Southern vernacular architectures recalling the homes she visited with her family as a child.

Across her writing and recorded speech, Buchanan articulates the nuanced relationship between her shack works and the found forms they engage. "I'm just now catching up in sculpture with what's been done!" she exclaims to McWillie in the 1995 recording.[21] Her earliest shack sculptures, small terra-cotta forms fired and painted with enamel were simplified and abstracted. In her typed artist statement titled "IMAGES FROM THE LAND / Georgia shack series" from circa 1984, she writes: "It is not my intention to produce copies of buildings that once dotted the Southern highways. . . . The surviving fragments are the inspiration for most of these sculptures. . . . I have, of course, rearranged the look of the dwellings to fit my feelings of their form as sculpture. The architectural element found in all of my work, I think, is present in this series."[22]

By the mid-1980s, Buchanan began building shacks through a more representational method, assembling roughly cut foam core to echo the asymmetrical, hand-built language of the original architectures.[23] In an undated typed statement, she described this as "a process of creating objects that relate to but are not reproductions of structures, houses mainly lived in now or abandoned that served as home or an emotional grounding."[24]

This practice of studying and interpreting shacks ultimately unfolded across mediums for the remainder of the artist's life, spanning sculptures, drawings, writings, artist books, and photographs. In her sculptural work, she experimented with scale, building techniques, and materials,

---

21. "Beverly Buchanan, Athens, GA, 8 July 1995," 96.
22. Buchanan Papers, Archives of American Art.
23. Following her years in Macon, Buchanan lived in Atlanta from 1985–87 before moving to Athens.
24. "Two Notebook Entries," Buchanan Papers, Archives of American Art.

incorporating found objects and regional scrap wood. Her years living in Athens full-time, from 1987 to 2003, marked a period of rigorous, place-based focus. Buchanan complemented her home-studio practice with regular excursions to document shacks in Athens, nearby rural counties, the coastal regions of Georgia and South Carolina, and occasionally in Florida and North Carolina.[25]

* * * * *

Like Buchanan, Judith McWillie committed her life's work to the situated documentation and study of overlooked aesthetic practices in the South. But the terms of her entry into this work were necessarily distinct, shaped by the specific dynamics of her white positionality within a structurally and culturally racist society. Born in 1946 and raised in Memphis, Tennessee, under Jim Crow's spatial and economic apartheid, McWillie grew up within a system that racially segregated public space while exploiting Black domestic labor to sustain white households. Within these conditions, the Black women who cared for McWillie as a child became central figures in her early life. When her mother fell ill, McWillie grew more intimately dependent on her caregivers, accompanying them to church and spending time in their homes.[26] The impact of these formative relationships and experiences in Southern Black cultural spaces laid the foundation for her engagement with Black geographies, despite ongoing segregation post-Jim Crow.

By the time she went to college to study art in 1965, the civil rights movement and its attendant backlashes were well underway. While the horrors of this historic period in Memphis were punctuated by the 1968 assassination of Martin Luther King Jr. (during McWillie's junior year), urban renewal persistently threatened Black Memphis residents with displacement and cultural erasure. Attentive to this spatialized violence as a young art student, McWillie turned her attention to problematizing the art historical framework that relegated the rich aesthetic yard traditions

25. For health-related reasons, Buchanan relocated to Ann Arbor in 2003, but retained her Athens residence through 2013, returning periodically and engaging in regional research during these visits.
26. As described by Judith McWillie in a series of interviews with the editors conducted between February 2024 and February 2026.

throughout Black communities in Memphis to "folk/outsider art."[27] In the acknowledgments section of *No Space Hidden: The Spirit of African American Yard Work*, McWillie narrates the beginnings of her documentary practice, recounting "yards that included the elaborate and colorful display of everyday objects were plentiful in African American neighborhoods in Memphis, Tennessee, where I grew up. . . . In 1969, I started to make photographs of these neighborhoods and collect narratives and folktales from friends in the north Mississippi Delta."[28]

Following her graduate studies in fine arts at Ohio State University, and a three-year period in which she returned to Memphis and continued to gather oral histories and photographs of yard art in the Mississippi Delta, McWillie moved to Athens in 1974 to teach painting at the University of Georgia, the state's flagship research university. From her new home base, McWillie continued to deepen her informal archival project, befriending vernacular artists locally and expanding the scope of her visits over the next decade to include Georgia, Alabama, Mississippi, Louisiana, North and South Carolina, Virginia, and eventually, states outside the Southern region.

In 1984, McWillie applied for a research grant from UGA to purchase "the first affordable home video equipment"—a Panasonic WV-3230 camcorder. Her intentions with this purchase were to "revisit practitioners and interview them more thoroughly, and also to document their neighborhoods and their relationships with family and friends."[29] McWillie upgraded her camera every few years as needed, and between 1984 and 2011, her videography grew to encompass one hundred and fifty unedited documentary videos that she later donated to the University of North Carolina Libraries' Southern Folklife Collection for public access. This extensive collection of videos offers hundreds of hours of visual and oral history, focused mostly on Southern cultural producers, both formally trained and self- and community-educated, working across visual and musical forms.

Taken together as well as individually, McWillie's videos evidence her critical priorities and methods, offering an indispensable resource for

---

27. Grey Gundaker and Judith McWillie, *No Space Hidden: The Spirit of African American Yard Work* (University of Tennessee Press, 2005), xv.

28. Judith McWillie, acknowledgments in Gundaker and McWillie, *No Space Hidden*, xv.

29. McWillie, acknowledgments in *No Space Hidden*, xvi.

witnessing the work of underrecognized Southern artists in the specific conditions within which they worked. For example, the recording *Lizzie Williams (his sister), Hawkins Bolden, J. McWillie, Xenia Zed, Memphis, Tenn., 3 July 1987* situates Bolden's yard sculptures in relation to the high-rise medical complex erected just feet away from his residence. As she interviews the artist and his kin, McWillie images Bolden's sculptures from slightly different angles and speeds of magnification, repeatedly panning her camera between Bolden's protective "scarecrow" sculptures and the looming seven-story building at the edge of his quaint yard. Her camera preserves both the oral histories of the artist and his community while producing a cinematic record of the charged tension between Bolden's yard art and the spatial encroachment of urban renewal. This situated portrait contextualizes his creative practice and home as a battleground, resisting urban renewal's forces of dispossession.

Like Buchanan's wide-ranging and counter-academic forms of study, McWillie's vast video archive constitutes a form of interpretative scholarship in its own right. As she said to Buchanan on July 8, 1995, "Even though I write those articles . . . I'm not that verbal."[30] Without formal training in video, documentary, or research, McWillie's cinematic methods echo Hito Steyerl's account of Juan García Espinosa's 1969 manifesto "For an Imperfect Cinema": "The imperfect cinema is one that strives to overcome the divisions of labor within class society. It merges art with life and science, blurring the distinction between consumer and producer, audience and author. It insists upon its own imperfection, is popular but not consumerist, committed without becoming bureaucratic."[31] In this way, McWillie's socially conscious documentary language is delicately calibrated between participation and restraint, balancing her self-insertion without erasing her presence to suggest a neutral gaze. Across her videos, the marked engagement of her sensitive eye combines with her questions, reactions, silences, and outbursts to render portraits of relational experiences while maintaining their complexities and tensions. In so doing, her videos subvert the rigid formalities of anthropological work, avoiding some of its attendant violences.

---

30. "Beverly Buchanan, Athens, GA, 8 July 1995," 73.
31. Hito Steyerl, "In Defense of the Poor Image," *e-flux Journal* 10 (November 2009), https://www.e-flux.com/journal/10/61362/in-defense-of-the-poor-image.

McWillie communicates some of her driving concerns in undertaking this documentary project in the March 21, 1985 recording *Videotape 2: N-2: Georgia, Sea Islands, South Carolina Coast. Highway 99, S.C. Highway 41. Gary Mack; Andy Nasisse's collection: D. Hall, Son Thomas, Bessie Harvey.* Set on the side of a highway's dense greenery in the coastal city of Brunswick, Georgia—not far from Buchanan's recently completed *Marsh Ruins*—the video documents McWillie's informal conversation with Gary Mack, a young Black man from the city. Together, they consider the discrepancies between the growing external interest in Black cultural work generated in the region and the extraction of local resources:

Gary Mack: They use 'em, you know. . . .

Judith McWillie: It never gets brought back into this community.

GM: No. Everything that's brought up in the community is taken out. Nothing's put back.

JM: That's it. Now, you hit on the reason for this whole project. Which is that there is a tremendous amount of interest across the board all over the country in the Black community in this area of the country—the coastal area of South Carolina and Georgia.

GM: Right.

JM: But there is this pattern of the artwork, the music, the notoriety, always being mounted elsewhere, far away, usually New York, Los Angeles, Chicago. And uh, I'm from the South and I teach at the university, and have noticed for a long time that there wasn't a lot *generated from here* where it could *stay here* and better people economically. But even so, just *preserve* the things that are *being lost* in this area. And it surprised me that, for example, the Sea Island Singers until two years ago had sung in every state of the union, in the universities there, except for Georgia.

* * * * *

Buchanan's motivations closely aligned with McWillie's, as both practitioners confronted the rapid threats to cultural preservation that anti-Blackness exacerbates in the US South. Throughout the 1995 dialogue with McWillie, Buchanan reinforces a mounting sense of urgency to "preserve the things that are being lost in this area." She repeatedly exclaims that "stuff around like that, it's disappearing." She goes on to define, "But what I mean by disappearing is that, um, by the time. . . If we see it one day, it may not be there next week."[32] This threat of disappearance drove Buchanan's own documentary impulse.[33] Her 1997 text "WHAT'S LEFT OF HOME" expounds on the feelings of loss that accompanied her lens-based practice: "Each time I go home and take someone with me, things, familiar landmarks from my growing up times, become more few and far between. Some things just outright don't exist anymore. . . . So, what pictures I take each time are a kind of dying history lesson."

This palpable urgency to historicize through photography is amplified through Buchanan's embodied feelings of precarity living with complex chronic asthma. Throughout her archive,[34] Buchanan narrates her negotiations of "survival," moving with equal measure between descriptions of her lived experience with chronic illness and the driving concerns and processes of her work.[35] Her typed artist statement dated March 20, 2002, begins: "Breathing treatment yesterday was a red-letter day. Limping badly, I found my way to rt 83 near Bishop to see a real old

---

32. "Beverly Buchanan, Athens, GA, 8 July 1995," 178–79.

33. Bryn Ashley Evans reflects on this quality of Buchanan's work, "Threats of loss make one precious, brood their own unique sensibilities." Bryn Ashley Evans, "That Spirit in Spite Of / Now Like It Was," *The Georgia Review* 79, no. 4 (Winter 2025): 943.

34. The use of "archive" here is meant to describe Buchanan's personal papers, largely consisting of ephemera, writings, correspondence, artist's books, and photographs, which she distributed among several of her close friends and colleagues. A significant portion was donated to the Archives of American Art at the Smithsonian Institution, while others are dispersed between smaller private and public collections.

35. Buchanan created a series of undated spiral-bound artist booklets titled *SURVIVORS*, consisting of printed photographs documenting vernacular architectures. Her 2001 spiral-bound artist booklet titled *HISTORICAL PRESERVATION THROUGH ART [BETWEEN MACON + JACKSON]* opens with her hand-written text: "A Word to the Wise. This artist has multiple medical problems. A trip requires 'packing.' Along with my insulin comes potassium for 3x a day pills. Asthma, inhaler, and mobile respiratory unit, walking stick, bottled water and a pistol." Buchanan Papers, Archives of American Art.

house as it was described to me."[36] In one impassioned passage from *Beverly Buchanan, Athens, GA, 8 July 1995*, Buchanan interchangeably references the rapidly shifting landscape and her own sense of mortality: "She'll take me with her, but we gotta do it soon! Because it's like, you know, last week I had bronchitis. And, you know, it's like you could be here today, and not here *tomorrow*. Or it could be bulldo[zed], with all the stuff with the Olympics happening. With all roads, and land being sold so fast, it could NOT BE THERE NEXT WEEK."[37]

Against this backdrop of incessant destruction, Buchanan's and McWillie's documentary practices endeavored to counteract erasure and loss. The forces of disappearance present in Georgia include direct, violent interventions like bulldozing, burnings, and related desecrations to people's homes; institutional neglect; legally mandated displacement; as well as the geographic vulnerabilities to catastrophic storms and hurricanes. What unites these processes is their origin in the plantation's regime of extraction and brutality, the legacy of which continues to structure the present, necessitating a practice of record-keeping and remembrance.[38]

While both artists enjoyed a kind of fluency in the dominant art world, they were committed to creating a record of aesthetic practices in the South, advancing an alternate orientation to art and material history.[39] Their projects further converge in their particular approach to theorizing visual culture, both positing the idea that someone's yard and home could act as a kind of portrait. Buchanan wrote through this configuration of portraiture repeatedly, most often in titles and texts that accompanied her shack sculptures.[40] In an undated loose note titled "Early Exposure," she described her first impulses

---

36. Buchanan Papers, Archives of American Art.
37. "Beverly Buchanan, Athens, GA, 8 July 1995," 157.
38. In a 2021 *New York Times* article about the Birmingham, Alabama, yard artist Joe Minter, the artist is quoted "I can hear the bulldozer coming . . . I've been waiting on someone to preserve this." The article contextualizes the threats to Minter's work in relation "to the destruction of many yard environments, including [Lonnie] Holley's in 1997 after a battle with the Birmingham Airport Authority." Hilarie M. Sheets, "Saving the Artwork of the South: Deep Investment, and a Drone," *The New York Times*, September 24, 2021, https://www.nytimes.com/2021/09/24/arts/design/joe-minter-gees-bend-souls-grown-deep.html.
39. In a lecture circa 2007, Judith McWillie described, "I want to make an aesthetic compendium of cultural forms that I consider to be beautiful in themselves."
40. Her 1996 exhibition at Bernice Steinbaum Gallery was titled *Visual Witnessing: Portraits of Shacks and Their Yards.*

as a child "identifying people by objects . . . and their houses + yards and gardens." This trifecta of house, yard, and objects, repeats in her "legend" for the large shack sculpture *SHACK SOUTH: Inside + Out* (1990):

> Things, therefore, are reminders of what it took to survive. . . . When someone made something, they left a visual mark. The community knew whose chair that was or who made that biscuit bowl. When John was asleep in "THE BED," he probably made it or inherited it from his Mother or Uncle. Washboard, enamel cup, all say functional. Exterior, because the yard was an extension of the "feel" of the house. If you don't see it, you know the ladder is SOMEWHERE.

McWillie intuits this haptic sensibility in Buchanan's work in the July 8, 1995 recording, echoing the idea of "the visual mark" when she shares "when I looked at your photos and at the shacks, they were all about *behavior.* They were all about the *people. The people's touch, on everything.*"[41] Buchanan expands on this concept in a transcribed interview with Eleanor Flomenhaft from 1993:

> At some point I had to realize for me the structure was related to people who built it. I would look at shacks and the ones that attracted me always had something a little different or odd about them. This evolved into my having to deal with [the fact that] I'm making portraits of a family or person which may recall individuals or families I had met. . . . I would look at a building and it would remind me of a person or a family. . . . I was forced to think not just of shacks as portraits of individuals, but to think of structure and culture.[42]

McWillie articulates a related insight when she tells Buchanan, "This book that we're working on is supposed to be specifically about, uh, homeground. Kinda like the way you *care for your surroundings*, uh,

41. "Beverly Buchanan, Athens, GA, 8 July 1995," 100.
42. Buchanan Papers, Archives of American Art.

reflecting what you believe in."[43] Given this attentiveness to surroundings, it is no surprise that the first eight minutes of *Beverly Buchanan, Athens, GA, 8 July 1995* are set within Buchanan's "homeground," in her carefully tended and abundant backyard garden. McWillie's camera jostles as she pivots up, down, and around—to the sky and trees, to the grains and pebbles of the ground, zooming in and out on the details of artworks, leaves, and insects before eventually honing in on one of Buchanan's repurposed cement sculptures sprinkled in birdseed and installed among the lush vegetation. In this symbiotic ecosystem, the sounds, movements, and traces of creatures and flora—birds, barking dogs, an ant on a sculpture, a peach growing in a thicket of greenery—harmoniously intersperse with Buchanan's art. It is here we are introduced to Buchanan's "visual mark" and the "feel" of her "homeground," choreographed in moving image through McWillie's responsive eye.

As the artists move inside, McWillie repeatedly turns the camera to Buchanan's shacks and other sculptures. They appear on video as distinct personalities, each asymmetrical form bearing its own particular posture, materiality, and coloration. Some huddle in groups, on shelves, windowsills, and fireplace mantels, while others perch alone, on the floor, on makeshift pedestals, or on swiveling platforms atop desks. When McWillie verbalizes her interpretation, "They really are, *bodies*. Uh. . . *people* bodies," Buchanan expresses frustration that her gallerist is more concerned with the financial stakes of the sculptures, unwilling to recognize their importance as living, personified companions.[44] She further activates the animacy of her sculptures when she relates to them maternally, "You know, it's like–it's like having ten children, and they all go different places. And unless you have a reunion, you don't get to see them all together!"[45]

* * * * *

43. "Beverly Buchanan, Athens, GA, 8 July 1995," 157. This book refers to *No Space Hidden: The Spirit of African American Yard Work*, published in 2005 by the University of Tennessee. Notably, the text centers quotations of artists narrating their own work, transcribed from McWillie's video recordings.

44. "Beverly Buchanan, Athens, GA, 8 July 1995," 123.

45. "Beverly Buchanan, Athens, GA, 8 July 1995," 100.

Another palpable presence permeates *Beverly Buchanan, Athens, GA, 8 July 1995*. Summoned through Buchanan and McWillie's shared remembrance, Mary Lou Furcron animates and structures the afternoon's unfolding. In their particularly spirited banter, Buchanan and McWillie conjure her voice in their back and forth impersonations of her characteristic idiom:

Judy McWillie: "*That's the way that is.*"

Beverly Buchanan: "*That's the way that is.*"

JM: "*That's the way that is.*"[46]

The second hour of the video is driven by a single action: Buchanan's attempt, and ensuing failure, to locate her photographs of Furcron. Wading through flat file drawers, piles on desks, from room to room, bookshelf to bookshelf, Buchanan addresses Furcron directly throughout this searching process. In her speech, there is no separation between the photographic representation of Furcron—through her person, her buildings, tools, and garden—and Furcron herself: "Mary Lou, I know you're hiding in here somewhere! I'mma find you! . . . Mary Lou, I know you're in here! *I know you are.*"[47] The weight of this personified "hiding" takes on a particular charge as McWillie recounts the grave consequences following a violent incursion into Furcron's privacy and land: "They cut down the woods between her and the highway, so she was gonna be *exposed*. And by god, Beverly, she had that stroke within a week."[48]

In a number of undated typed texts that function as fragmentary artist statements, Buchanan described the spatial relationship to privacy that Furcron embodied: "I've noticed an attraction to 'enclosed' black women. It might have started with Mary Lou Furcron (Now 100 yrs. plus)." In her text titled "Private Spaces," which is not specifically about Furcron, Buchanan theorizes a sacred relationship to privacy inseparable from raced and classed positionality, writing: "When constructing a modest dwelling for poverty-stricken and or unemployed minorities, particularly Southern Black people, one wants to keep in mind two, I believe, very important

46. "Beverly Buchanan, Athens, GA, 8 July 1995," 139.
47. "Beverly Buchanan, Athens, GA, 8 July 1995," 184–85.
48. "Beverly Buchanan, Athens, GA, 8 July 1995," 209.

concerns. One, is the desire for private areas or 'personal space zones.'"[49] This concern with opacity resonates in *Beverly Buchanan, Athens, GA, 8 July 1995*, where Furcron exerts a commanding presence even as she remains elusive, never appearing directly and defying easy description.

As their conversation shifts to focus on Furcron, Buchanan and McWillie grapple with the difficulty of assigning language to Furcron and her creative practice. Describing the day Buchanan first met Furcron, she narrates, "It was a case of astonishment at first sight. . . . There were no words. . . . I couldn't write about it. . . . I can't do words here." McWillie replies, "Well, words even do damage. That's what's so difficult about trying to do anything connected with Mary Lou. I mean, other than a transcript, I don't know."[50] McWillie expounds on this problem of language in her 1988 book review of *Folk Art and Art Worlds*: "The terms used to name them—'primitive,' 'naive,' 'eccentric,' 'outsider,' 'isolate,' and/or 'unsophisticated'—refer not to their [the artist's] motives but to the orientation of consumers who plainly view them as 'something other.' Throughout this process, the folk artists themselves are curiously absent from the dialogue, even in significant books like this one."[51]

Listening to Furcron's self-narration, like McWillie suggests, is essential in order to avoid reinscribing the damage words can do. In the oral history preserved in the 1987 video *Mary Lou Furcron, Vesta GA.*, Furcron positions her techniques within descriptions of her family relationships and childhood influences. Lovingly reciting a long list of relatives who lived nearby and whose memories are retained in the land she cultivates, Furcron's storytelling elucidates her embodied, ritualistic, and material approach to remembrance. She notes the roses that her mother tended, how her father sowed cotton seeds under a pear tree, and her grandmother's connection to a particular pecan tree.

As Furcron discusses the inherited gardening methods she continues to practice, she clarifies the stakes of her craft: "You got to have your heart

---

49. Buchanan Papers, Archives of American Art.

50. "Beverly Buchanan, Athens, GA, 8 July 1995," 199.

51. Judith McWillie, "Folk Art and Art Worlds (Book Review)," *The Pennsylvania Magazine of History and Biography* 112, no. 2 (April 1988): 316.

and soul out there in that field with what you're doing, and if you don't do that, you just out there. You don't make nothing out of it. That's the way that is." She goes on to share, "As long as I've got the plum trees, I'm alright." Recounting childhood memories, she describes contributing manual labor on the family farm "as soon as you get big enough to get out there in the fields," alongside enchanted memories playing tag in the moonlight, "running and hiding, tagging each other . . . just like it was daytime." As Furcron traces her connection to the land through anecdotes, she retells her father's idiom, "we live on the mercy of each other."

Another way through the problem of language is to critically investigate the existing "official" language that has been applied to describe Furcron. Though Furcron lived on the margins in almost every sense, her striking hand-built architectures gained a word-of-mouth reputation culminating in a newspaper feature in the *Athens Banner Herald* on Monday, January 30, 1989. Headlined "A House of Sticks," the article includes a photograph of Furcron posing in front of her home beside a carefully manicured rose bush, captioned: "78-YEAR-OLD MARY LOU FURCRON BUILT HER OWN HOME FROM SURROUNDING BRUSH NEARLY 20 YEARS AGO. The Furniture Inside The Home Was Also Constructed From Nearby Timber and Remains Intact Despite The Years." The article goes on to characterize Furcron's hand-built home as "the primitive hut."

The term "primitive," flagged by McWillie as a word "that does damage," undercuts the author's attempts to celebrate and spotlight Furcron's creative ingenuity by dismissing her design intelligence as inherently inferior. This racist operation is co-constituted with and magnified by the ableist framing of Furcron's mental health later in the article: "Ms. Furcron suffered from mental illness several years ago and had to sign some papers before she was sent to the state hospital in Milledgeville for a brief stay. Today she still refuses to sign any papers, she added, for fear that it might precipitate another trip to the mental ward."[52]

In sharp distinction, Buchanan and McWillie's dialogue, rooted in reverence and attuned to structural inequities, challenges the pathologizing

52. Karen Veal, "A House of Sticks," *Athens Banner-Herald*, January 30, 1989.

operations that were routinely used to incarcerate practitioners like Furcron.[53] Conscious of language's potential to violently categorize, they maintain a vantage point that rejects the belittlement and erasure embedded in official testimony, fostering deeper recognition of Furcron and her work.

* * * * *

Saidiya Hartman writes, "The effort to 'brush history against the grain' requires excavations at the margins of monumental history for the ruins of the dismembered past to be retrieved, and turning to forms of knowledge and practice not generally considered legitimate objects of historical inquiry or appropriate or adequate sources for history making."[54] It is precisely the "illegitimate" nature of Buchanan and McWillie's exchange that destabilizes the damage words can do. Their call-and-response impressions, personal anecdotes, feminized gossip, fragmentary emoting, and apparitional addressing constitute an indirect, subjective, relational language that exceeds official narrative.[55]

In their impassioned dialogue, Buchanan and McWillie enact a counter-history that subverts the official narrative's framing of Furcron's mental health. Instead, Buchanan and McWillie's stuttering banter gestures toward the traumatic history that shaped Furcron's life. By discussing the lived experiences that led Furcron to leave Philadelphia, where she had moved with her family in her youth and worked in a factory, they offer context for appreciating Furcron's preference for her solitary space "enclosed" by the trees. What surfaces is a history centered on Furcron's embodied, temporal incompatibility with factory labor:

53. In her 2013 text *JB Murray's GPS*, McWillie describes how economically marginalized Black Southern creative practitioners like Furcron were regularly subjected to this racist, ableist, classist carceral operation. Referring to J. B. Murray, another artist in rural Georgia that McWillie befriended, she writes, "An elderly African American man who had been incarcerated in the Central State Mental Hospital for 'acting religion.' In those days it was not unusual for elders with meager resources to find themselves in such places." Judith McWillie, *JB Murray GPS* (Cavin-Morris Gallery, 2013).

54. Saidiya V. Hartman, *Scenes of Subjection: Terror, Slavery, and Self-Making in Nineteenth-Century America* (W. W. Norton & Company, 2022), 24.

55. Hartman refers to such speech acts as "ways of knowing disguised as jargon and nonsense." Hartman, *Scenes of Subjection*, 13.

JM: You know how she went to work in a factory?

BB: Yes!

JM: Okay. And-and then they fired her, you know, because she was "too slow."

BB: Yes! "Too slow!"

JM: And when-when they said to her, uh, you know, "You're fired." She goes, "*But, that's the way I work.*"[56]

Taking their unofficial, word-of-mouth exchange seriously opens an understanding of Furcron's lived experience and creative practice as inherently at odds with capitalist production. This misalignment must be read through chattel slavery's structuring role in capitalism, and the historical processes of pathologizing and punishing noncompliance within the plantation that carry forward into present-day carceral frameworks in the prison and "the mental ward."[57] Buchanan and McWillie refuse the logics of racial capitalism in how they speak about Furcron, instead honoring her account without question.[58] They summon her, giving her own language primacy. When Furcron, present through their dialogic impressions of her, says "That's the way I work," she refuses the regulatory and exploitative demands of the factory.[59]

Buchanan and McWillie's conversation further illuminates a dialectical investigation into, and undermining of, the term "poverty":

JM: You know there's always a kinda ironic thing, about when stuff like this is destroyed because. . . Most people look at it and just see poverty.

56. "Beverly Buchanan, Athens, GA, 8 July 1995," 141.

57. Micah Khater notes, "In the antebellum South and Caribbean, doctors and slaveowners deployed medical terminology to prescribe violent treatments for 'slave ailments,' like running away (drapetomania), being obstinate (rascality), or eating dirt (cachexia africana)." Micah Khater, "No Use to the State: Phrasing Escape and a Black Radical Epistolary of Disability in Early Twentieth-Century Alabama Prisons," *Disability Studies Quarterly* 43, no. 1 (2023), https://doi.org/10.18061/dsq.v43i1.9662.

58. Cedric J. Robinson's term "racial capitalism" refers to how "the development, organization, and expansion of capitalist society pursued essentially racial directions." Robinson, *Black Marxism, 2.*

59. In *Mary Lou Furcron, Vesta GA.*, Furcron narrates: "If I went to Philadelphia I'd jump up and get in the trolley and go to work every day."

BB: Yeah, yeah. . .

JM: And one of the things I loved about Renée Stout—The first day she was in town, we went to see the *House and Home* show, and went immediately to the Mary Lou Furcron stuff. The first thing Renée said was, "You know, this isn't poverty."

BB: No!

JM: Bingo.

[. . .]

BB: That's right. No, it's not poverty.

JM: Unh-uh, it isn't. God almighty. But it's those, it's *those details*, you know? It's *the stacked stones*.[60]

In place of the scarcity that capitalist language insists upon, Buchanan and McWillie dwell in the wealth of "details" to be found in Furcron's "self-fashioning."[61] Where the *Athens Banner Herald* article named Furcron "the lady dressed in rags," McWillie and Buchanan co-generate a profoundly reverent and tender attention, as they describe a sweater Furcron perpetually mended:

JM: You know, the thing that used to just take my breath away was that sweater. . . . That was really about eight sweaters.

BB: Yes it was.

JM: And *every* hole was—

BB: And her shoes, the shoes, the things that she put together for shoes, as a shoe!

JM: But that garment, that sweater garment with those colored threads around those holes, you know, sewing one over another.

BB: It was a wonder. It was a wonder.

JM: Yeah.

---

60. "Beverly Buchanan, Athens, GA, 8 July 1995," 178.

61. Hartman writes, "I hope to illuminate the practice of everyday life—specifically, tasks of resistance and refusal, modes of self-fashioning, and figurations of freedom." Hartman, *Scenes of Subjection*, 13.

BB: A work of art.

JM: A miracle.

BB: A miracle! Yeah, a miracle![62]

Jubilantly declaring Furcron's mended sweater "a work of art" is a further act of refusal against the imposed categories seeking to separate and hierarchicalize aesthetic practices. Comparing Buchanan and McWillie's flowing exchange in *Beverly Buchanan, Athens, GA, 8 July 1995* with Buchanan's 1990 interview with Delores Brandon on National Public Radio's *Crossroads* program exposes the stark contrast and tired frameworks Buchanan often had to navigate in traditional interview contexts, where there was an imposed demand to define her relationship to "folk art." Throughout Brandon's questioning along these lines, Buchanan seems to be refusing the very terms of the questions:

Delores Brandon: Do you feel connected to the folk artist? Or do you see yourself as quite different?

Beverly Buchanan: Oh, I think all Southern artists have to deal with that. And I certainly do feel connected. We all have to do it. I think that's one of the things, that we, that all of us, as Southern artists have in common anyway, is that we have to do it. We have to do our work. It's almost a compulsive thing too, so that might be the real connection.

DB: I don't, I don't quite understand.

BB: Well, um, you know, I can use found objects by choice, on the one hand. But I can also go and buy materials to use. And, characteristically folk artists use what's available. So what I'm saying is that I can use what's available, and I can also readily use what's not available.

DB: Right. But in terms, of say, there's a kind of distinction made. I don't know, one is—

62. "Beverly Buchanan, Athens, GA, 8 July 1995," 156.

BB: It usually has to do with education. That somebody has, that I have studied. And, you know, I'm not sure that what I did at the Art Students League is any better than what I'm doing now. [*laughs*] You know, that's usually the distinction that's made. But my distinction would be that I can find materials or I could buy materials, and have access to bought materials. Where folk artists may not, or may not even want to do that. That their idea might be to use what they can find even when they can buy something. I'm not sure. I don't know what Howard Finster buys now, is what I'm saying. I don't know whether he still uses found stuff, or he buys stuff. It doesn't matter.

DB: Right. So you don't really make a big distinction?

BB: Not really, no.

DB: Between folk art and so-called fine art?

BB: No.[63]

In contrast, the conversation in *Beverly Buchanan, Athens, GA, 8 July 1995* offers a deeper engagement with Buchanan's work and influences precisely because McWillie and Buchanan are aligned in their refusal and their reverence.

* * * * *

In a present-day interview, McWillie reflects on the video she recorded with Buchanan thirty years earlier: "Mary Lou is a central presence in that video. She was our common love and common experience, and that made the conversation go the way it did—because she was central. The sharing experience always yields more ridges of different kinds, as opposed to people talking at each other from their own worlds."[64] With their orientations toward Furcron acting as a connecting force, McWillie and Buchanan's conversation provides a rare situatedness for Buchanan to speak in more nuanced language about her decision to return to the South and locate her work in a Southern context.

---

63. Transcribed from an audio file in the Buchanan Papers, Archives of American Art.
64. "Judith McWillie: Present Day Reflections," 272.

Rather than asking Buchanan to categorize herself for or against "folk art," McWillie is receptive to Buchanan's work on its own terms, positioning Buchanan's engagement with Southern vernacular form as a relational aesthetic practice, drawn from a collective language. McWillie insightfully reflects, "Now, when you see stacked stones in the photo, and then *your* sculpture, and it's all related to, uh, *a shared experience*."[65] This prompts Buchanan to narrate her work through generatively affective terms that an interrogation about "folk art" could never produce: "It was just that there was nothing up there that looked like that. But here, there are things that *feel* like that. So I went from just ideas to-to ideas *and* feelings. Ideas and feelings. I think that was the connecting factor."[66]

As she narrates to Judy the artistic necessity of returning to the South, due to her work's incongruence with the dominant art world's available framework, Buchanan continues, "I couldn't put . . . an art world label on it."[67] McWillie employed similar language in a 1992 *Artforum* review of fellow Georgia artist Lonnie Holley's work, writing: "His vision defies classification in Western terms."[68] She finds the defiance of dominant terminology in Holley's work arises from "its dialogic origins . . . rooted in the dynamics of social reciprocity." This refusal of the singular, individuated artistic voice recalls Édouard Glissant's embrace of a diasporic orientation, in which "one consents not to be a single being."[69] McWillie echoes Glissant in her perception of "a shared experience" in Buchanan's work, illuminating Buchanan's devotional engagement with vernacular form as a "feeling"-based practice of attuning, noticing, caring, recognizing—an inherently social practice.

Buchanan's and McWillie's work, and their exchange on July 8, 1995, demonstrates how feelings are better suited to such alternate orientations

---

65. "Beverly Buchanan, Athens, GA, 8 July 1995," 101.
66. "Beverly Buchanan, Athens, GA, 8 July 1995," 103.
67. "Beverly Buchanan, Athens, GA, 8 July 1995," 103.
68. Judith McWillie, "Lonnie Holley's Moves," *Artforum International* 30, no. 8 (April 1992): 80–84.
69. Édouard Glissant, quoted in "One World in Relation: Édouard Glissant in Conversation with Manthia Diawara," trans. Christopher Winks, *Nka: Journal of Contemporary African Art*, no. 28 (2011): 5.

to art itself. Feeling through sculpture, feeling through the camera, feeling through nonlinear conversation. Feelings hold the generative and inevitable role of influence, not as a linear trajectory of artistic movements in the academy, but as a way of being present to relation, a process of receptivity and reciprocity. An "emotional impact," as Buchanan describes to McWillie, leads to a merging with and relating to, as opposed to a separating from.[70]

Recounting the story of her 1989 sculpture *Tribute to Mary Lou Furcron*, which she made directly following her first visit to Furcron's home, Buchanan tells McWillie: "There weren't words. And I came back that day and made the shack. . . . In honor of her."[71] The sculpture translates the feeling, and the feeling is reverence. Love. Recognition. Buchanan "had to return home" to find the social worlds and situated materialities of Black Southern makers, like Furcron, that her practice honored.[72] The tensions and possibilities of bringing these tribute forms to a hegemonic art world context are elucidated when McWillie later remarks, "It's almost, Beverly, like when you made these, and you put them in the gallery, it was almost like it was *permission*, for people to love them. Who *didn't know* whether to love them or not."[73] What is at stake, in the life's work of both artists, is this commitment to creating the grounds for such love to be possible.

Twenty years after McWillie and Buchanan recorded this video, Buchanan passed away. *Beverly Buchanan, Athens, GA, 8 July 1995* is the longest publicly available video or audio recording with her that exists. An affective power, born of care and love, pulsates through the entire

70. "Beverly Buchanan, Athens, GA, 8 July 1995," 138.
71. "Beverly Buchanan, Athens, GA, 8 July 1995," 199.
72. In her 1988 drawing *Blue Sky Shack*, Buchanan wrote, "I think that artists in the South must at some point confront the work of folk artists not so much in the terms of the work but of the persons and the work as being of and from the same place with the same influences, food, dirt, sky, reclaimed land, development, violence, guns, ghosts and so forth. . . . I had to return home to find out that I might have something to say that I was not saying 'up there' which had to do with a kind of celebration of the spirit of people I had known who lived in dwellings called 'shacks' and who could be recognized by what they wore and how they walked and by the flowers they grew in their front yards." Andrew Edlin Gallery, New York, https://www.artbasel.com/catalog/artwork/74794/Beverly-Buchanan-1940-2015-Blue-Sky-Shack?lang=en.
73. "Beverly Buchanan, Athens, GA, 8 July 1995," 180.

121 minutes of recorded footage and sound.[74] A "home-made theory," made live inside Buchanan's home and garden on an ordinary day in July 1995, between two artists for whom the ordinary is anything but.[75] When the video fades to black, Buchanan is mid-sentence, narrating prednisone dependence and jovially laughing. The photos of Mary Lou Furcron remain elusive. The tenderness and heartbreak of this perfect ending are, indeed, inarticulable. The video holds what cannot be said.

---

74. Akemi Nishida writes: "I use the idea of affect to describe the invisible, inarticulable, between-the-lines feelings and senses that care activates. As much as care can be thought of as a concrete action, it can also be understood as what circulates among and through us and transforms us (for better or worse). It is the invisible force or energy that impacts us as much as we emanate it and influence others." Akemi Nishida, *Just Care: Messy Entanglements of Disability, Dependency, and Desire* (Temple University Press, 2022), 22.

75. Aurora Levins Morales writes: "We create [homemade theories] out of our shared lives, [and it] really help[s] us to make sense of everything that we are and all that we find to love." Aurora Levins Morales, "Genealogies of Empowerment," in *Telling to Live: Latina Feminist Testimonios*, ed. Luz del Alba Acevedo et al. (Duke University Press, 2001), 26.

Editors' Note

The translation of *Beverly Buchanan, Athens, GA, 8 July 1995* from video to print involved multiple interpretive interventions.

The 121-minute video is marked by spatial, rhythmic, and stylistic shifts. Our first intervention was to break the video into ten scenes, mimicking the structure of a playscript in order to create approachable sections of content. We determined the scenes by following the internal logic of the video's movements, wherein we understood something differentiated and self-contained was expressed within the bounds of a certain passage. Each scene title is followed by timestamps marking its start and end points, corresponding to UNC's streamable video file. The video link is included on page 309.

A short introductory text opens each scene, describing the ambient and affective textures that follow. Within the transcription, italicized text inside brackets selectively describes facial, gestural, or vocal expressions; spatial shifts; camera movements; objects, images, and visuals in the setting; and other aspects of the video's operations.

Because the spirited exchange between Beverly Buchanan and Judith McWillie functions in sharp contrast to the dialogue of a formal interview, our editorial orientation necessarily differed as well. Rather than alter or reorganize Buchanan's and McWillie's voices for concision and regularity, our transcription asks the reader to acclimate to their speaking patterns, as one might when reading dialogue in a novel. We placed critical value in preserving the informal and regional textures of the artists' individual voices and relational dynamics. In order to maintain important emotional qualities in their conversation, we chose to selectively preserve repetitions, interruptions, and the occasional stutters. We applied capitalization, varied punctuation, and italics to emphasize the textures, volumes, and rhythms of each speaker's delivery.

Recognizing that speech and transcribed text *do* different things, our edit also privileges readability. We aimed to strike a balance between narrative flow and affective information, and thus consolidated some of the original speech's fragmentation through minor deletions without removing extended passages of text. Additive clarifying language is indicated through the use of brackets without italics. We did not signal omissions.

Throughout the text, Judith McWillie is referred to by her nickname, Judy. All individuals mentioned in the dialogue are listed with short biographies in the "People" section, beginning on p. 276. The "Places" section (p. 286) provides a map of the locations throughout Georgia referenced in Buchanan and McWillie's conversation. Numbered endnotes (p. 288) provide additional context, clarification, and explanatory information that supplements the dialogue.

Just as transcribed text and spoken language function differently, printed video stills operate distinctly from moving images. In their finitude on the page, the reproduced stills we included reflect the range in McWillie's embodied, gestural cinematography. Our sequencing experiments with how the interplay of image and sound might be translated into a relationship between image and text. Stills are presented in chronological relation to each other and the transcription, with occasional deviations in support of the compositional demands of the layout.

Beverly Buchanan, Athens, GA, 8 July 1995

a video by Judith McWillie

Scene 1

The Garden

00:00:04–00:08:02

We are situated in a lush garden in full bloom. Green foliage fills the edges of the camera frame, creating a sense of enclosure and privacy. A thick songscape of birds and insects reverberates over the sumptuous scenery, teeming with life. Judy, the only person present, is behind the handheld camera, which jostles lightly as she moves through the space, attentive to the interactions between flora, fauna, sculptures, structures, and sunlight. She pans through the garden in an extended orientation, using the camera's zoom to magnify quiet details: rocks hidden in the edges of herbs and flowers, an ant crawling across a metal sculpture, birdseed scattered across cast cement stones. Through dappled light, she follows birds pecking on the ground, on the roof, and from bird feeders installed at different heights. The birdsong is occasionally punctuated by the barking dogs and honking horns of the neighborhood.

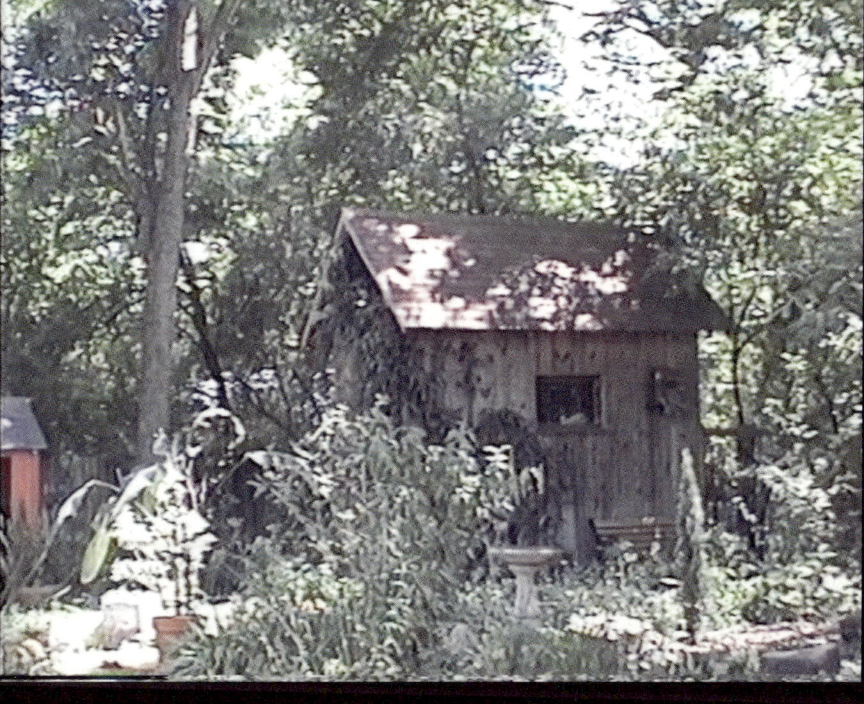

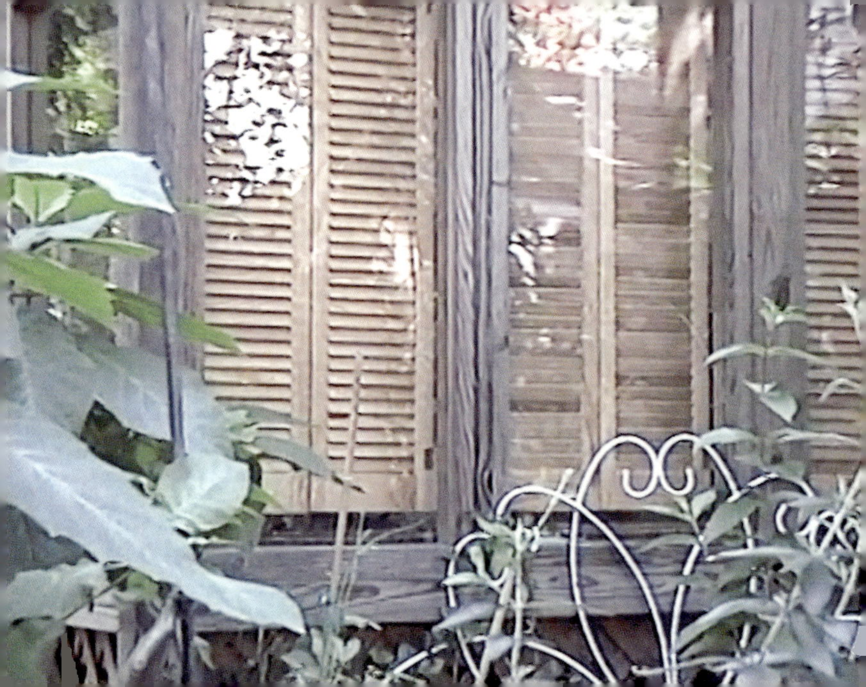

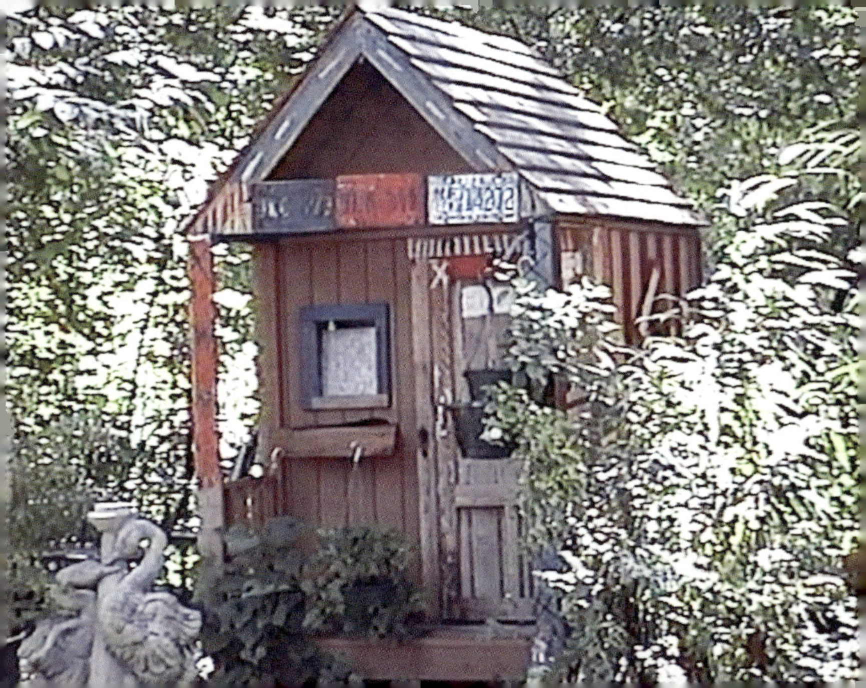

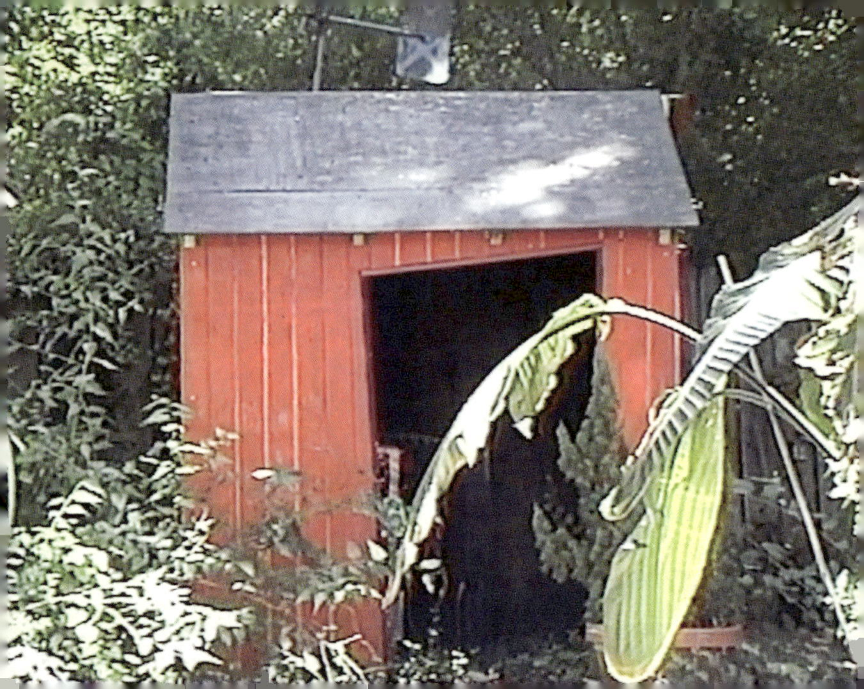

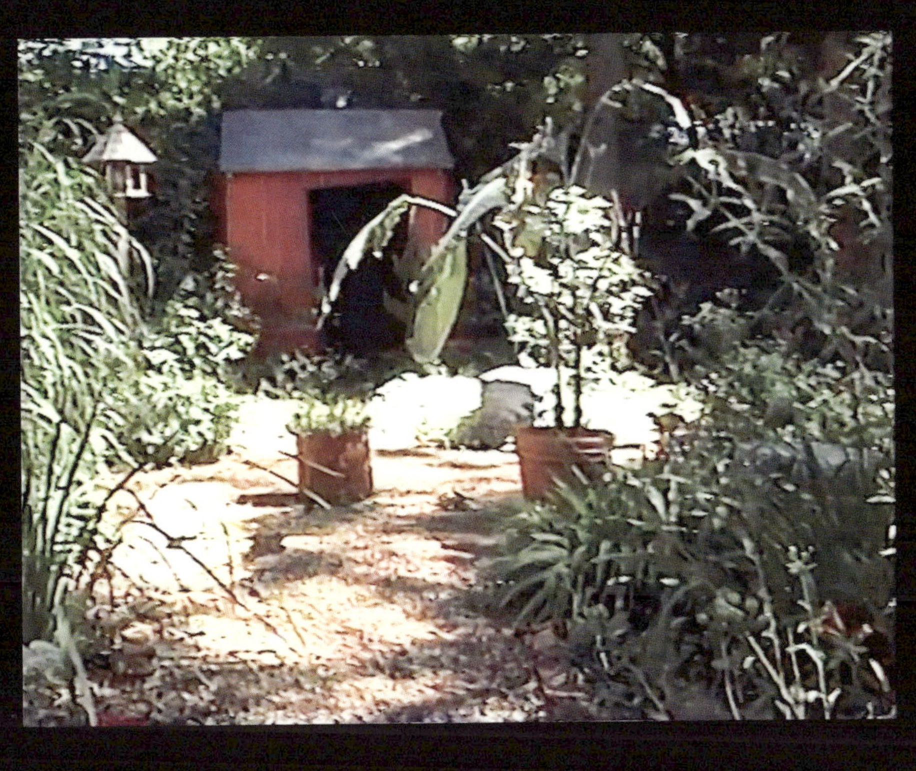

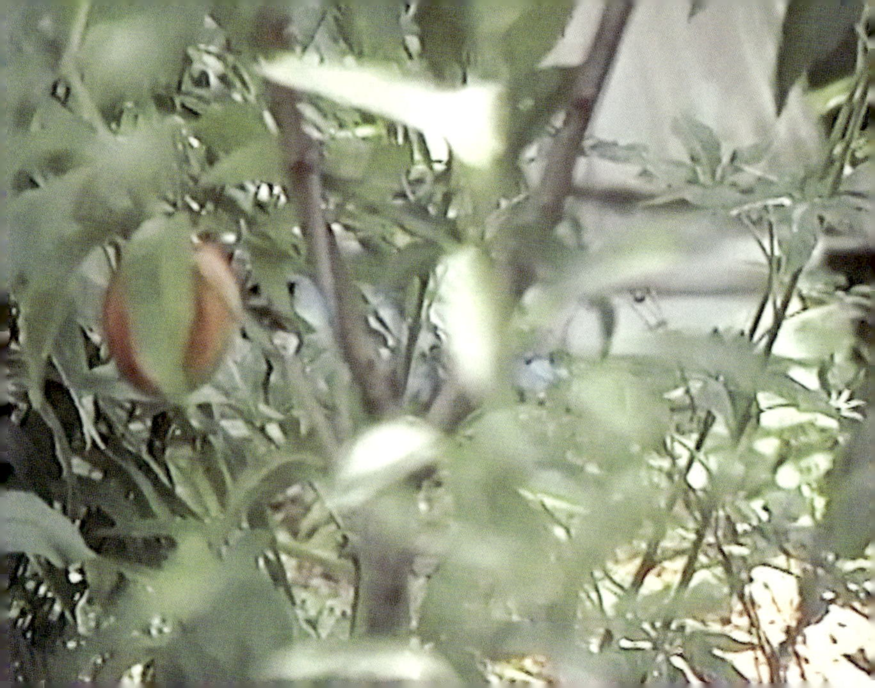

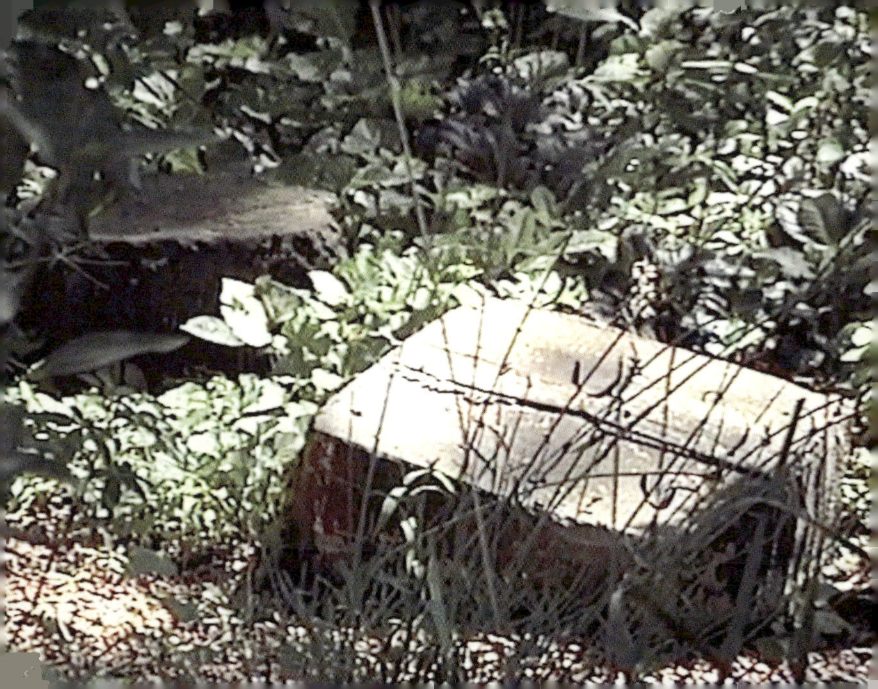

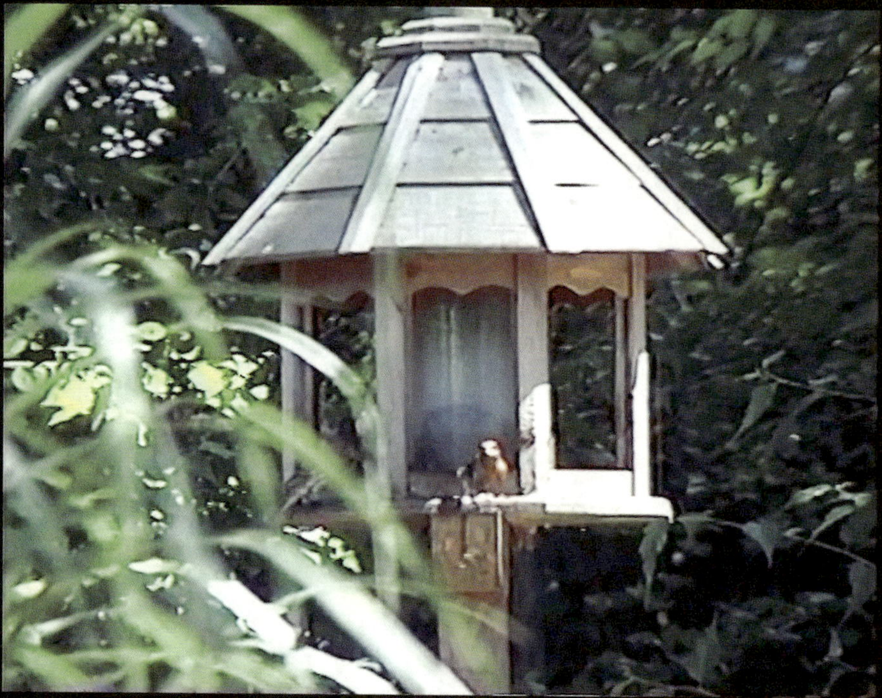

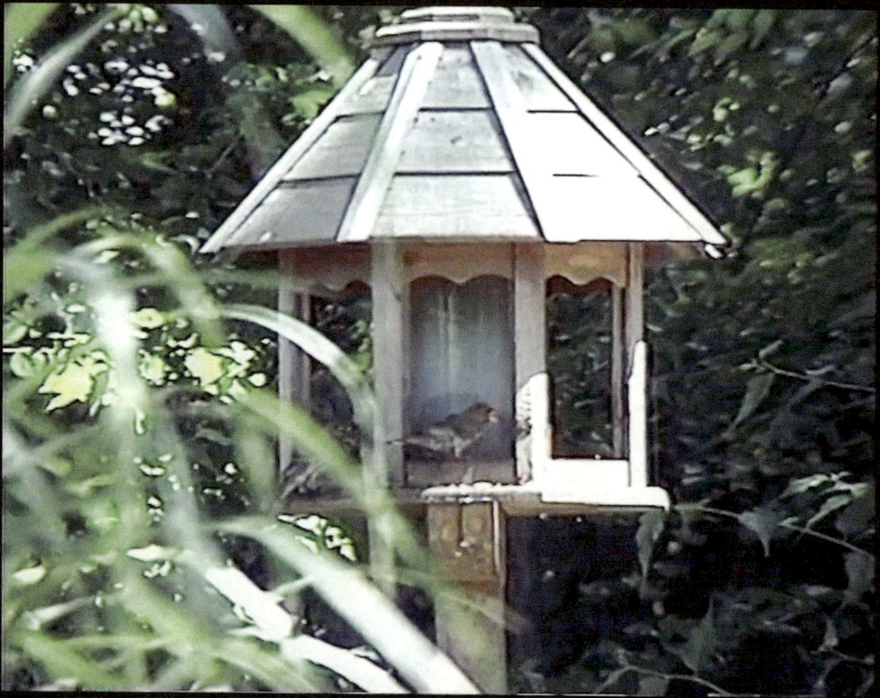

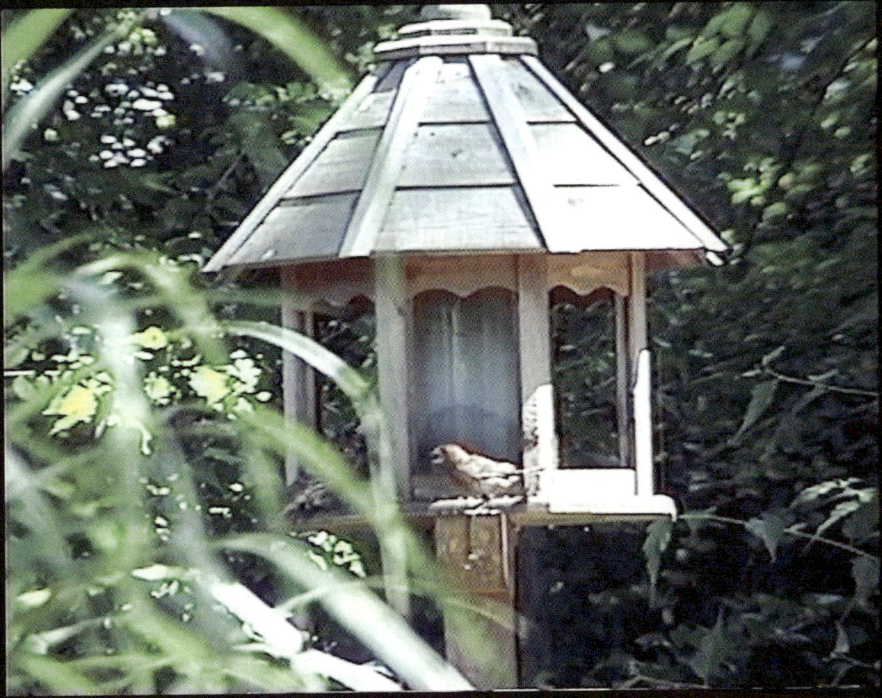

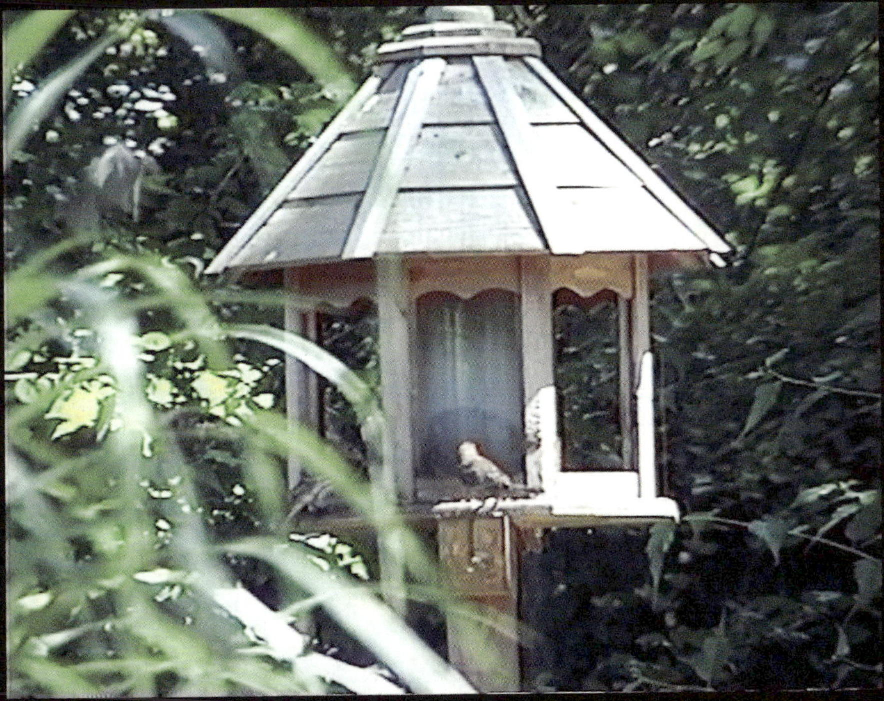

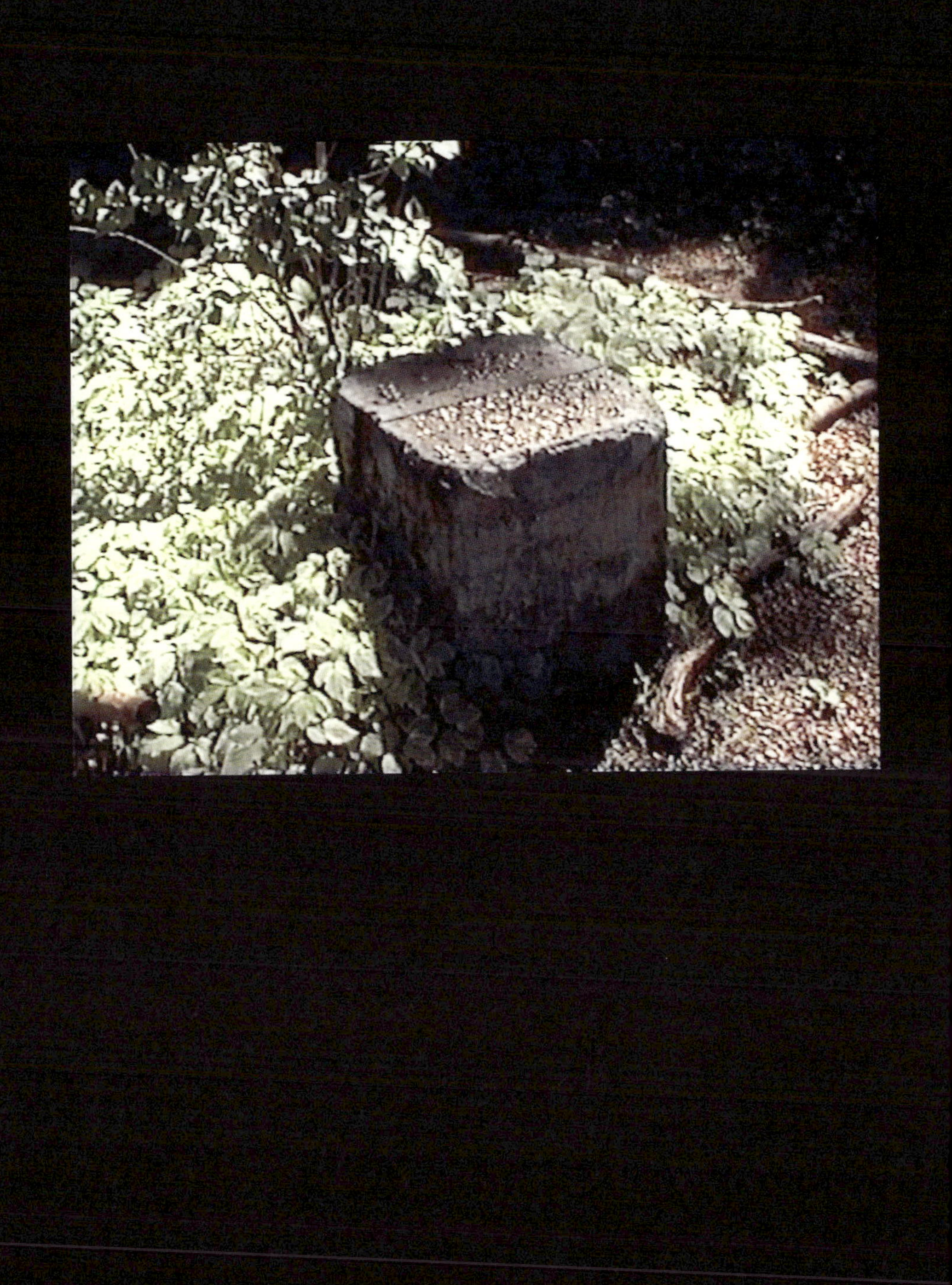

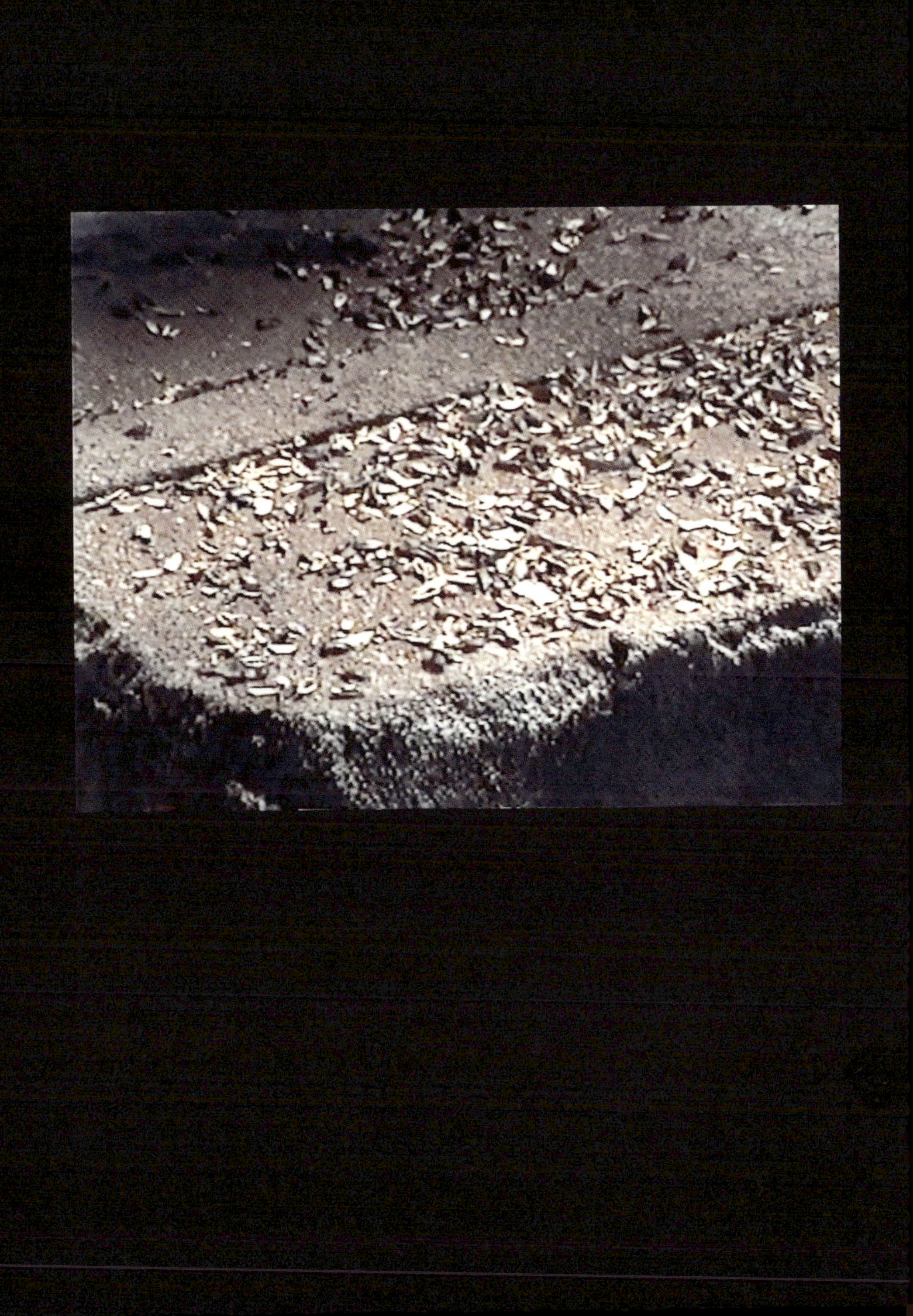

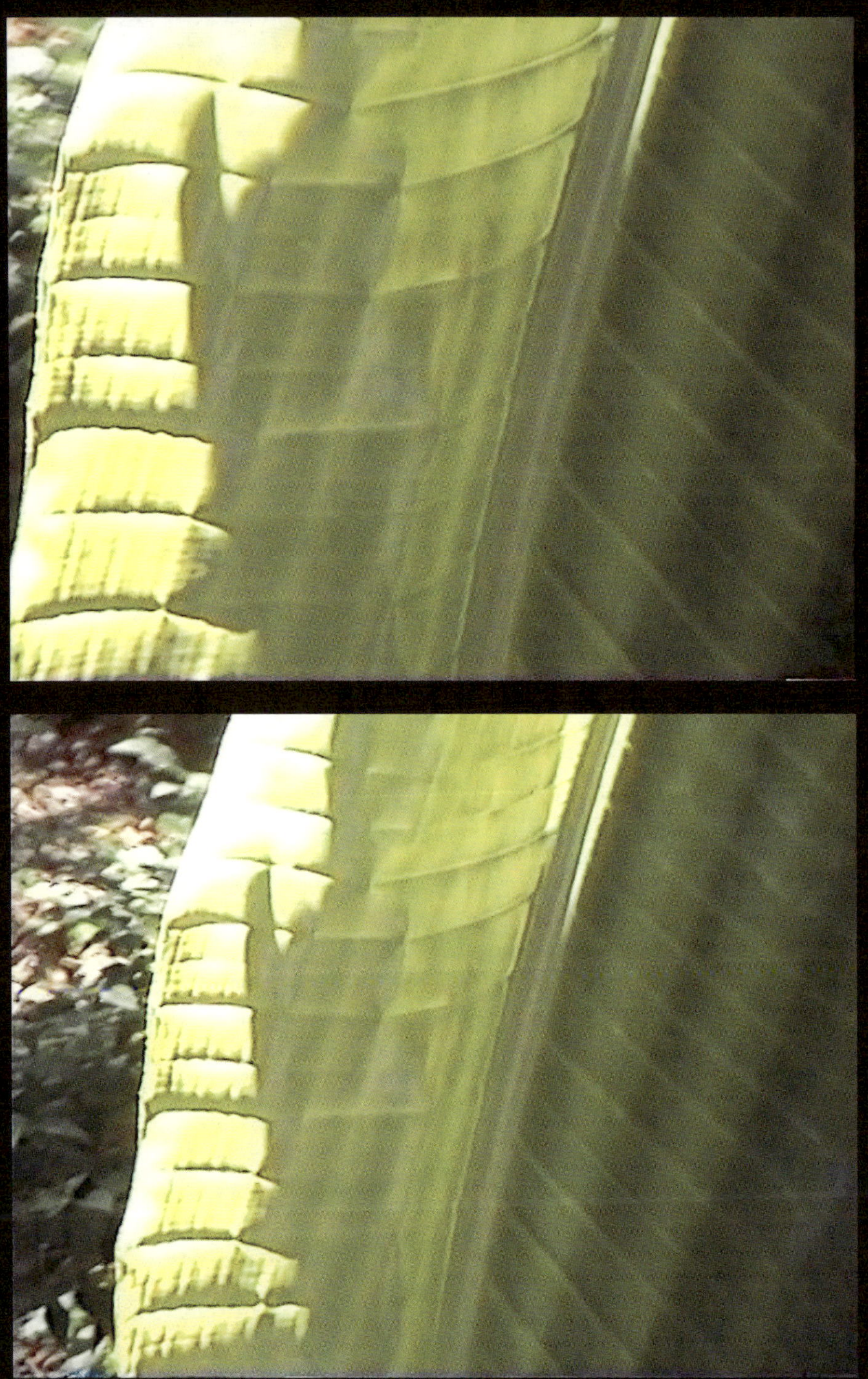

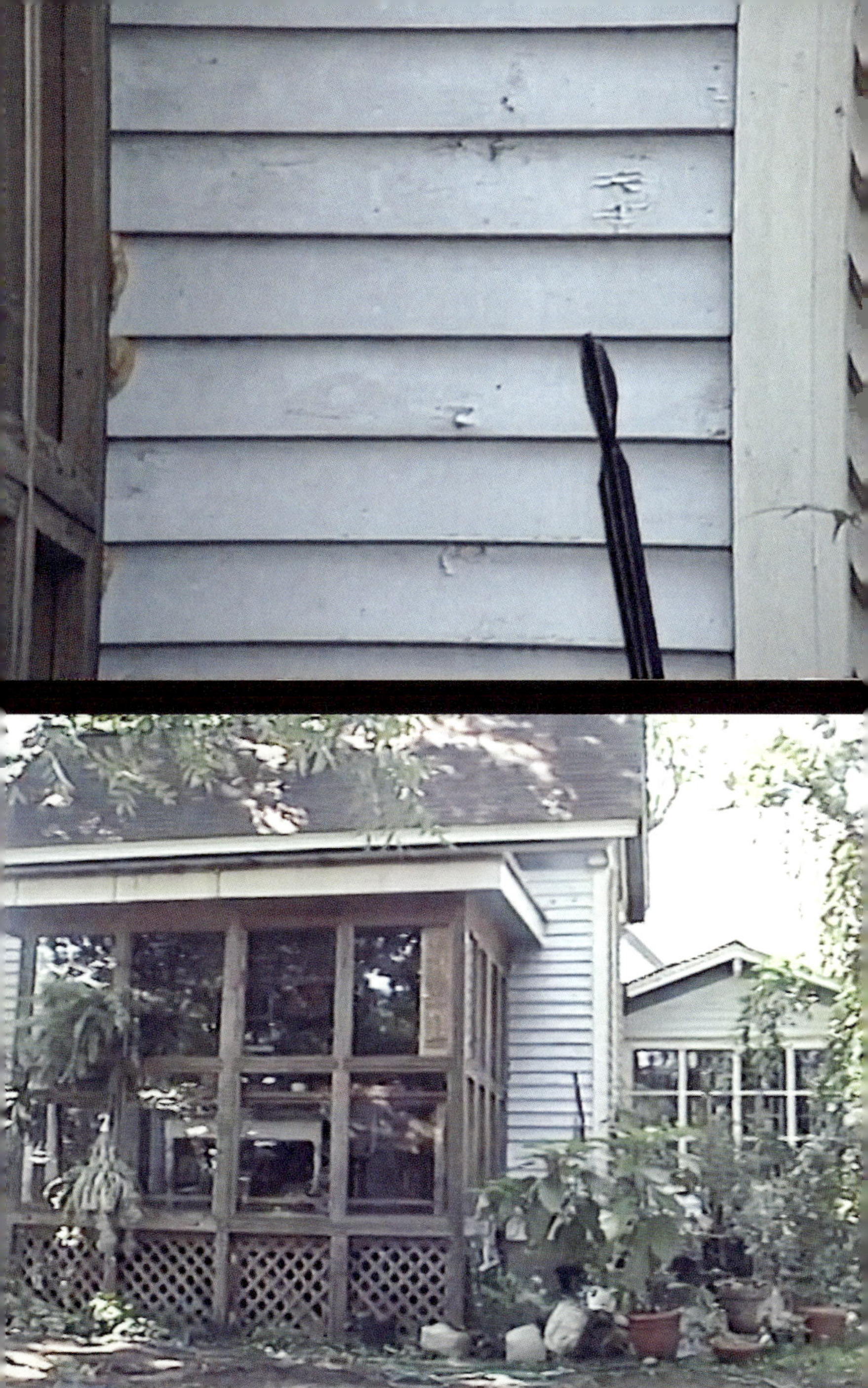

Scene 2

The Driveway

00:08:03–00:09:06

Beverly's forest green Toyota Tacoma pick-up truck is parked in dappled light in the gravel driveway, the neighboring houses just visible behind tall grasses and trees. As Beverly exits the truck, Judy leaves the camera at the edge of the driveway on a tripod and walks to greet Beverly. We hear her footsteps crunching the gravel as she emerges in the frame. Beverly and Judy's voices come in and out of legibility in fragments as the stationary camera records their exchange from a distance.

Beverly Buchanan: [*opens the truck door*] I apologize.

Judy McWillie: [*walks toward the truck*] Hey.

BB: I was out at Jimmie Daniels Road, and I said, "What time is it?" ... Said "It's ten to" ... And I said, "I've got ten minutes to get home!"

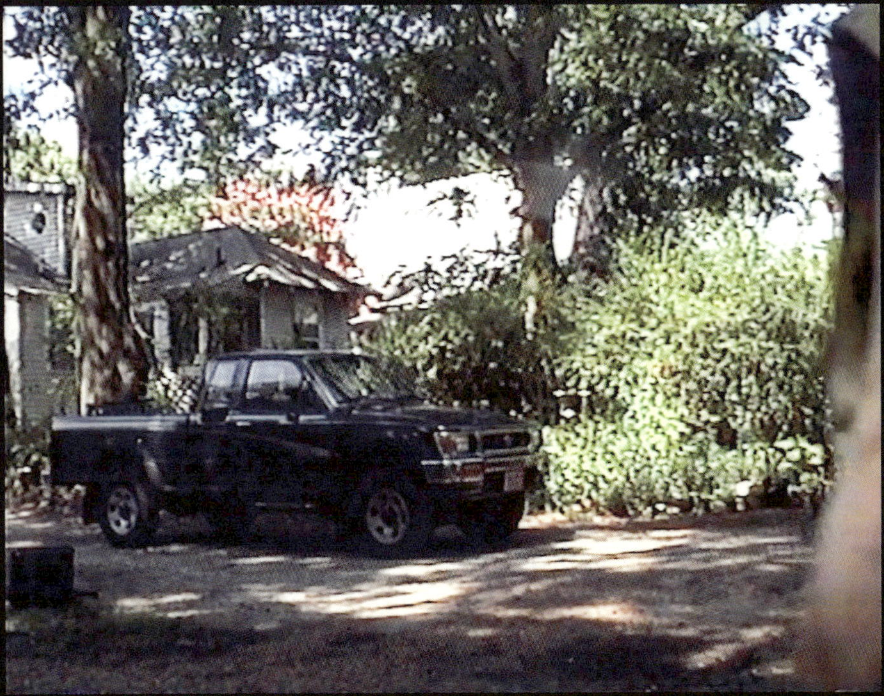

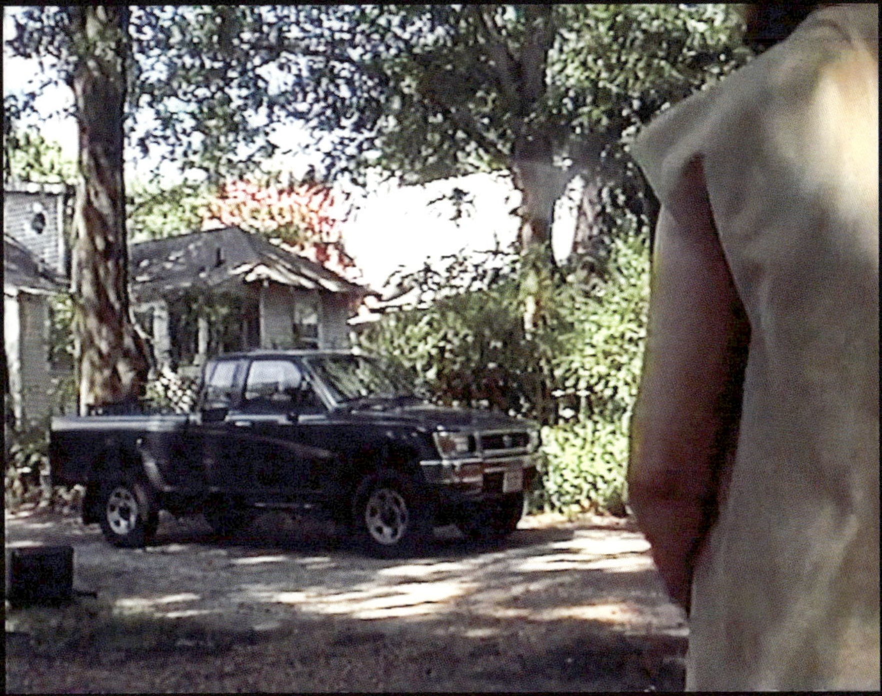

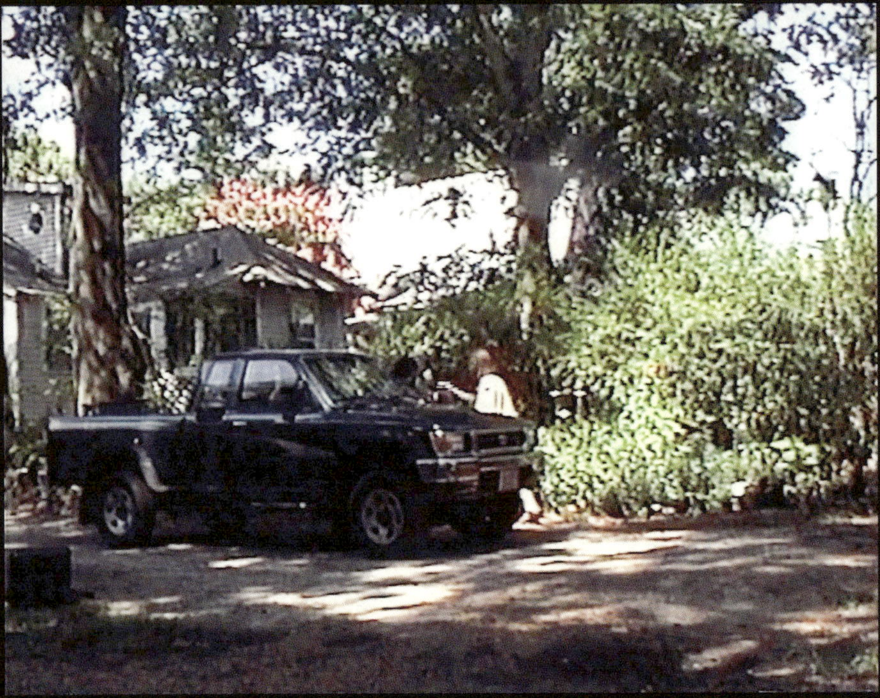

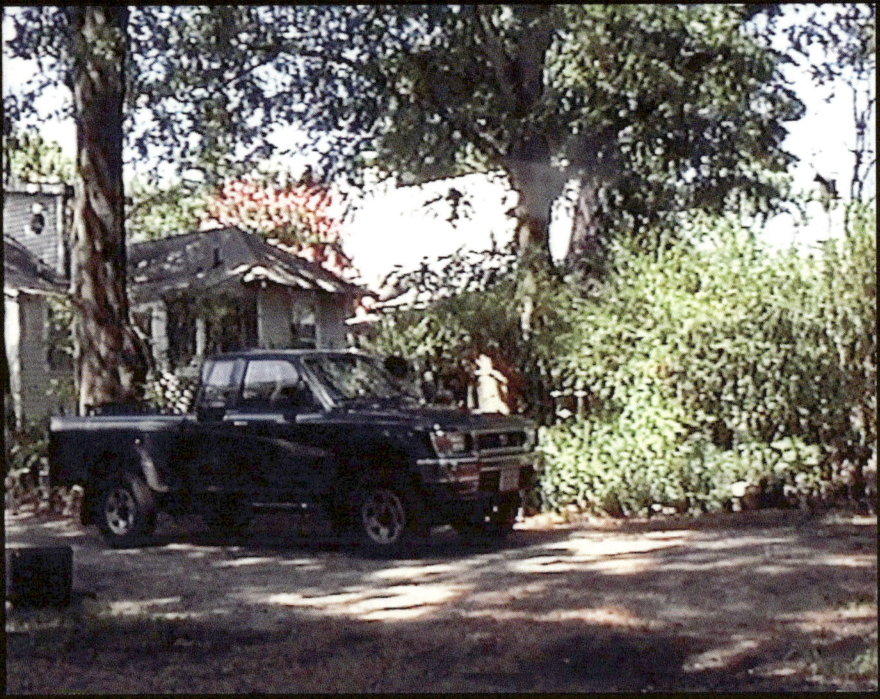

[Judy reaches the truck and holds the door open. They stand together at the truck door, conversing]

BB: I'm so sorry. I said, "And all these cop cars over here by McDonald's, what's going on?"

[Inaudible dialogue. Judy waves at the camera]

BB: If she–if she–if she gets there, I hope she just looks around for ...

[Judy leans on the truck hood speaking inaudibly. She seems to be reassuring Beverly. She then walks back toward the camera, smiling. As the sound of her footsteps on gravel grows louder, the scene cuts out]

Scene 3

Inside

00:09:07–00:16:21

We have entered Beverly's home, and immediately we are immersed in a space of making. Piles of materials, found objects, and sculptures in various stages of process are everywhere—on shelves, on dressers, in seemingly every corner. We shadow Judy's movements as she orients within and observes her surroundings with her camera. When her eyes rest, ours do too.

Beverly and Judy stand in the hallway and begin conversing. At the end of the hallway, green garden light floods the dimly lit space through large studio windows. The ambient hum of a fish tank's trickling water permeates the soundscape.

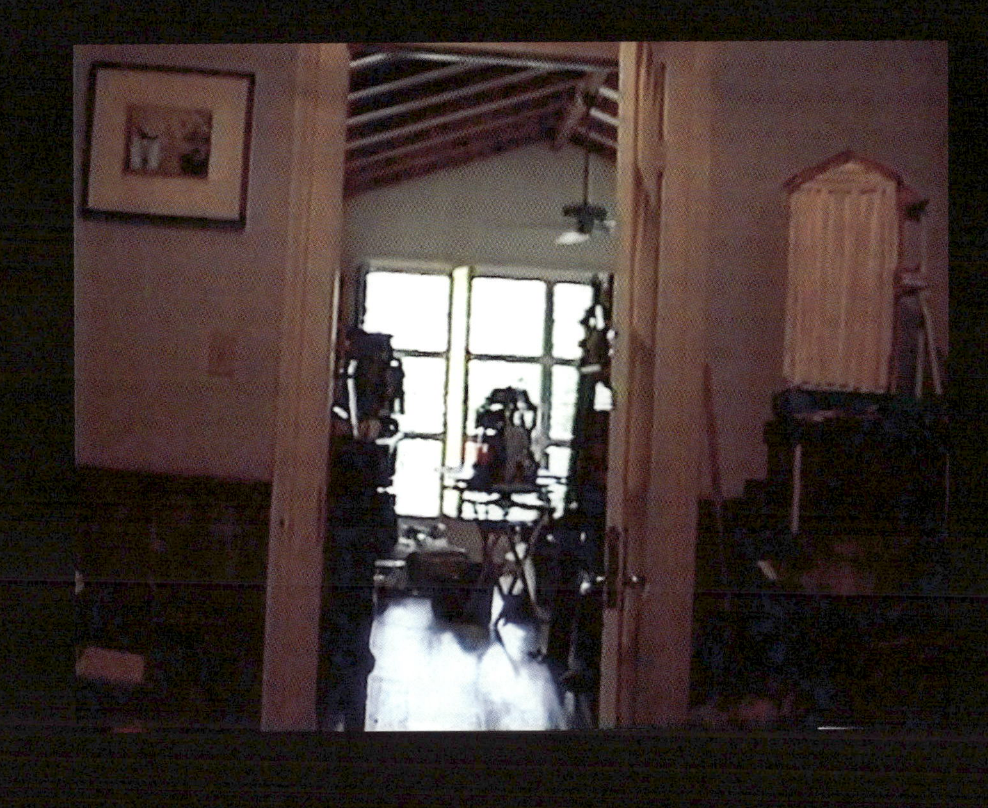

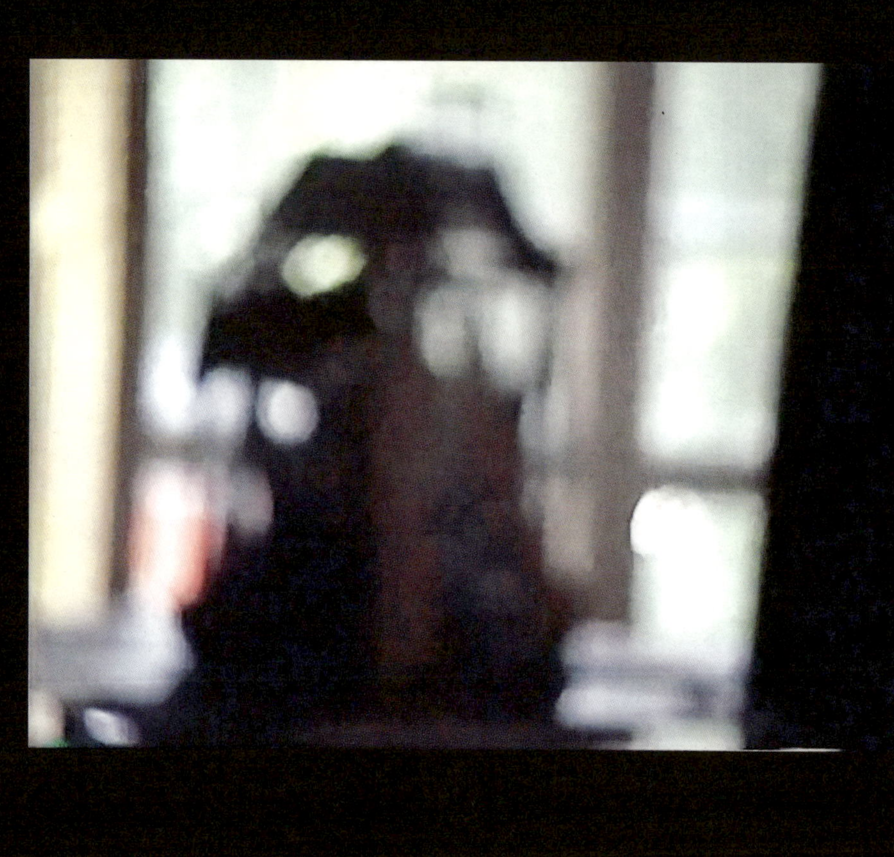

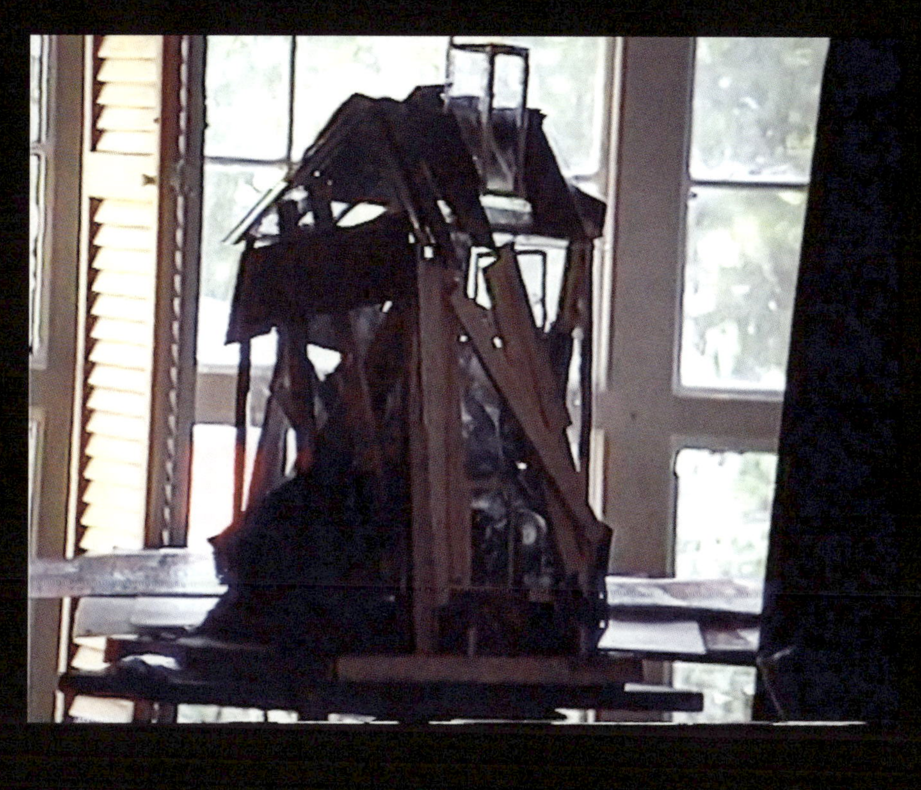

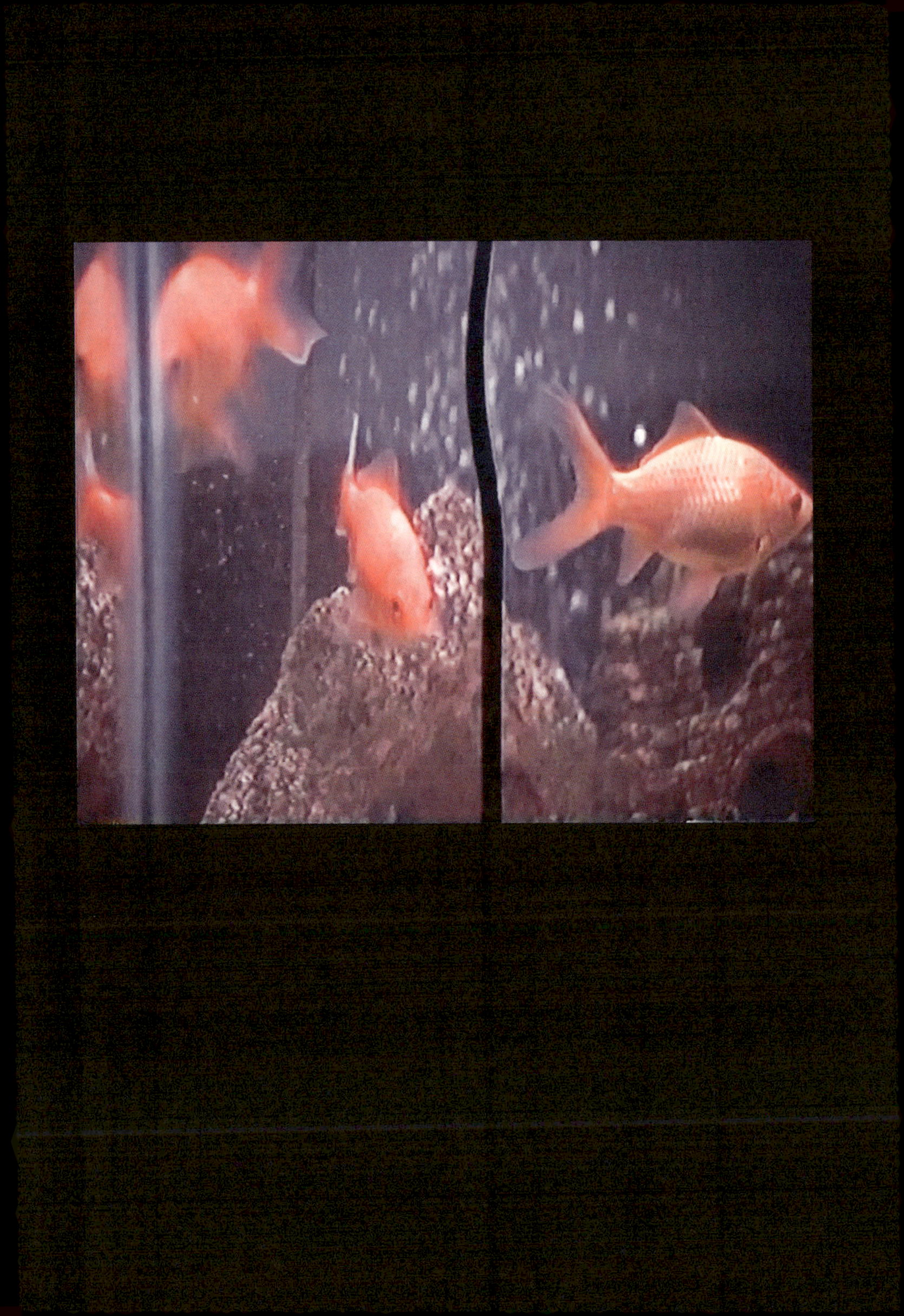

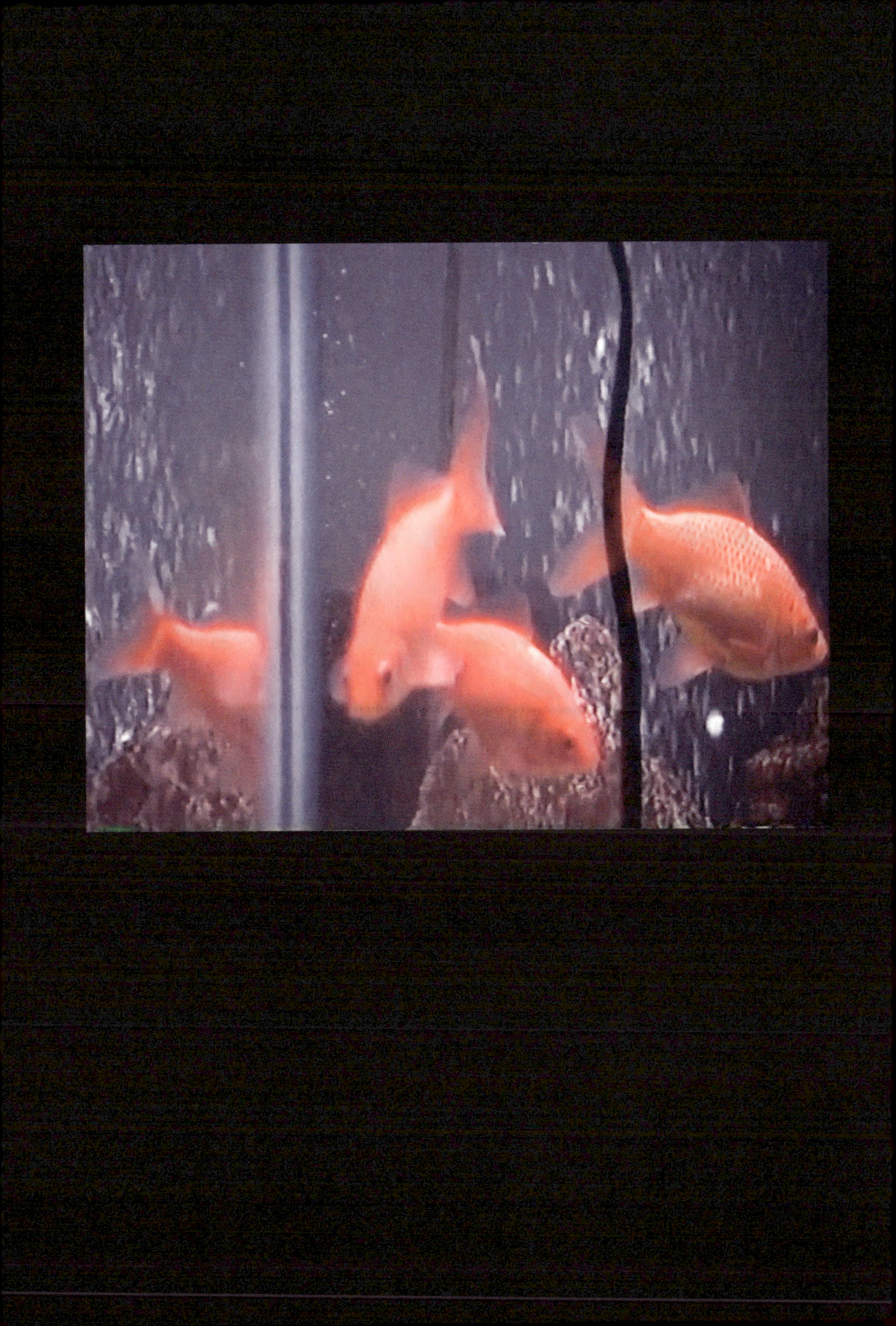

Judy McWillie: Beverly, what's that thing in the backyard that is made out of metal, that has a flag on the side of it? Is it the inside of something, or is it a—?

Beverly Buchanan: It's my mailbox, let me show you.

JM: It's your mailbox!

BB: It's the metal version of this.

[*Judy pivots the camera to focus on the sculpture Beverly refers to, which rests atop a cabinet near the front door. The sculpture is roughly the shape and size of a mailbox but asymmetrical and made from scrap wood*]

JM: God, it's wonderful.

BB: It's the metal version of this, and what he did was, he did not follow completely this. [*touches the sculpture*] And, I'm trying to think, where was it shown? I've forgotten where it was shown. But the guy who made the metal shack that was in Atlanta,[1] on what's now Ralph David Abernathy [Boulevard], down from the Wren's Nest.[2] He's here in Athens. He made that. And so he made the metal version of this.

JM: Oh man.

BB: And it's never been, I don't think it's been shown anywhere at all, Judy. [*crosses the hallway*] Um, this is what they're gonna take to Duke.

[*Beverly comes into view facing the camera, and places her hand on a large glass cabinet filled with toy cars*]

Roger Manley came and selected things for a separate exhibit of *House and Home: Spirits of the South*.[3] He wants to see what artists collect, so he... [William] Christenberry collects calendars 'cause his grandfather collected calendars.

JM: Mm-hmm.

BB: Max Belcher said he didn't collect anything. Manley said, "I don't believe that. He can't have a pristine house!" I said, "Well, I don't know, I've never been to Max Belcher's house, so [*shrugs shoulders*] I don't know!"

[*Laughter*]

So I said, "Well, it's kind of peculiar." I told him, "I *assemble* things."[4] I said, "I'm not sure that I..." I said, "I *really do* have one collection. I collect cars. I swear to you I collect cars!"[5] [*gestures emphatically with hands*] I said, "But other things I kind of *assemble* if I like them," you know?

JM: Yeah.

BB: I said, "I used to have, um, a Black doll collection. And I kinda quit doing that 'cause I found some things that were so *offensive* that I just didn't wanna have them." [*shakes head*] And I said, "So I just, I'll get something if I think it's *interesting*." But, I really do collect cars! I really do! And this is just a *small* portion of my cars, and in here is just stacked full of cars! [*points excitedly at multiple large cabinets*] So he wants to borrow *this whole thing*. The base, and this. This was my mother's, but this came from Billy Evans. And so, he said, "I want you to put all your cars—" I said, "My cars won't fit in here, man!"

JM: [*laughs*] You collect them since you were a kid?

BB: Probably, but I started out drawing cars. I drew cars, I would draw cars... [*laughs*] I did! I drew cars! [*starts walking toward the front door*] Isn't that pitiful? ... What is this? Can I–can I see if the mail is here? Would you mind?

JM: Oh yeah!

[*Beverly briefly exits the front door, while Judy scans the piles of toy cars with the camera. Beverly returns with mail in hand*]

JM: It's gonna be so wild because, you know, even though I write those articles, I'm not–I'm not that verbal.[6] It's real strange. But I know you'll understand if I just—

BB: I do understand. I enjoyed your video *so much*.[7] It was the best I'd ever seen because your *eye did what my eye would like to do*—focus on *exactly* what you focused on.

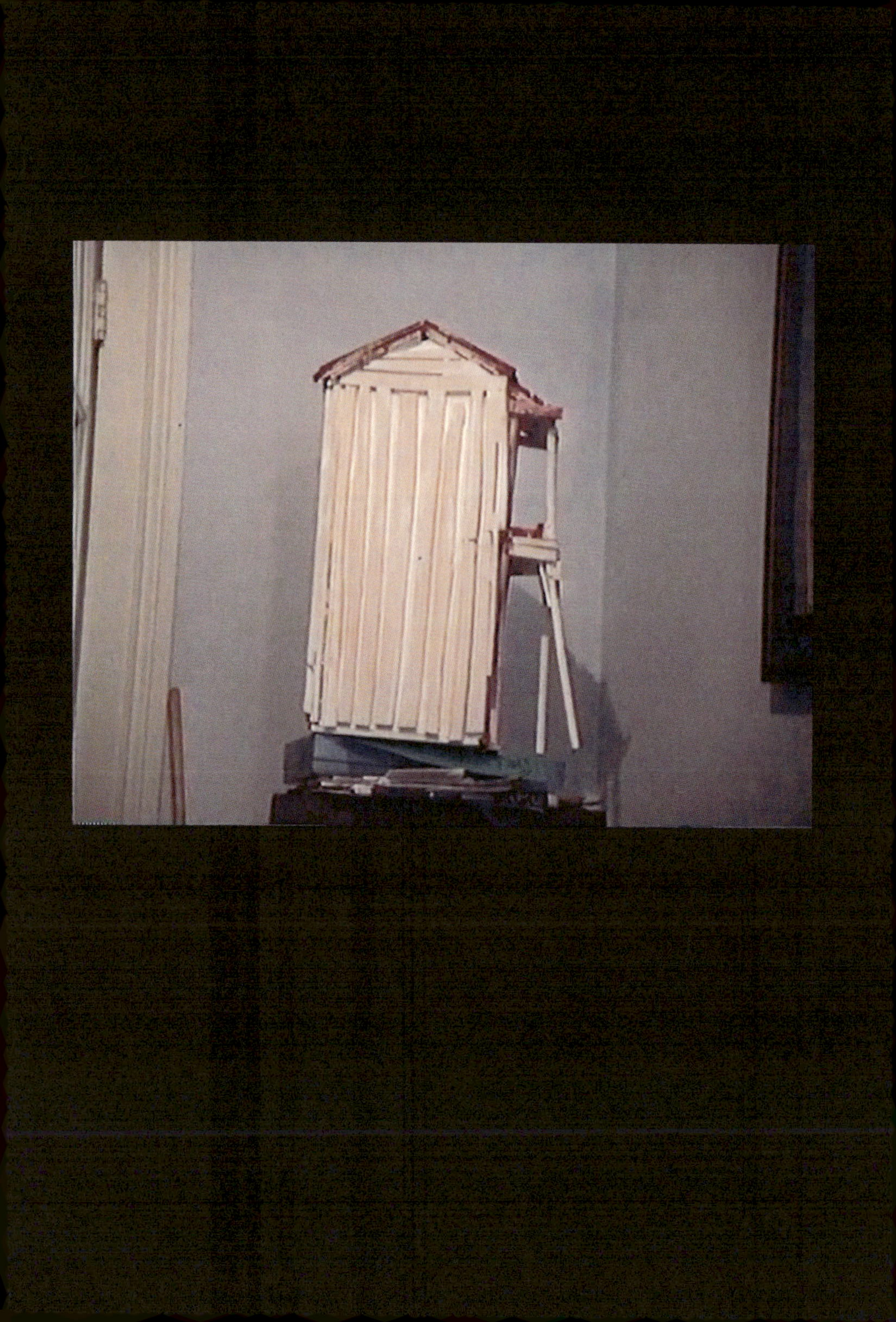

JM: God, the *beauty* of those things.

[*Judy pivots the camera to face a white shack sculpture, viewed in profile, sitting on some boxes in the corner of the hallway*]

BB: I'm serious! I was just so impressed. And I was just real proud of that. I thought, "Well good for her because..."

JM: [*zooming into the shack sculpture*] But you know, Beverly, it's like... I mean, those things are so beautiful that, I don't know, I'm still trying to deal with the fact that it's all...

BB: Yeah! I'm gonna sit here. You wanna sit? You can sit wherever you wanna sit! You can sit in the back. You can sit—

JM: Can I go in there and look at that thing on the—?

BB: Absolutely! The plexiglass thing?

JM: Yeah!

BB: Yeah, I've never done that before.

JM: [*gasps in admiration*]

BB: And it's, it's sort of a response to the, uh... A year ago, I was down in St. Marys. Patti [Phagan] and I went to St. Marys for the 4th, and stayed at the bed and breakfast. And that's when we tried to find Sunbury.[8] And I'll show you one or two photos that I took. And I wanted to tell you our experience.

JM: You found it?

BB: No.

JM: Okay. I can tell you how to get there.

[*There's a jump cut in the video and the conversation abruptly pauses. The video resumes inside the studio off the hallway, where Judy records closeup views of Beverly's shack sculptures. The plexiglass shack sculpture they spoke about sits on a TV-dinner table in the middle of the room, and the walls are lined with sculptures arranged on shelves and other furniture*]

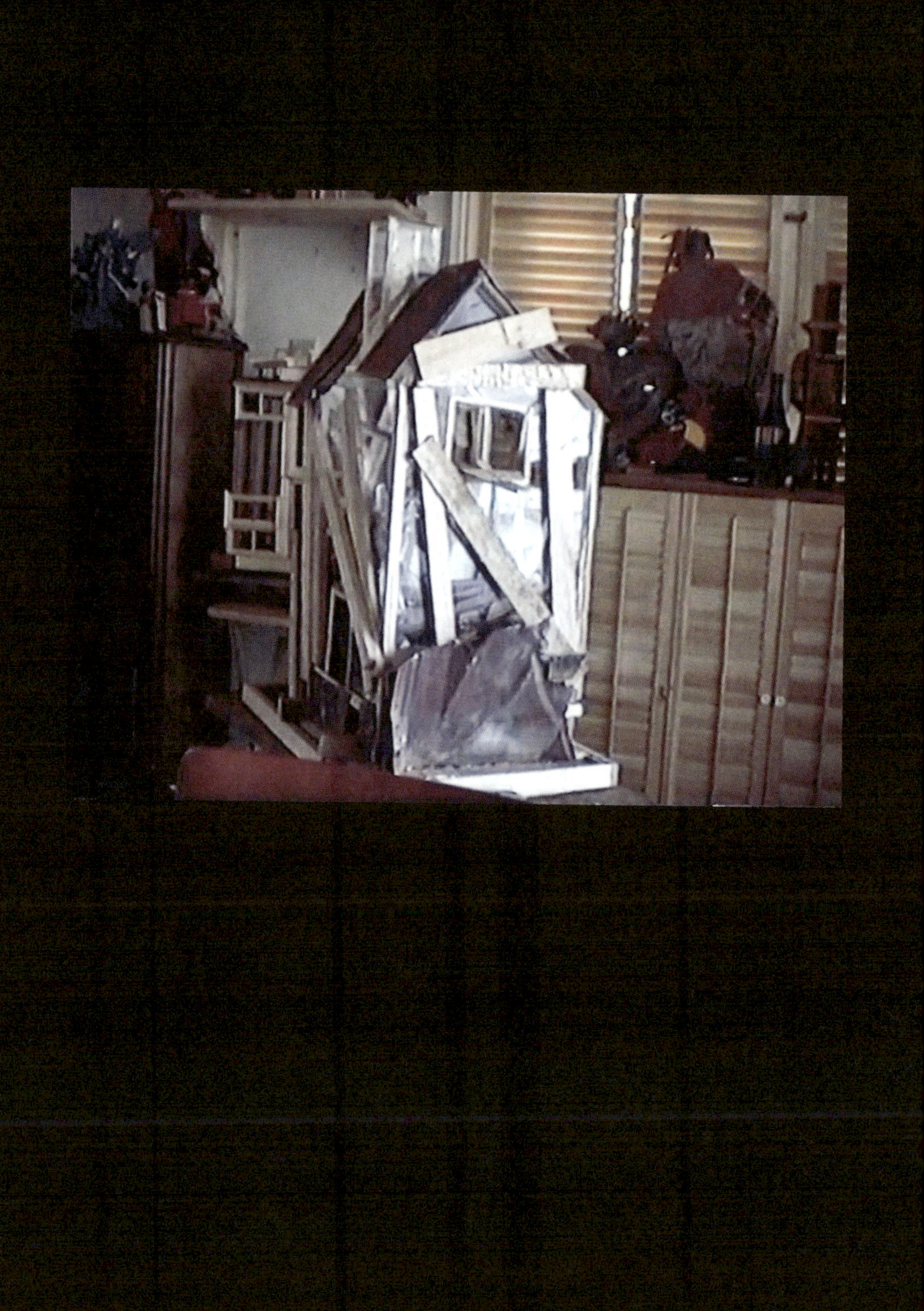

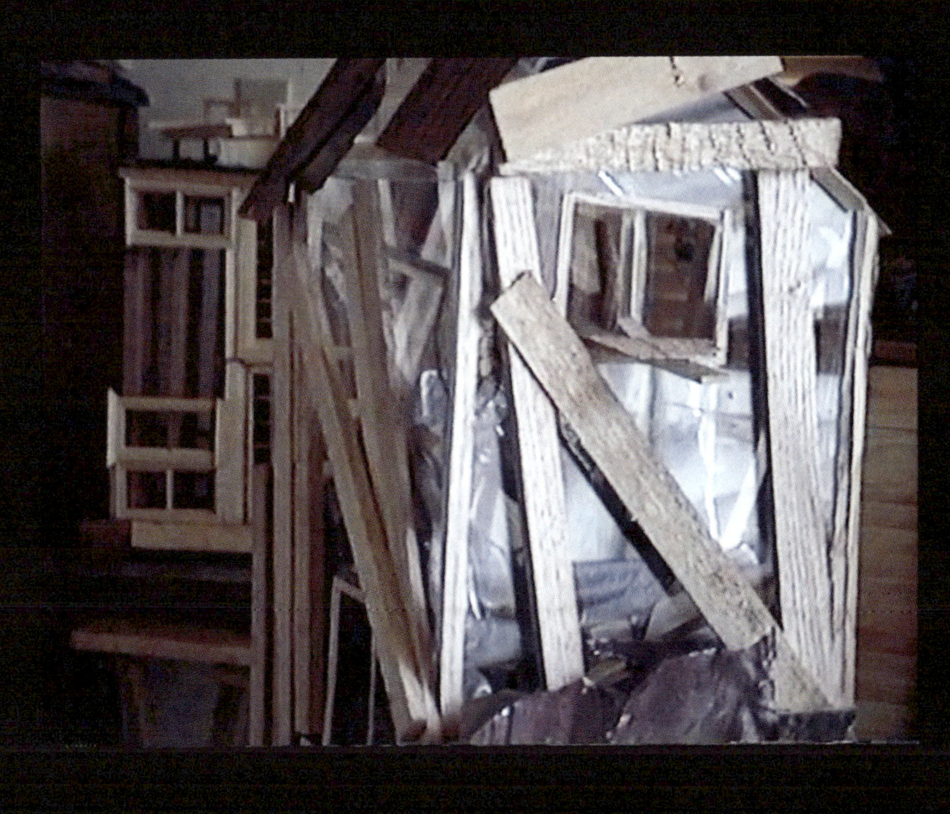

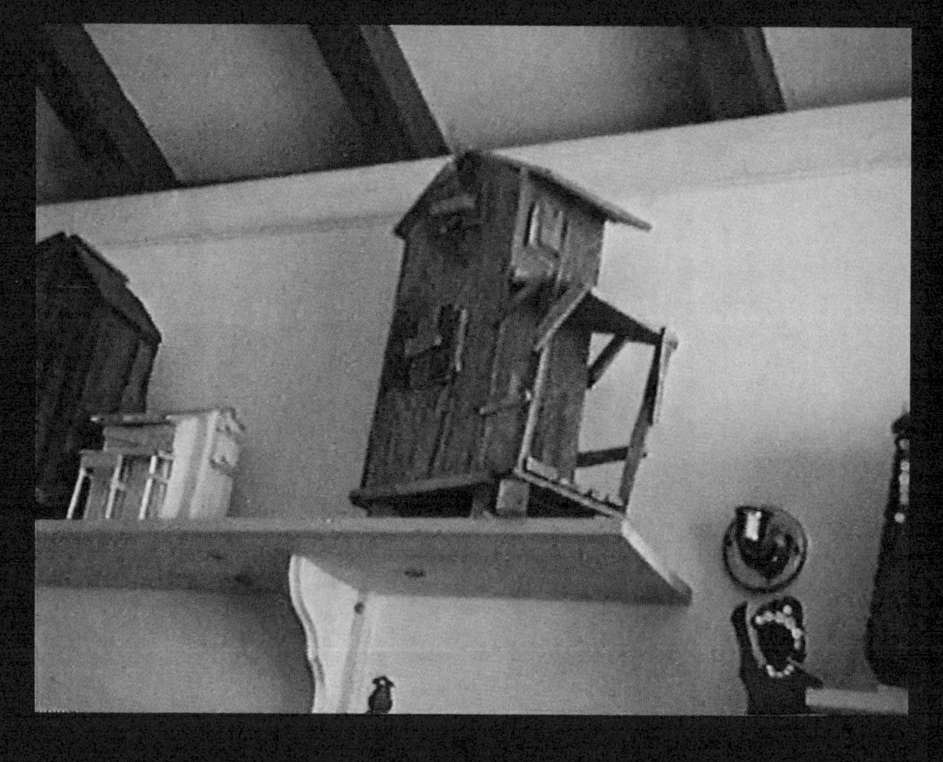

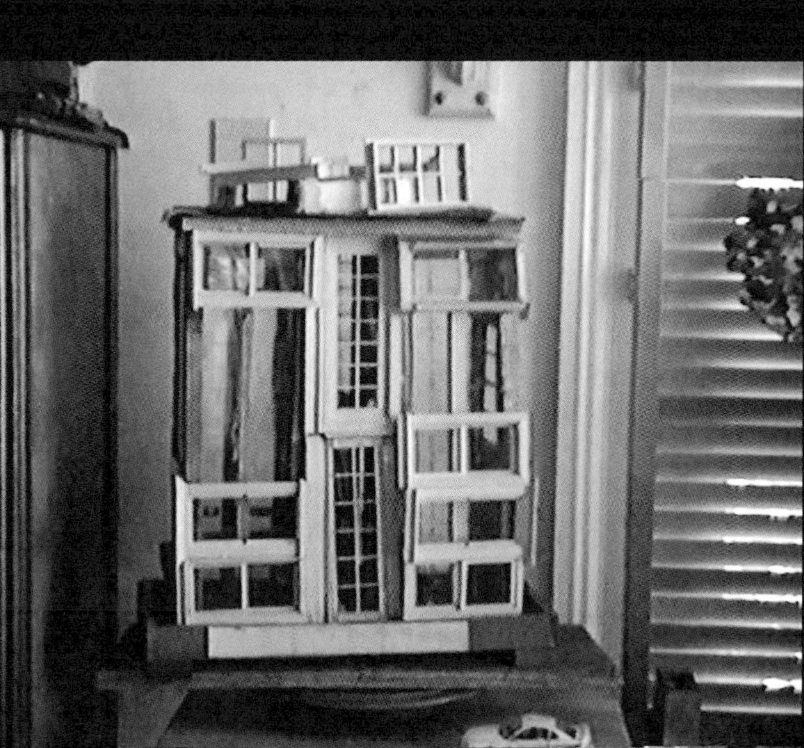

[Judy returns to the hallway and continues to record shack sculptures installed amongst the hallway furniture, as the conversation resumes]

JM: See, all the shacks were in New York [at Bernice Steinbaum gallery] the last time I was here.

BB: So I'm behind in shacks. Let me show you the two that are gonna go up to New York.

JM: Okay.

BB: The one that's in the kitchen on that pedestal is. And the only reason it hasn't gone up is, I would think it would be cheaper for me to send *two at one time.* [Bernice Steinbaum] wants *six shacks* right now. I told her I had completed *one.* And that I, of course, couldn't afford to send it to her. [*chuckles*] She then said, "Oh, we'll-we'll pay for it on this end." And I just tried to let that go in one ear and out the other 'cause I didn't wanna get really, extremely upset about that statement. [*raises eyebrows, and heads into a room off the hallway*]

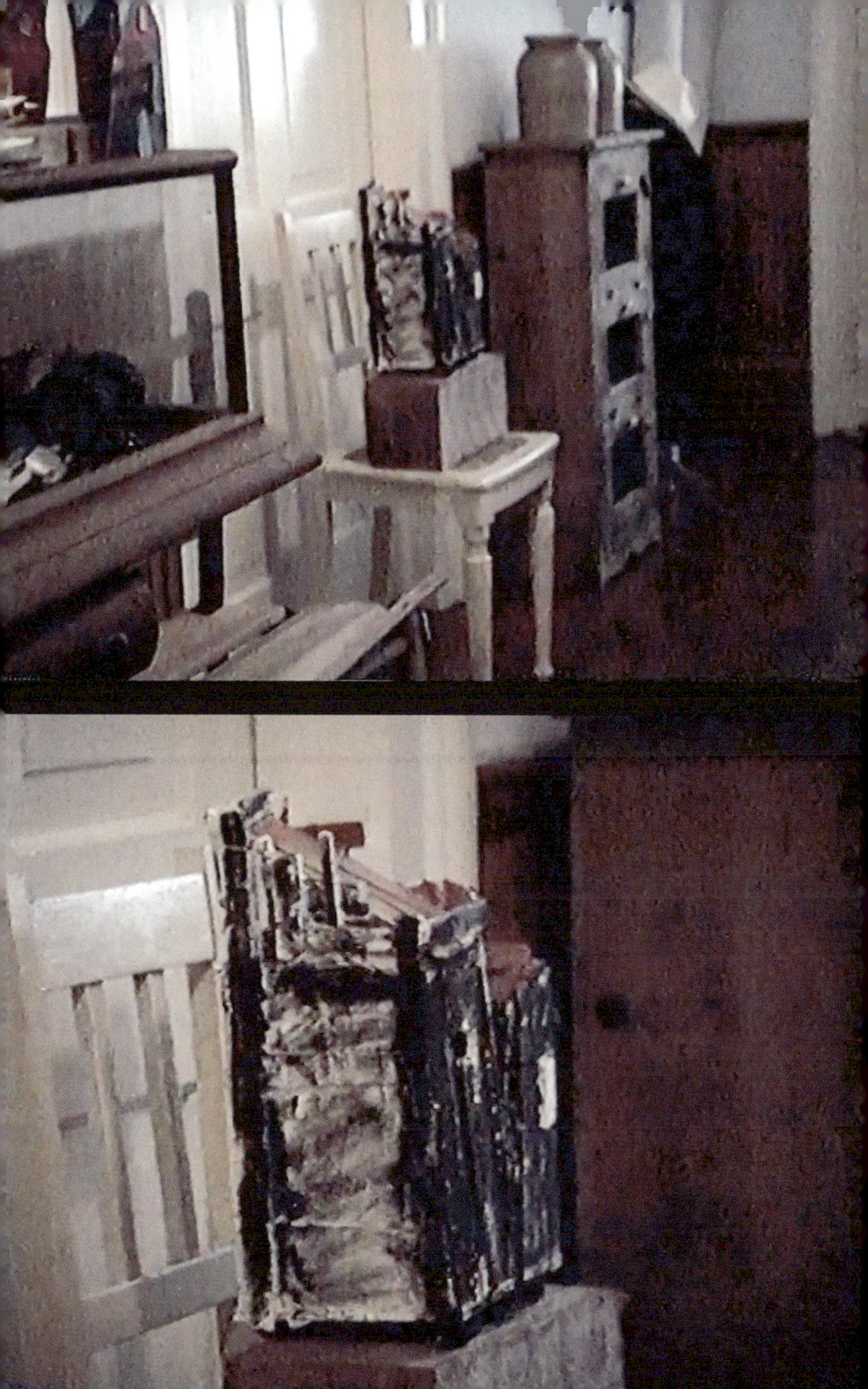

Scene 4

The Desk

00:16:22–00:45:41

We follow Beverly to an extra bedroom, where a mixed-media shack sculpture sits on a lazy Susan atop a large wooden work desk. Art supplies, found objects, and smaller works in process are scattered about the desk and room. Behind the desk, tall windows illuminate tropical houseplants, a treadmill, and an African mask on the wall. A decorative fireplace lined with ceramic jugs flanks the desk on one side. When Beverly and Judy eventually each take seats on opposite ends of the desk, they engage in a long conversation about Sunbury and Beverly's influences. We are introduced to each speaker's distinct storytelling style, including Beverly's highly animated facial expressions and hand gestures.

As the scene opens, the shack sculpture on the desk commands the room like a character, its silhouette jagged from the angled and roughly cut scrap metal, lumber, and sticks that constitute its form. Beverly walks to the sculpture and begins to rotate it, while Judy zooms in to frame Beverly's hand on her shack.

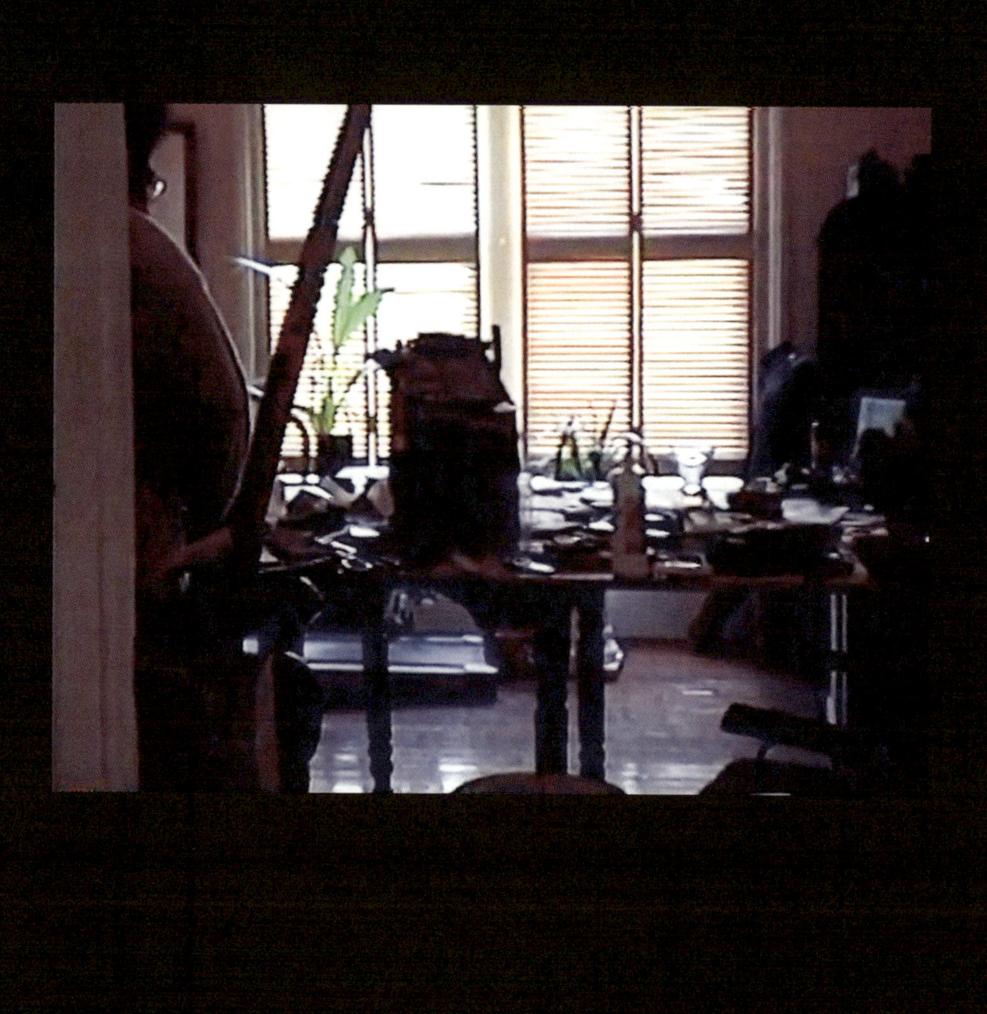

Beverly Buchanan: And the second one is this one, and I'm having problems with it because I... I can't seem to get past... [*rotates the sculpture on its lazy Susan*] It's like it's what I want, but I can't get past... I've *now* gotten past, but I had a hard time with this part of the roof, 'cause I wanted it to have a certain look, and it hadn't gotten that. And I started adding on a kitchen area... [*spins the sculpture*] And I hadn't done that before. And I'm using wood glue, *and* the glue-gun glue. 'Cause the wood glue really does make it hard and stable, so that if somebody hits against it, it won't fall apart. It will fall apart if you just use glue-gun stuff.

Judy McWillie: [*sighs*]

BB: But it's just now looking like I want it to look. The tape was just to hold it up until it set. [*stops touching the sculpture*] But, [Bernice Steinbaum] doesn't understand it. And I know she doesn't understand. It's like, I'll go, "Well, okay, I think I can put it outside and photograph it now." And then suddenly I go, "No, not yet." And that's *my* decision. And she, you know... I'm sorry! It's tough, tough, tough, you know?

JM: That's right. It's like one time I did an awful thing. I sold a painting to somebody, before it was finished.

BB: I know. I've done that. We've *allll* done that, okay. It's nothing to be ashamed of. It's, you got to do it!

JM: Well, I saw it two years later, and it sure as hell was unfinished! I mean, the time factor is what you kill.

BB: Yes! That's right.

JM: Yeah. God...

BB: I know. I do know.

[*Beverly walks to the windows and opens the shutters. Light pours in*]

BB: We can sit down any time you want to. I was just gonna open [the shutters] 'cause this is what got done with some of the grant money. Was to have that light come in. Wonderful light.

JM: You bet! [*chuckles*] God...

BB: Even just with one open, it's... incredible light. [*stands at the desk admiring the windows*]

JM: Sure is.

BB: This was my painting room. I used to paint in here, and then... [*walks back to the windows and opens the second set of shutters*] It takes so much to get things arranged the way you want.

JM: Oh it's terrible.

BB: This house was not a studio. This is a house! And so you have to make it... It's just marvelous light. It really is. It's like...

JM: Yeah it is. You got those tall windows like that.

BB: Yeah! It's just, it really is. I was...

[*As Beverly trails off in contemplation, Judy zooms in on a colorful folded paper work on the desk. It features an expressively drawn self-portrait, with line drawings of shacks in the background. As Judy zooms back out, Beverly stands by the desk, facing Judy and the camera*]

BB: [*moans*] No, we never did. We didn't find Sunbury. We found a Baptist church that I thought was Sunbury, but it wasn't. I didn't see any remnants of what I thought I might see.

JM: Well there's two churches. One is the Palmyra church, and it's off on a side, dirt road.[1]

BB: Uh-huh.

JM: And then the Sunbury church, when you take that exit off I-95—

BB: Yeah, that's what I did, yeah.

JM: Okay. You make a left, and you just keep going and going and going, you know, east. And then there's a fork in the road, and there's a little sign that says "Sunbury Missionary Baptist Church." Okay.

BB: [*sighs*] We didn't see that. We took a right instead of a left.

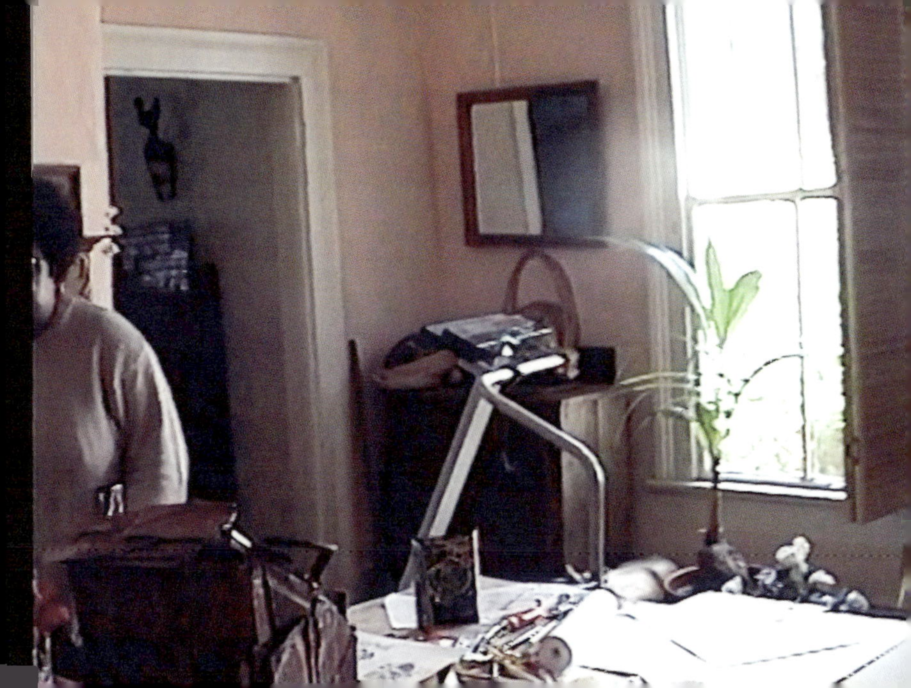

JM: Okay. You take that left fork. And the church is there, but almost everything is gone, except Rachel Bowens's handprint is still there.[2] And Reverend Hesikiah Allen, that beautiful diamond grave with that slash through it.

BB: I didn't see it. We didn't see it. These two guys...

JM: Well, man, and then, the historic site. See, I think it was back in '86. A local woman named Amanda Cox and Deacon Paige Stevens of the church organized a day, and we brought down [Robert Farris] Thompson.[3] And, uh, he gave first a talk in the church, and then a lecture in the afternoon. And, at that time, a lot of stuff had disappeared—

BB: Yeah. [*nodding and smiling*]

JM: But it started coming back. So the historic site has it. But there's nobody at the historic site that knows what they got.

BB: Uh-huh.

JM: And, um, there's *some* photographs. We put together all the photos we could find. So the church has an archive of those, and the historic site, so—

BB: We went to the *other* church—

JM: You went to the Palmyra church.

BB: —and talked to some of the people in that area. And what was disheartening for me was one young man... It was like, it wasn't quite a trailer park.

JM: Yes. A trailer behind a tiny shotgun house, do you remember that?

[*Beverly takes a seat at the desk, facing Judy*]

BB: I don't remember the house. I remember following this young man, and Patti was driving. I was just so excited to be in the area! I followed him... It was like a circular drive or something. And I stopped at this one house that had these incredible, uh, painted white rocks in a–in a straight line, and in a circle formation. And the house! [*exhales*]

I hesitated. I thought, "I wanna know what happened to this stuff, if I'm in the right area." So I walked on up to the house and knocked on the door, and didn't get a response. I stayed there, like, two seconds. And something said to me, "Go next door." Okay. And, I could see people next door. This young man walked in the house, so I started talking to him to ask him about these pieces. He had *no idea*. Not only did he not know what I was talking about, he could have cared less. And that attitude just, it-it-it shook me. Really, standing there talking to him, I could hardly... And he said, "I don't know anything about it. Maybe some of the women inside may know."

JM: Well there's a lot of changes that have gone on just in the last ten years.

BB: I'm sure, I'm sure.

JM: But next to the house, I mean, next to the church—and you'll see it next time you go—is a little house with a screened porch with green painted, uh, woodwork on the outside.

[*Judy walks in front of the camera as she takes a seat across from Beverly. The camera is stationary on a tripod, separate from her*]

BB: Okay. See, we were at the wrong church.

JM: And that was Eddie Bowens's house, who was Cyrus's cousin, and he died at age one hundred and one—

BB: Oh my lord. [*sighs*]

JM: —a couple years ago. And his wife Mary [Bowens] is still around, but that house is now being kept for some kind of, there's plans for a museum.[4]

BB: See, we were at the wrong church. He didn't know anything about it. And that just really got to me. [*places hand on heart*] But these two women came out, and I think one was his mother. I started asking, and she said, "I don't know. Whatever happened to all that stuff? I don't know if it got bulldozed over or not." And my heart sank. My heart sank.

JM: Okay. Well, as far as I know, first time I went there was in '83. And at that time, everything was freshly painted and *beautifully kept*. Um, the grave marker on Cyrus Bowens's grave himself was round railroad ties nailed to a cross with a dolphin skull on top. And it was all painted white, freshly painted.[5]

BB: Yes, yes. A lot of stuff was painted.

JM: And the dolphin skull you could see had had silver paint under it.

BB: Uh-huh, mm-hmm.

JM: And then Rachel Bowens's monuments, and a bunch of others. Boston was one family name. And, uh, the *ladder*. Just a-a pipe that was like a ladder, sticking up.[6] And, basically the only thing that's left is the upright concrete markers. And at the little church, the Palmyra church, there are two Cyrus Bowens head markers. And they've got green glass in 'em, and it's shaped like a triangle. And inside is typewritten Xs and Os.

BB: Okay, I think I did see that. I didn't take a picture of it. I took a picture of something, just a round object, unusual looking stuff. And I thought, "I'll-I'll show you that, that I photographed."

JM: See, it's so... Oh god, it's all so delicate because—

BB: Yes! *I'm sure it is.* God... [*sighs*]

JM: For example, one day, I mean, I-I heard that his daughter moved back. She's now deceased. And so, I found her house.

BB: Mm-hmm.

JM: Uh, she had had both legs amputated 'cause she had diabetes.

BB: Yeah...

JM: Her name was Eva Mae [Bowens]. And I got an interview with her.[7] Uh, but *just that week*, her brother had died.

BB: Yeah... [*sighs*]

JM: *Just that week.* And she had been to South Carolina. And the brother was the person that Cyrus passed it all down to. So he was gone by—

BB: I understand. [*nodding*]

JM: Okay. And so now Eva Mae's house is still there, but it's very run-down, and there's now a trailer behind it. But if you stand in front of it, and you see the trailer, immediately to the left, across the road, is where Cyrus Bowens's house was. And it's a dense woods. But *somewhere, under all that underbrush*, is a concrete slab with a footprint.

BB: Mm-hmm, okay. [*smiles*]

JM: *It's his.*

BB: Okay. Well, I think we *were there* in the area. I really do. And I just think we didn't know it, but we had this feeling. Because the funny thing that we did was to go down Old Sunbury Road, that even a logging truck probably hadn't been down in ten years! [*shakes head*]

JM: Yes, lord...

BB: And it was so scary, but exciting at the same time! There were two entrances to Old Sunbury Road. One, I think we made a left turn off the expressway and then saw it. Or else we made a right turn, and saw the sign and started down in my old pickup. [*points out the window*] Well, the road was kinda muddy, and it began to rain. And we got scared, because that kinda mud, I grew up with that kinda mud, and I thought, "Oooh no." At some point, we turned around—we hated to turn around—we turned around, and came back out. And then started down the road to the left again. And, um, we went through this old cemetery that I think part of it was the DAR or something like some—

JM: Yes, yes, yes.

BB: —very historic cemetery.

JM: Yes, uh-huh.

BB: Part of that cemetery, Old Sunbury Road came out into that. [*gestures perpendicular roads with hands*] The other end of Old Sunbury Road came out into that! So we said, after driving around that cemetery, "Let's go down that part of it, see if we can hook up with where we were." We never did, but we felt a little bit better, 'cause we were a little bit more sure of the truck, that we weren't gonna get stuck.

And, we could see a little truck down that road, and thought, "How did he get down there?" [*laughs*] You know, the mud! This wasn't a four-wheel-drive truck that I was in then, but it was bigger than [the truck] I saw. And this guy came out, and I swear I had seen him before. It was like I had seen him here in Athens or something. And he was in a little Toyota truck. He looked like someone I had seen in Athens. And I thought, "I wonder if that's a student?[8] I wonder if that's somebody who..." And he turned around! I thought, "Now if he turned around, I'm not gonna go down there 'cause that means..."

But we went back to the bed and breakfast in St. Marys, and these two idiots walked in there. [*impersonates man's voice*] "We-we were worried about you. You know, you two take off every day, and we don't know where you're going." We said, "Well, we're just driving. We just... [*shrugs shoulders*] We didn't come down here to hang out at a bed and breakfast, you know? We came out..." [*laughs*]

So these two guys were just so cute. I said, "We tried to find Sunbury." "THE OLD GRAVES!?" I said, "Yeah." "WE FOUND IT!" I said, "I'm gonna kill you and throw your body right out on the street in St. Mary." [*puts face into hand, chuckling*] I said, "I have been through this *all day*, roaming around, and you mean—" "OH YEAH! WE FOUND IT!" Patti and I wanted to kill them, you know? [*smiles*] It was hysterical! They found it. Or they found some remnants of it. They found what we didn't find.

JM: This was over the 4th, just last year?

BB: Yes! Last year. It was a year ago!

JM: Well, that sign I think is still there 'cause I was down there in April, and, uh, the sign is there. But the church is kind of modern. It's a cinder block church, and they got new doors on the front. But I swear to god, the first time I ever saw it, there was that wooden veneer on the door, right? Beverly, I swear to god, there was a lightning bolt cut out of the wood. Perfect lightning bolt! I've got pictures of it. Where the wood had been, uh, hit by lightning, *or something*, and-and had torn off, or blown off of it. It was—

BB: Yes.

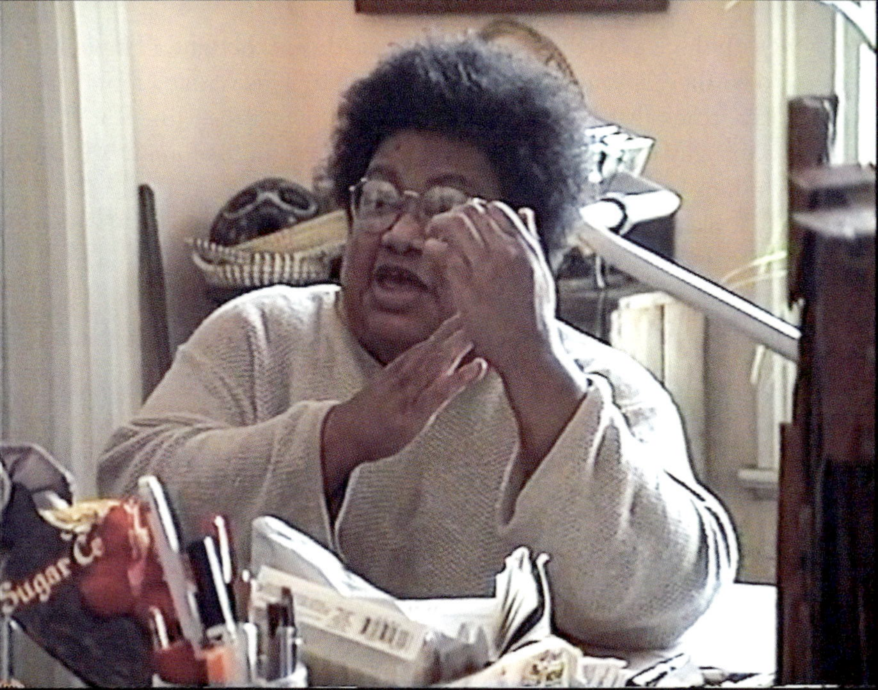

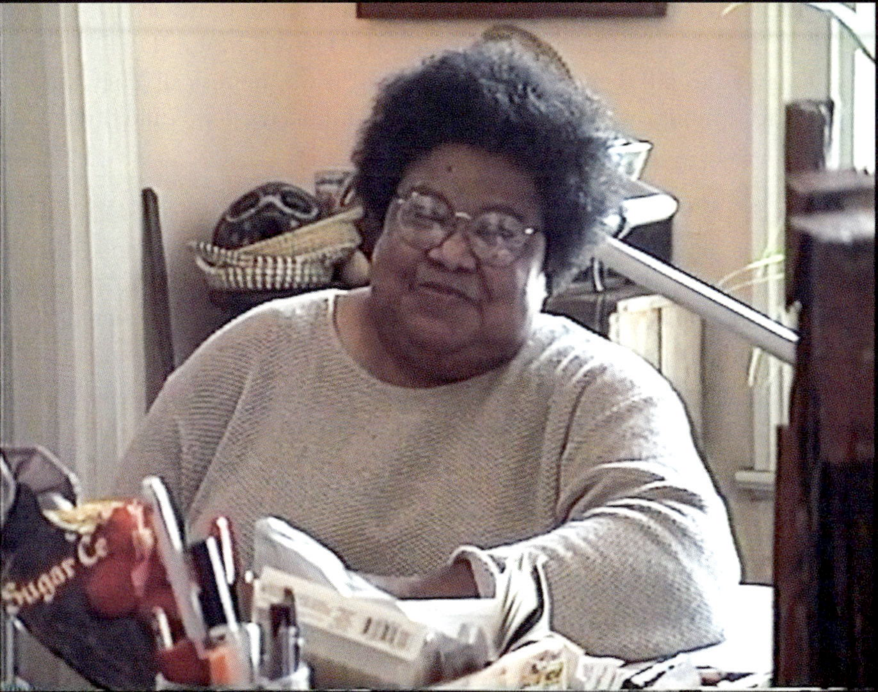

JM: And, uh, the person that knows about everything is Paige Stevens, and he's the deacon, one of the deacons, if he's still alive.

BB: We went to the wrong church! See, these guys, when we described to them, like I told you, where we were, they said, "No, no, no. You should have taken..." There was one road that we didn't take, and they said, "That's the road you should have taken." [*points forward*] And now I know what they meant.

JM: Well, sadly, except for the Rachel Bowens monument, and Reverend Allen, it's *mostly gone*. And, of course, the reason—

BB: That's alright. I just wanted to be in the area, you know? I just wanted, just to be there. I didn't think much was left at all. But *now* I know what road... We kept going up and down these little roads, and this one road that we did not... We should have turned, veered off to the right after it. I could see the road, and we just decided, "Well, there's nothing down that road."

JM: Yeah, yeah.

BB: And that was the road. [*smiles*] And [those two guys] went [down] that road, and that's how they...

JM: And when you go just past the church and the cemetery, there's a road that veers off to the right, a dirt road. And that's the road that [leads to] Cyrus's house, and where Eva Mae lived.

BB: We didn't do that. We were just so shook up about being on Old Sunbury Road, dirt road, when it started that heavy rain. And you know, the next day was when we started back to Athens, and came up [Georgia State Road] 16. And the rain really got very bad, and we weren't sure we were gonna make it to Macon. Got to Macon, and one old lady walked into the restaurant and recognized me, I think, and just said, [*impersonates high-pitched tone*] "Are you...?" She said she was gonna go to the beach in Florida. It was raining so bad, she decided not to go. And I said, "Oh, I think you ought to go." She said, "Well, are you visiting now? You're not here anymore." I said, "No, ma'am. I'm in Athens."

JM: My god, she remembered you from Macon.

BB: Oh yeah! She said, "Well, um, are you gonna spend the night?" And I said, "No, I think we're gonna go on to Athens." That's when she told us that the bridge at High Falls is out. And Patricia and I stood up because her parents live in that area. I thought, "You're joking," and the both of us stood right that minute. And I said, "No, I think we better go." She said, "Well, go on!" That was wonderful.

[*Laughter*]

And I think we must have been the last people to cross the Ocmulgee River before they closed off that bridge.[9] If we spent the night, we wouldn't have been able to get out of Macon!

JM: God, that was those floods over there![10]

BB: Right! I called Mary [Porter]. [*points out the window*] Mary was next door, and I called her, and asked what the situation was in Athens. And she said, "Well, we've got some rain, but it's not flooding." I said, "Well, I hope to see you maybe in two hours if we can get over the Ocmulgee River." And we did. We were probably the last—I'm serious. The-the water was up. I had never seen the river that high. It was at the level of the bridge when we crossed it. [*gestures water level*] And that told me right then, I thought, "Oooh, we just made it out of here," you know?

JM: Yeah...

BB: So it was a year ago.

JM: Wow. Yeah, it's pretty, uh, it's pretty un... I don't know what you call it down in there, you know? There's a family named the Blue family, that lives actually farther toward Brunswick. And they're ten miles down one of those dirt roads, but there's a cemetery *in their backyard*. All their people are buried there.

BB: Are buried, yeah. [*nods*]

JM: And, uh, it's-it's... There's just a lot to see, of the grave things, everywhere, in that area.[11] But it has *really* changed, and I-I don't know if—

BB: Yes, I bet. You wouldn't wanna see it really.

JM: [*Judy crosses in front of the camera*] Yeah. I-I don't know if Deacon Paige Stevens... I think he's still around there 'cause his house was still, you know, looked like somebody was living in it, but I didn't stop this last trip. And he knows the *whole* thing. And the Bowens family were *all* deacons of the church. And the funny thing is the cornerstone of the church is a Masonic symbol. Like, maybe it doubled as a lodge or something. And with the, uh, the names of the families. Eddie Bowens was the last, and, uh... 'Cause he died, actually, I think after Eva Mae. No, no, she died after Eddie. That's right.

BB: There's a lot of stuff that's, um, that is rapidly being lost. I mean, Prudence Lopp is a real estate appraiser, and so I get to ride with her as she's going around this area. So I get to see *a lot of stuff that's so incredible.* And it's nice because I can look at it, sketch it, or photograph it.[12] And she's doing the driving, and that's helpful for me. But there's *so much* that has influenced my work, you know? [*gestures toward the shack sculpture on the desk*] I'm adding on things that didn't exist! I'm adding on, not that they didn't exist before, but I'm paying more attention to extra rooms and extra...

JM: Mm-hmm.

BB: [*points to the shack sculpture*] Like, this little piece was started in 1989. And I'm adding onto it, and-but that's the way people do houses!

JM: Yes!

BB: [*touches the fireplace*] This house was built almost a hundred years ago, and it's been added onto. So that is not an unusual situation. I'm just now catching up in sculpture with what's been done!

JM: [*laughs*]

BB: I mean, by adding on one or two, or adding on a room here. [*points to the sculpture*] I'm late doing that, you know? [*laughs*]

JM: You know, Mary Lou Furcron told me that the house she lived in was an old kitchen.

BB: Oh, I'll bet!

JM: She said it was, originally, a smokehouse kitchen.

BB: Yes, I bet. 'Cause that was so common to have the kitchen separate from the house, and, um...

JM: But, uh, I have to tell you. That *House and Home* show was the first time I saw *all your work* together, and...

BB: And even that's limited.

JM: Yeah. But it, it *did* something, you know... I can't say, I mean, you can't say that you *understand* an artist's work, but the *dimension* of what you've done, in that show, comes through.

BB: Let me tell you why it surprised me. Now, the show that's *just my* work will be here next year in Brenau.

JM: Okay.

BB: The sixteen-year retrospective, uh, survey.[13] And that includes... [*points toward the backyard*] You saw one or two of the *Blue Stones* in the back out there?

JM: Yeah.

BB: Okay. Well, those I made in Macon, and that material was left over from... There are... sixteen stones? [*laughs*] In Florida, in Miami, at the Earlington Heights Metrorail Station in Miami.[14]

JM: Is that what you put together at Jekyll Island?

BB: No. No. The piece in Miami is that color, that blue.

JM: Okay, mm-hmm.

BB: And it's white Portland cement mixed with a blue dye, blue pigment.

JM: Mm-hmm.

BB: The piece down there [near Jekyll Island] is, uh, still in the marsh. In fact, I'm gonna show you photos that I took last year of that piece. I mean, it looks great. It really does. [*smiles*] But this show that's coming to Brenau has everything, has a lot of aspects that are not in the *House and Home* show. That almost didn't happen because, uh, Jock Reynolds had never seen... Some of the photos that are in this show, he didn't know existed.

JM: That were in the *House and Home* show.

BB: Right. He didn't know existed. He was just exposed to the photos that the gallery had. And that was basically Mary Lou Furcron at her house. So he just saw one or two... [*shrugs*] He saw, I think, Leon and his dogs.[15]

JM: That reminds me. There's a woman from *Life* magazine that's gonna call you.

BB: Okay.

JM: Uh, she called me two weeks ago, something about swept yards. And I told her, uh, that you had the best photographs.

BB: Of Mary Lou?

JM: Of anybody. No, just of anybody.

BB: [*laughs*] Oh dear lord...

JM: And so, uh, I told her she could see them at Bernice's, but she said, "I'll call her after the fourth when I get back from vacation."

BB: Okay. Bernice doesn't have these photos.

JM: She doesn't?

BB: No. I have them, or Photo Express.[16] Between Photo Express and me, we... But Jock had not seen a lot of them. Sharon [Sanderson] was keeping all the negatives and stuff, helping me keep stuff together. And I said, "Go out to Sharon, and let her look for the negatives of what Bernice had." That's what it was.

JM: Okay.

BB: And so when he went out there, Sharon said to him, "Let me show you some of her other photos that she doesn't show anybody. She doesn't care if nobody sees them. She just takes these for herself." And he said, "Alright." He said he could not believe it! Sharon told me that he said, "I don't believe I'm seeing all this stuff. Why didn't—who? No one has ever seen..." Sharon said, "No, she didn't show 'em to anybody." And so, from that, he had her print up—She said she must have made one hundred prints of different things to send him. And from that, he selected [prints] for [the exhibition], you know?

And, of course, he had to keep in mind he had already selected Christenberry's work, and Max Belcher. So he had to kinda put in extra things of mine that he hadn't planned to in the first place, 'cause he hadn't seen them! You know? So he didn't know about that. And the gallery didn't have that because they weren't really keen on photographs. They were concentrating on my sculpture and the drawings.

But when I saw this show up in Andover, I was speechless because of the relationship that the three of us had without knowing it. [*forms a negative space between hands*] I'd only seen, I'd seen a few of Christenberry's works, 'cause Lucinda [Bunnen] had some of his work. But mostly in catalogs. And the three of us together [Max Belcher, William Christenberry, and I], we met there for the first time. We'd never met each other. The three of us could not put into words what we were looking at. We just kinda walked around and looked around, looked at each other's work, and just shook our heads. Because the *enormity of the impact* of it really kinda got to us.

JM: That's right.

BB: That doesn't happen to me in my shows. It really doesn't. It's like I've seen this work now, but I *never* see all my work together. It's like here's this one piece, there's one in the kitchen. [*points to different sculptures within and beyond the frame of the camera*] The next time I see these, this may be in one show, and the other one may be in another show.

JM: Exactly.

BB: You know, it's like–it's like having ten children, and they all go different places. And unless you have a reunion, you don't get to see them all together! You know? [*laughs*]

JM: That's right. That's right. But, the uh... god, I mean there's so many things on my mind from that show. But the main thing for me was that when I looked at your photos and at the shacks, they were all about *behavior*. They were all about *the people*.

BB: Yeah. [*nods*]

JM: *The people's touch, on everything.*

BB: That's right.

JM: Behavior. The stacked stones, for example.

BB: Yeah.

JM: The foundations.[17]

BB: [*smiles*] Yeah. I've done that a *long* time. I did that in New York, and I probably didn't know what I was doing, but I did that and made stacks. I stacked stones in New York.[18] I did. [*gestures verticality with hands and laughs*] And it got to people. People *felt something* that wasn't New York, but they didn't know what it was. They said, "This is not New York, but it's, it really gets to me. I can't stop looking at it."

JM: Right. And the strange thing, this is hard to put into words.

BB: Yeah, it's hard! It's hard.

JM: Uh, okay. Whenever you mention something like modernism and all that, minimalism, people think that you're using it to bolster, you know, to boost vernacular art or something. I don't mean it in that sense. What I'm trying to get at is that, for me, you know... What's his name? Richard Serra, Carl Andre.

BB: Mm-hmm.

JM: Those people. They seem to me they were screwing around with the system. You know, "If I can take, uh, cheap bricks into a London museum and somebody put[s] on precious gloves to carry 'em, then I'm doing something with the system." But, I couldn't get any further than that with that art. Now, when you see stacked stones in the photo, and then *your* sculpture, and it's all related to, uh, *a shared experience*.

BB: Mm-hmm.

JM: *That's the difference*.

BB: Yeah. Yeah. [*nodding*]

JM: And that's why... I think that the similarities—you know, the fancy term they use is "the syncretisms"—might be what some of the people in New York are relating to.[19] You know, they're looking at that and they're saying, "Well, god, I mean, how do I relate to this? Is it like minimal sculpture? Or is it, you know, through some art lens? Some art historical lens?" But then, when you see the photos, and all these things that you looked at that led to the stuff you *did*.

BB: Mm-hmm, yeah.

JM: Or things you found, that you had *already done*.

BB: Yeah!

JM: That you had done in the *abstract*, and then went out and *found*!

BB: Yeah, that's right.

JM: That's it!

BB: That's right. That was scary. That was scary. [*smiles*] It was scary. And then I got over being scared, because I started to think about how I, what I was feeling at the time. For example, when I first started making stacked stone pieces, or, they weren't stacked. They were really meant to be, um, separate. The reason that I started cementing them together was... [*sighs*] an awful thing to have to admit, but it was fear of having things stolen. In other words, galleries said, "We can't show these individually this size because someone could walk in and pick up one of these, and put it in their pocket and walk out. You're gonna have to find some way to..." And so I had to try to find some way to do that, and also maintain the integrity of what I was trying to do.

JM: Mm-hmm.

BB: But my first stone pieces were called "frustula," fragments.[20] And I remember taking some small pieces to a park in New Jersey, and sitting them on other stones, and photographing them on top of other stones. And I would change the arrangement of them, and all that kinda thing. And then people would go to different places, take photos of stones, and come back and say, "Look, this looks like your work."

JM: Yeah.

BB: The *really strange* thing that happened with the stones was a friend of mine, Arden Scott, went to Scotland, and came back and said, "I wanna show you some photos I took of some stone pieces in Scotland." No, no! "Some photos of some things that I've shot." That's all she said! And so I sat, and she showed me these. And my reaction was, "Have you been in my studio?" [*frowns*] She came to [my studio in] Macon, and played the pipes in Macon. And, you know, you could hear them all up and down Cherry Street. Bagpipes inside is not the thing to do. [*smiles*]

I said, "Now, see, that piece is by my window. When did you shoot that?" She didn't say anything. She must have shown, like, twenty-five slides. About every other piece that she showed, I would relate to it. *It was like I was a part of that.* And she shut off the projector and said, "Every one of these pieces is in Scotland." [*humorously exacerbated*] I said, "What? It's not possible!" She said, "My family and I were just floored, 'cause I had photos of *your* work in *your* studio, and we were looking at stones that look like you made them right here!" I said, "I-I-I," I was speechless.

JM: They were just stacked—?

BB: Yeah. I was just absolutely speechless. And then the same thing about "black walls." That I did these paintings and called them *Black Walls*, and then I *saw* black walls.[21]

JM: Exactly.

BB: Very scary kind of stuff. But I think it was like, looking at Serra's work, looking at other people's, you had to have a system. Intellectually, you had to have *an idea* for things, which was okay. And so, I understand what their idea was about. I was just not prepared for the fact that *my idea*... It wasn't that I disagreed with their idea. It was that I had to find my own relationship to what I was, what I thought I wanted to do. And it wasn't working. And it didn't work until I came South. Well, it began a little bit in New Jersey. I just didn't-couldn't call it something. [*smiles, wide-eyed*] But I could call it something once I got back home. Back home.

[*As Beverly gestures with excitement, the shack sculpture in the foreground rustles*]

JM: 'Cause you started making them—?

BB: 'Cause I started making them up in New Jersey!

JM: And New York?

BB: Yeah, right! It was just that there was nothing up there that looked like that. But here, there are things that *feel* like that. [*opens arms outward*] So I went from just ideas to-to ideas *and* feelings. Ideas and feelings. I think that was the connecting factor.

JM: But it's a–it's a reversal of a process, and I think this means something. A lot of people go out and say, "This looks like art." But you make art, and you say, "I don't know what this is, but I'm gonna *find it out there*."

BB: Or I'm gonna just do it.

JM: "I'm gonna find it in the world."

BB: Yeah.

JM: Okay. And it's like... It works. Works that way.

BB: Well, it was... I wasn't unhappy doing it. It's just that I didn't, I couldn't put a label on it. I couldn't put, um, an art world label on it. I just called them "fragments." I called every one of them I did "fragments."

JM: So those were the first things you did when you were up there?

BB: Yeah. [*smiles*]

JM: God... But what about the pieces that were in the catalog? Were those the ones on Jekyll Island? Those are the ones that...

BB: Well, they're in the marsh between Jekyll and St. Simons.[22]

JM: Yeah.

BB: I got to go to the back here and—

JM: Okay, alright. Let me turn this off.

[*Beverly abruptly rises from the desk, and walks out of the room. Judy follows suit, rising from her seated position into the camera frame. She walks in front of the camera, before the video cuts out*]

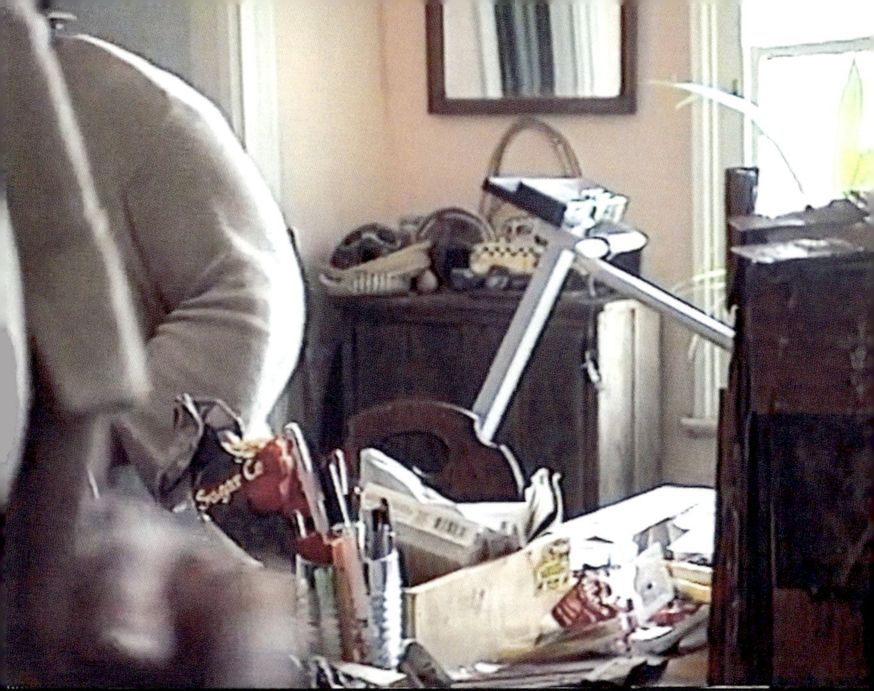

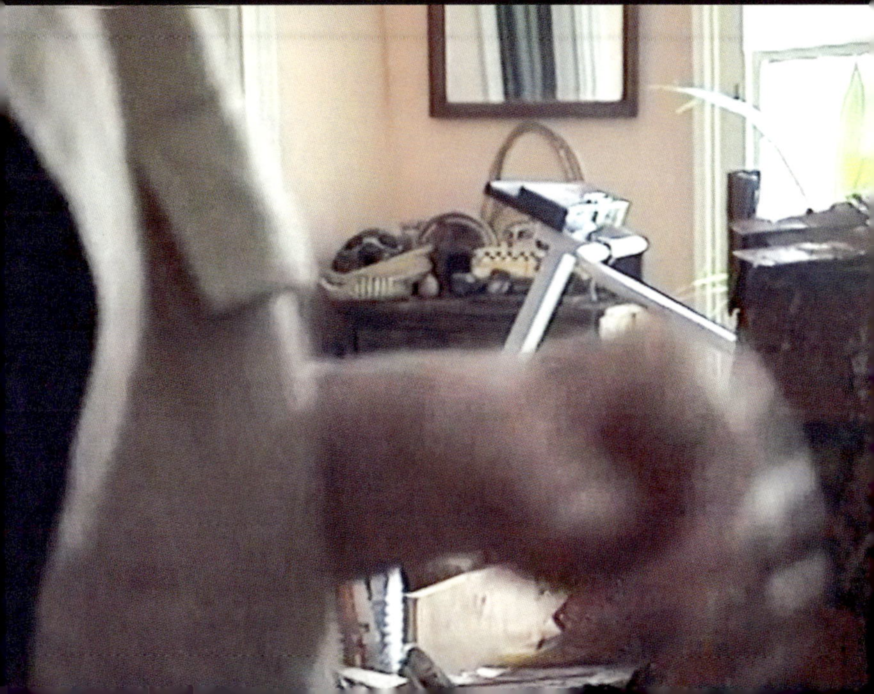

Scene 5

The Studio

00:45:42–00:52:46

Beverly and Judy have moved to the main studio room, with its large windows facing the garden. Inside the studio, both artists are on their feet moving about throughout the scene. Beverly directs their movement and conversation as she guides Judy through a show-and-tell of sculptures and photographs. Judy's camera is frequently off-kilter as she follows Beverly's lead.

The scene begins mid-conversation, facing the plexiglass shack sculpture once again. Beverly touches it as she discusses the significance of its transparency. A distinctive assemblage of plexiglass, diagonal wooden strips, scrap metal, and found objects, the sculpture's transparent walls filter the light from the studio windows.

Beverly Buchanan: [*spins the plexiglass shack sculpture*] After the flood, seeing people walk down the highway. We saw this one lady with one suitcase, and a dress swung over her shoulder, and that was *all she had*. And we knew. It was like, "Oh lord." [*places head into hand*] It was like, this could be your rel[ative], your next-door neighbor, you know? And then walking by, seeing pieces, seeing houses. You could see money. You could see parts of floors. You could see... There's a knife in here, and-and there's a little stove in here somewhere. Their possessions were *there*! In the middle of *nothing*! With *no shell* around them.

Judy McWillie: You mean the houses had fallen in? 'Cause the water had, uh...?

BB: And the winds had blown away the exterior walls![1] [*points to the sculpture's transparent walls*] And floods had just kind of fossilized things, *right in their spot*. Tables, chairs, were right where people left them. [*with a downcast expression*] You know? And so this was sort of a response to that. It's like I wanted you to be able to *see inside*. There's a sewing machine in here. It was just, it just really got to me. It got to everybody. It really did.

[*As Judy zooms into the shack sculpture's doorway, Beverly walks to the coffee table and picks up a pile of eight-by-ten-inch color photographs. She holds up a photograph of her 1981 sculpture* Marsh Ruins *to show Judy. In the image, two large gray lumpen mounds peak out through marsh grass, blue water behind them*]

This is the piece that's down there between Jekyll and St. Simons.

JM: There you go. That's the one.

BB: That's the tabby piece.[2]

[*Beverly picks up another stack of large color photographs, removes them from their sleeve, and begins flipping through them*]

And this is what I saw in, uh, Brunswick last year. So I took some photos... Oooh yeah. I think this was, this was one of the trees that I just... [*sighs, holds up a photograph of a live oak tree draped in Spanish moss towering over a parking lot, with 1990s-era cars around its trunk*]

JM: Mm-hmm.

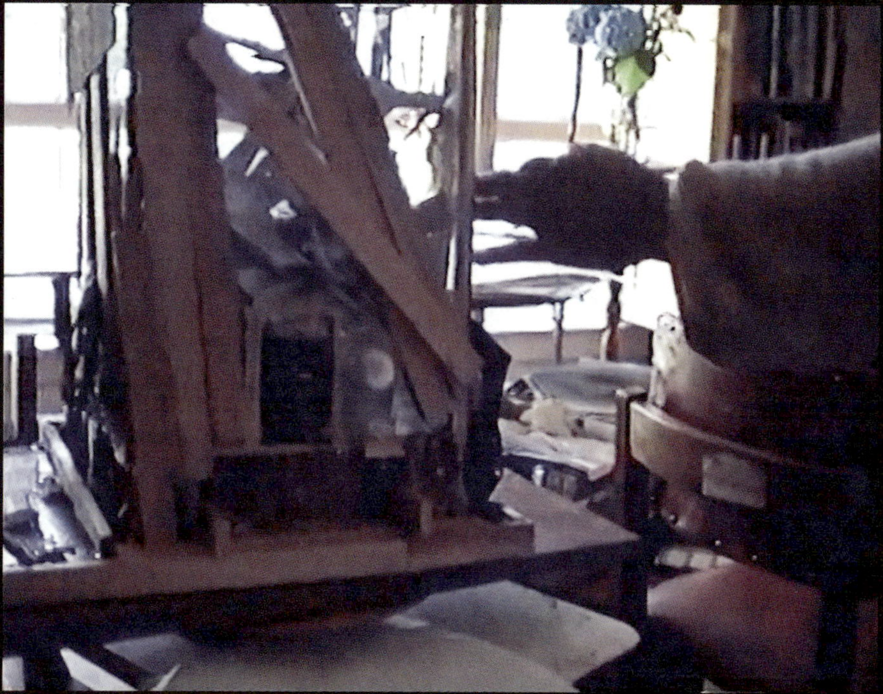

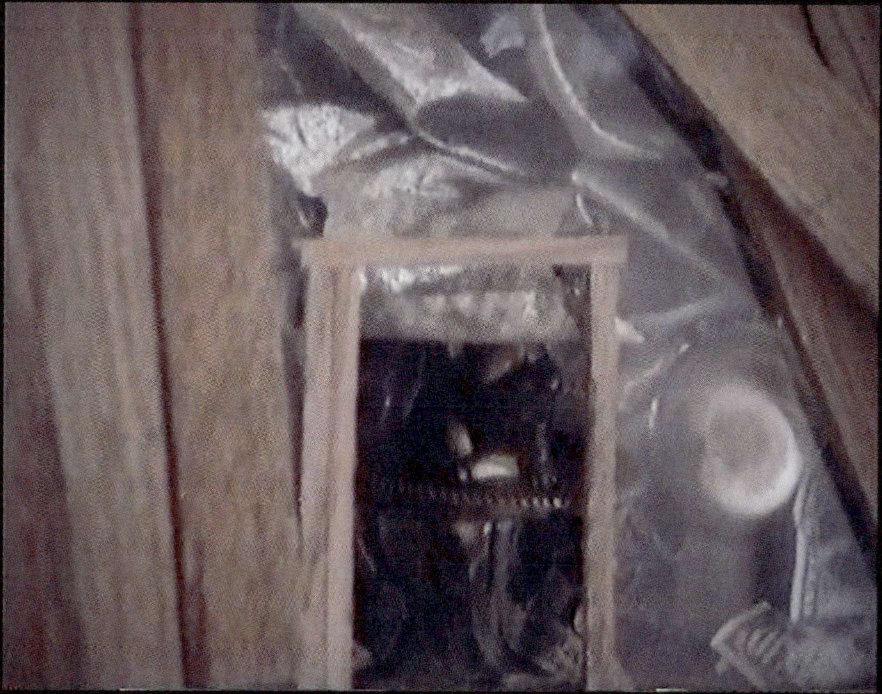

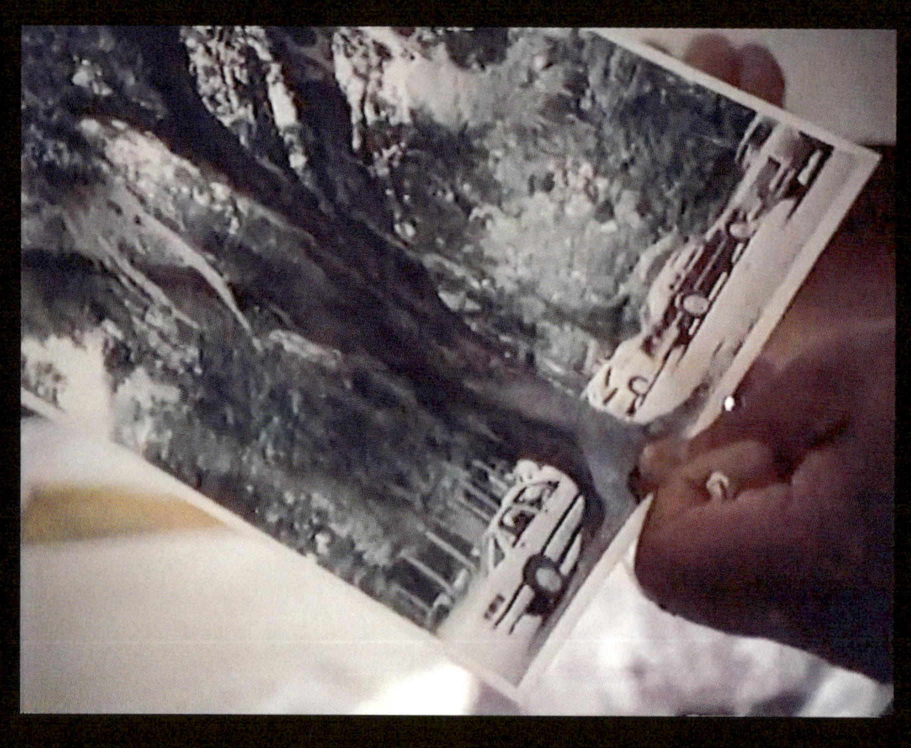

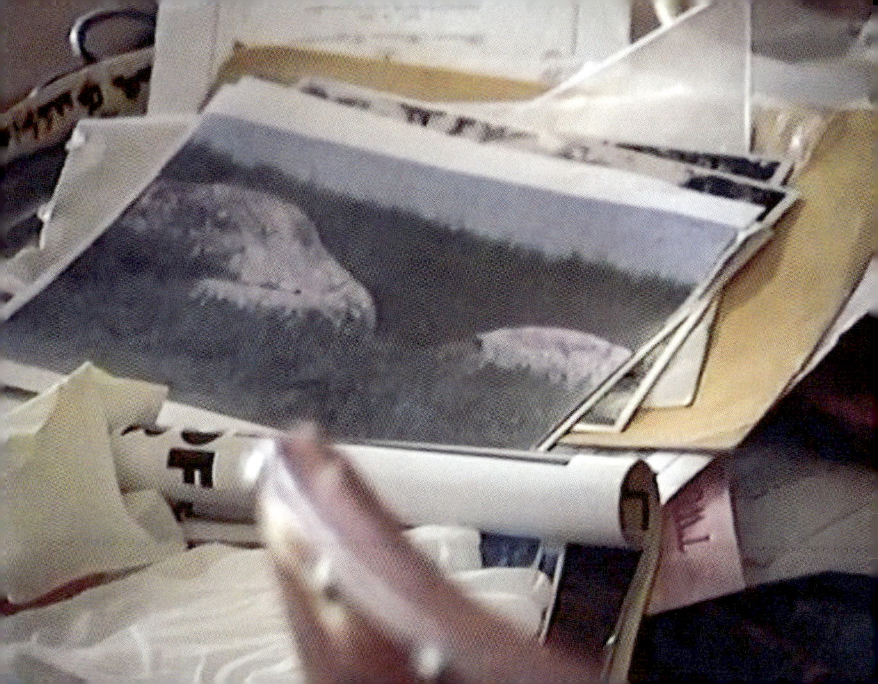

BB: [*continues to flip through photographs*] What else can I show you? Oh, this is also [the] coast. "Does somebody have a green house?" Well, yes! Somebody has a green house! [*laughs*]

JM: It, it's still amazing to me that you started making art in New York, and then it led you, as it were, home.

BB: Yeah, it's amazing to me too. [*places the stack of photographs down*] It really is! [*cackles*] It's amazing to me too.

JM: [*laughs*] I mean, god...

BB: Yeah, I got started up outdoors in the Bronx. First outdoor show was, uh, '60, '66, I think. And one of the people that I exhibited with was the late Hannelore Baron. And, a bunch of us later got in galleries, and we would see each other. And that was just really strange. It really was. 'Cause we just never expected that. But we got started outdoors, on a church fence! [*laughs, continues looking through photographs piled on the coffee table*]

JM: On a church fence?

BB: Yes!

JM: In Brooklyn?

BB: In the Bronx.

JM: In the Bronx.

[*Beverly pulls out a photograph and holds it out in front of herself, displaying it for Judy. It's hard to make out exactly, with long rectangular boxlike forms and a smaller irregular form jutting out from the grass*]

BB: This is what I saw at... That was the only thing that was near that church at Sun—

JM: At Sunbury, yeah.

BB: I didn't know what that was.

JM: Oh! Now, that's it! *That's* the graveyard, yes.

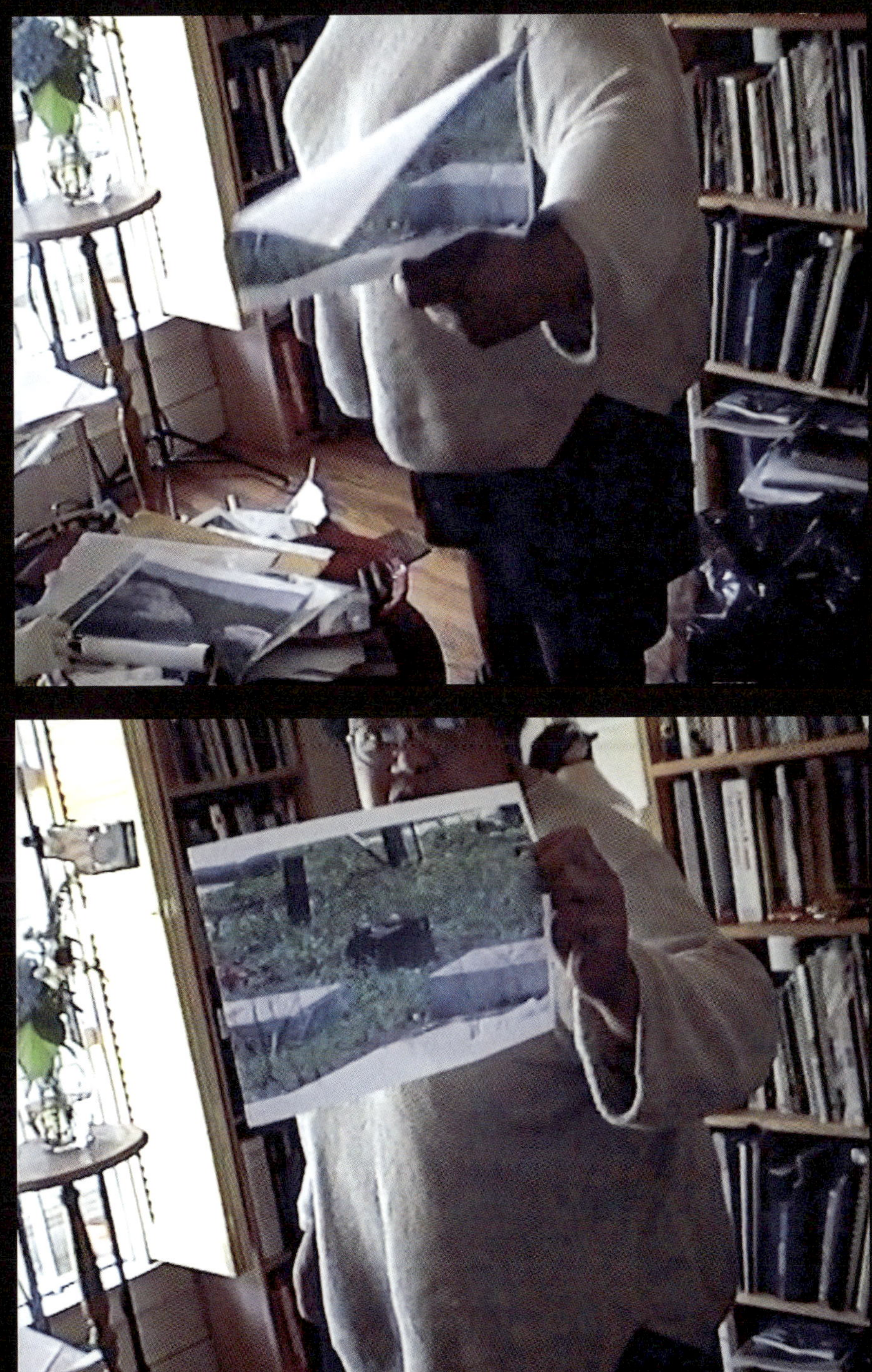

BB: You're joking! You're joking!

JM: No, no. Let me tell you about that.

BB: [*sighs*] Judy! Oooh Judy!

JM: That is *the base* of something that, as far as I know, has never—I've never been able to turn up a photograph of it. But in addition to those bird, serpent, human wooden things that you see reproduced everywhere, he made a *little man*.

BB: I didn't see them.

JM: No, no. Those were stolen in the 1950s. But-but Eva Mae Bowens told me that *besides* that, he had made this kind of realistic sculpture of a *little man*, and that's who stood on *that base*.[3] I've never even seen a picture of that little man.

BB: [*sighs*] Oh, wait 'til you see this. [*places the photographs down, walks to the hallway*] Well, wait a minute. [*from the hallway*] But I wanted to show you—the facility is right here! You need to see back here, 'cause back here is where my bed is, and where the other kitchen...

JM: [*laughs*] Should I follow you back there, or should I wait?

BB: Well, let me go use the restroom.

JM: Okay. [*laughs*]

[*While Beverly's away, Judy records more details inside the studio. Her handheld camera peers inside the plexiglass shack sculpture, filled with various metal scraps*]

BB: [*shouting from the hallway*] Those metal pieces are what I cut... Those figures are what I've cut out recently from metal plates that Charles Radcliffe brought me. Some of these old ceiling tiles, ceiling metal things.

[*Judy films the view out the window, slowly zooming into a butterfly flying amongst the blooming foliage and blue glass bottles of a bottle tree in the backyard*]

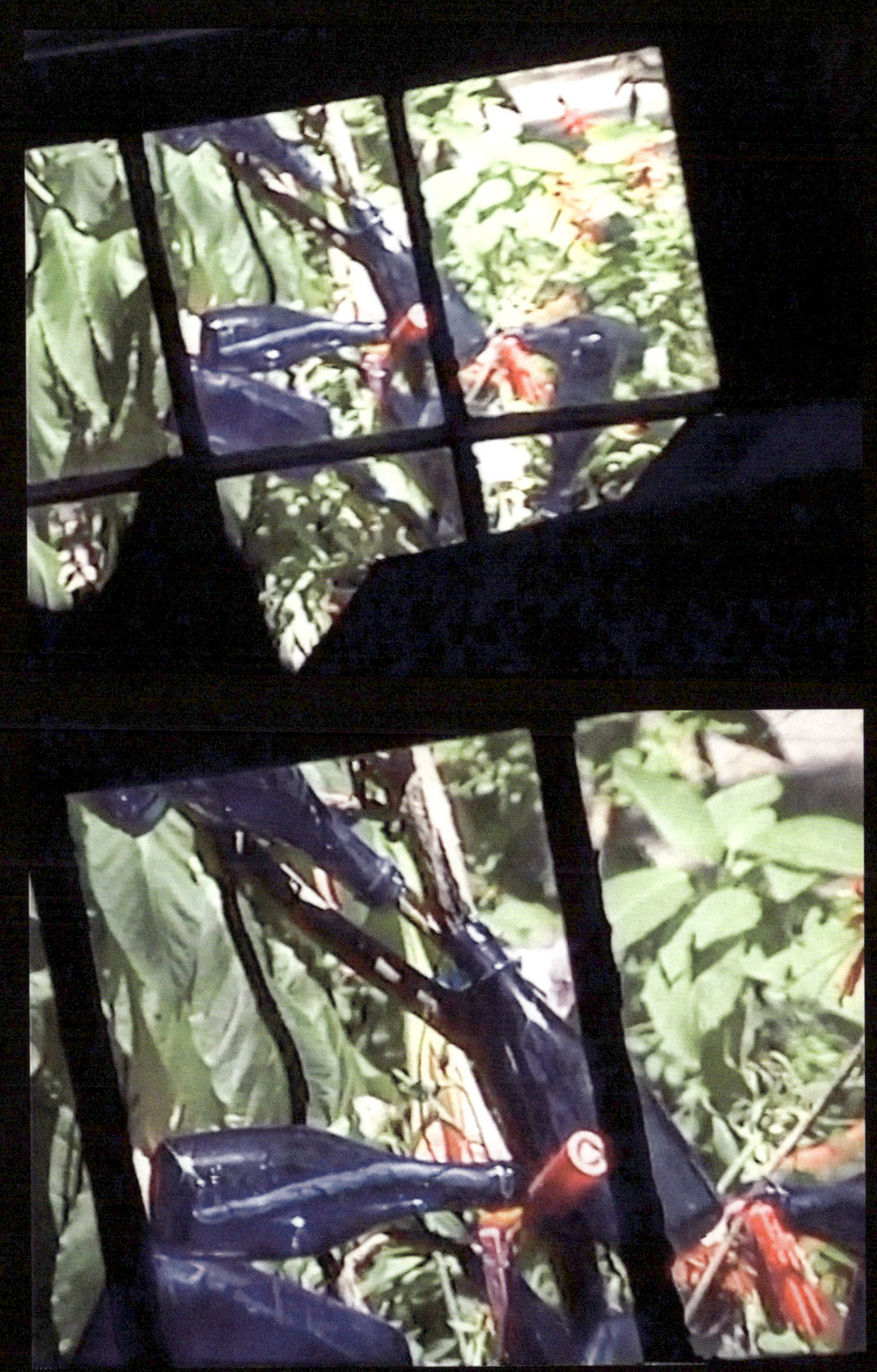

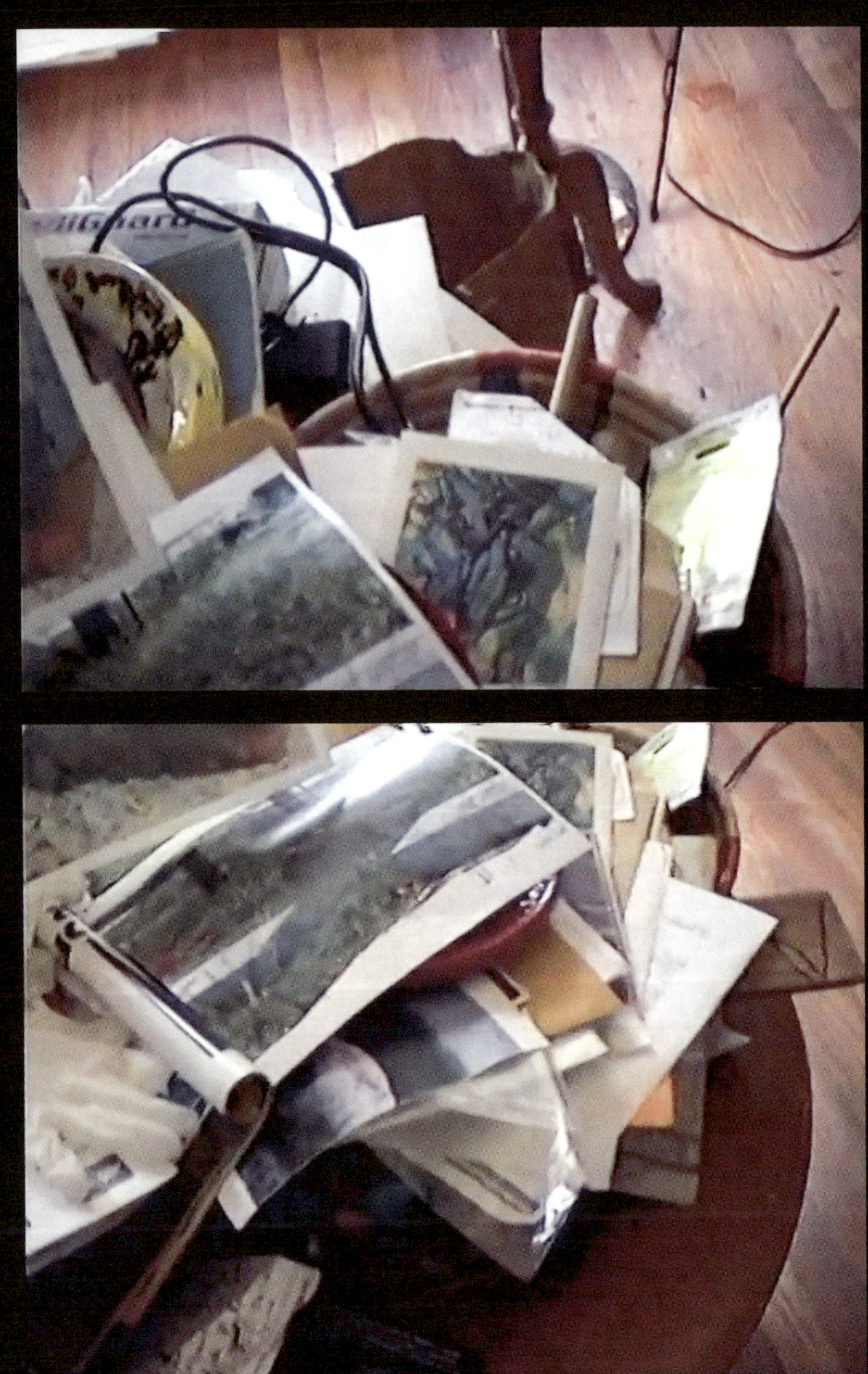

[*Beverly returns to the studio, and continues to show Judy her large color photographs, placing them onto the coffee table*]

BB: Oh, there were things I was trying to drag out to show you, but I'm overwhelming you all at once! This was when, this was what one of those stones are. And this was the last day of casting down in Macon, before the stones had to be taken down to Florida.

"Do you have anything left over in there?" "Yes, ma'am." I said, "How much?!" He said, "About half a yard." So I said, "You're kidding! Meet me back at your concrete station. Before you wash your truck out, let me see if I can find some *container*! For the rest of this stuff." [*laughs*] So I found these boxes! And so I cast, you know, he backed his truck up, and we poured the... So that's how those, that's how I managed to save...

[*Judy crops in on the photograph, which shows Beverly in the process of removing cardboard molds, revealing freshly cast cement boxlike forms tinted blue*]

JM: That's the blue pigment? 1986?

BB: Yeah! And that's something good about having a data bank on your camera. I borrowed that camera, so whoever took the picture had a data bank to-to, um...

[*Beverly's voice trails out, and the video suddenly fades to black, then starts again. Judy adjusts the camera, and as she pans across the studio to face Beverly, she images the piled-up materials stacked upon the coffee table. Beverly stands at her bookshelf, taking down a red book, the catalog for her sixteen-year survey exhibition* Shack Works]

BB: Did I give you one of these? The catalog for the...

JM: Oh, no, thank you!

BB: Well, see, I had been walking around with it, and so when I saw you that day over at Continuing Education, I immediately went, [*taps pockets as though looking for something*] I got one of these for Judy.

JM: Aww, thanks.

BB: Yeah, you need this. Oh, Judy, I swear I thought you had that! [*walks to the opposite bookshelf, thumbs through books*] Did you get a *House and Home* catalog?[4]

JM: Oh yeah, you bet!

BB: I'm sorry, you shouldn't have had to buy that.

JM: That's okay. I wanted... [*laughs*] It's gotten all dog-eared.

[*Beverly reaches up the bookshelf, and pulls out a green magazine with big lettering that reads "MS. PORNOGRAPHY"*]

BB: This was the *Ms.* magazine.

JM: [*cracks up*] Oh, I've got that. You must have had a good time with that!

[*Laughter*]

BB: Ooooh! "She's doing pornography now!" "No I'm not! This was just a special issue!" Ahhh... [*rolls eyes, places the magazine back on the bookshelf*]

JM: [*laughs*] Well, at least they didn't have to go past the first page if they didn't want to.

BB: Ahhh, it was just...

[*Sighing, Beverly pulls out a stack of thin, self-published artist booklets. They're made with eight-and-a-half-by-eleven paper printed with photographs, and bound with black spines and clear plastic covers*]

BB: This is what you don't get to see from the show that is coming to Columbia [South Carolina] soon, that show in the red [*Shack Works*] book. And I put together little booklets like this just to kinda, you know, just to say, "This is what kind of stuff I've been doing."[5]

JM: Mm-hmm. But the Brenau show is gonna be a whole survey, then?

BB: Yes. And the Brenau show has catalogs like this in it, that you *can't see*! They won't let you look at 'em! They won't let you open the case and look at them.

[*Beverly places the booklets back on the bookshelf, and turns toward the hallway*]

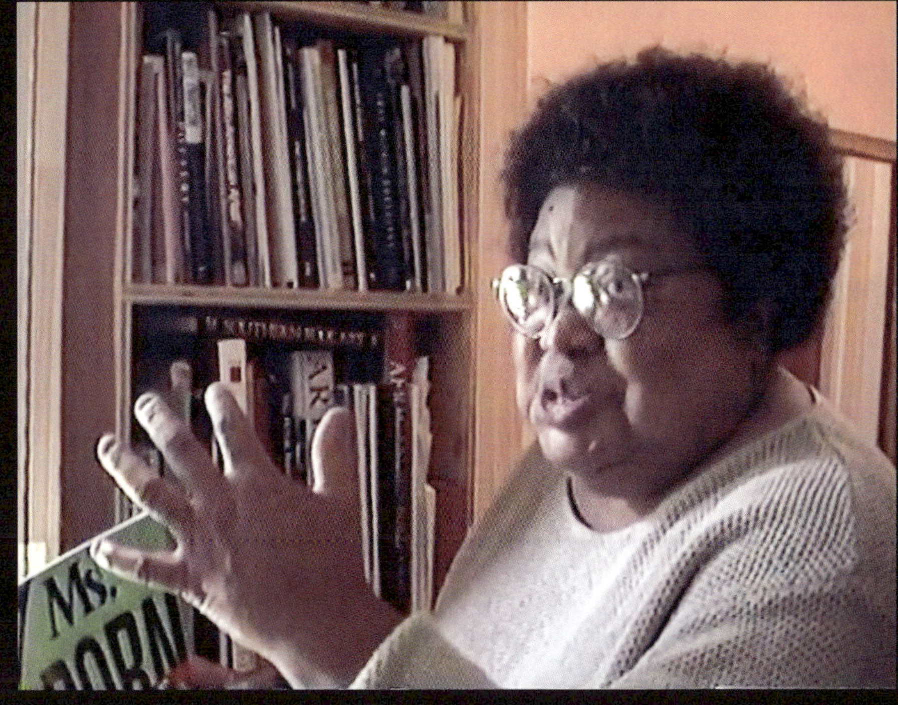
Ms.

Scene 6
Wandering

00:52:47–01:00:09

Exiting the studio, Beverly leads Judy down a hallway through another section of the house. The two converse as they wander from room to room, making their way to the studio kitchen, the sunroom, and then back. Their conversation twists and turns accordingly, responding to the artworks, objects, posters, plants, architecture, and light they encounter along the way. Both artists seem giddy and playful in the process. Through Judy's handheld camera, the space feels labyrinthine and disorienting.

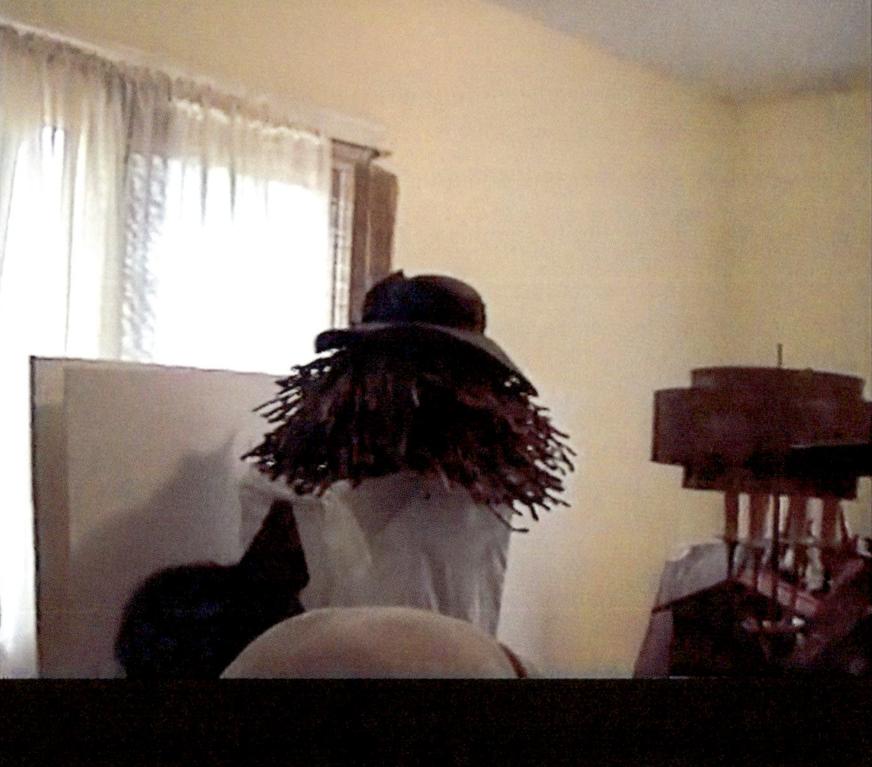

Beverly Buchanan: I wanna show you back here where, uh... I've still not gotten things really together much. But back here, I wanna show you this one piece that I did, that I would hate to have to sell.

[*Beverly enters a room off the hallway. It's packed with furniture and sculptures. A life-size figure, boxlike, with abundant hair and a black straw hat, stands in the center of the room*]

BB: It's a figure.[1] [*walks toward the sculpture*] And she used to be out in the front of the house.

Judy McWillie: I remember *her*! When she was out there, I—

BB: Was she? Oh good! She's gonna go back out there, because I miss seeing her out there.

[*Facing away from the camera, Beverly embraces the figure's rectangular waist and rotates her*]

She's gonna go back out there. It's just that I had to, you know, it's one of these things that you have to get stuff together and... [*exhales, returns to the doorway to face Judy*]

JM: You know, the other thing about the shacks, in particular, is how they're, they really are, *bodies*. Uh... *people* bodies.[2]

BB: [*leans in the doorway, nodding*] Yeah, I kinda think so. Kinda think so.

JM: Yeah. They're bodies, of people.

BB: Yeah!

JM: And they also, I'm thinking of one—

BB: That's why it takes so long for me to, you know? And that's hard to explain, when somebody's trying to sell your work. You can't explain that. [*shakes head*]

JM: Well that's the kinda thing that they discover on their own, if they hang in with the work a long time. But the other thing, of course, being an old Catholic, is *tabernacles*.

[*Beverly buckles over, chuckling*]

JM: I mean, there's one really simple [shack sculpture] in the *House and Home* show that's real monolithic. You know that one?

BB: [*nodding and chuckling*] Yeah! You know, my father was a-a... I went to Catholic school from kindergarten to eighth grade. It ended in eighth grade.

JM: No shit!

BB: [*cracking up*] Of course I did!

JM: [*laughs*] Yeah, life sort of ended in the eighth grade for me because then they split us up, and we went to high school.

BB: Well, we didn't have a high school. There was only *one* Black Catholic school in Orangeburg. One Black—one *Catholic school.* And it was Black kids went to it!

JM: Mm-hmm.

BB: White kids didn't have a school to go to! [*grins*] And I went from kindergarten to eighth grade, and after that, you had to go to public school. High school then started in ninth grade, so my kindergarten through junior high was spent in Catholic school.

JM: Ho hooo mannnn!

BB: And all that that says. [*grinning and nodding*]

JM: Ho hooo okaayyy!

BB: Oooh yeah, I could probably say the act of contrition on my head! [*smiles, clears throat*] I mean, I'm still sure. I mean, it's-it, that influence is always there.

[*Beverly walks over to a poster on the wall. Judy rotates the camera to face the poster, an enlarged photographic portrait of a white woman in a distinctive top hat*]

JM: Who's this?

BB: That's Pat Passlof. [*laughs*] Pat hates this photo, but she came to one of the shows in New York. We were, we got to be friends in New York. She was the Elaine de Kooning connection. She and Elaine de Kooning and-and Willem de Kooning.

JM: Mm-hmm.

BB: And Milton Resnick is Pat's husband. And they were just heartbroken when Milton and Pat weren't allowed to see Willem de Kooning.

JM: When? You mean after he was sick?

BB: Yeah.

JM: Where do they got him now? Is he still at the house, or is he, uh...?

BB: I don't know, I don't know. But Pat—

JM: You know, I never thought he had Alzheimer's.

BB: I don't know what he's got.

JM: I mean, I thought he was just *zoned out*. I mean, I saw him in 1980. A lot around 1980.

BB: Really?

JM: It's been a long time, but-but he just, he didn't seem senile. He painted all day.

BB: Woowww!

JM: At night, he liked to watch TV to unwind before he'd go to bed.

BB: No kidding.

JM: And he saw the *Grand Ole Opry* for the first time, and—

BB: For the first time! [*laughs*] For the first time!

JM:—he was so excited. And this friend of mine, Connie Evans, she was with me, and she played—

BB: [*laughs*] For the first time!

JM: —she played the spoons. And-and he kept saying, [regarding] the *Grand Ole Opry*, Roy Acuff and all, "*Is this some kind of tradition in this country!? This is marvelous*!" [*laughs*] I thought, "This guy's okay!"

BB: [*laughs*] That's not senility! That's right! [*wagging finger*]

JM: This dude's all right! This dude's fine!

BB: That-that's not senility. That's right. [*nodding*]

JM: And they were already saying he was senile.

BB: Ooooh, I *really* don't know. I never talked to them about that. They just made that comment. But they were my Elaine de Kooning connection. I mean, I was in Macon. I drove up to—

JM: I'm gonna–I'm gonna turn this off for a second.

[*There's a jump cut in the video. When it restarts, Judy and Beverly are still standing in the same spot. Judy spins the camera toward the other end of the hallway, revealing a hybrid kitchen/studio with very tall ceilings. Beyond the kitchen, the sun-room is bursting with green*]

BB: —off for a while if you want to.

JM: Oh no, I love it. [*laughs*] I gotta pick up all this stuff in here!

[*Beverly walks toward the kitchen. Judy follows behind her, panning the camera along the walls of the hallway, pausing for a moment on a large black-and-white photograph of Beverly's 1979 work,* Ruins and Rituals.[3] *The photograph shows three large blocky cement sculptures installed amongst trees in a wooded area*]

BB: But, um, that's how Roy Lichtenstein is. Roy Lichtenstein is just a regular, *very nice* man.

JM: Yeah!

BB: 'Cause I had been having trouble, for the piece in Miami, getting an insurance company. And he had suggestions. And then Betye Saar was *just wonderful* helping me to find somebody!

JM: I love her!

BB: Because they wanted me to have a million-dollar insurance policy. You got to be joking! You had to insure the piece until they could, uh...

JM: Oh, she's great, Betye Saar.

BB: This is the kitchen area for the studio.

[*Judy's camera lingers on a potted plant resting in the kitchen sink, then tilts upward, tracing the verticality of a tall clerestory window. A spider plant hangs at its peak*]

JM: [*in awe*] Whoooaaaa.

BB: And, of course, I sleep back here because it's, um, it's cat-free. [*laughs*] It's animal-free!

JM: The cats get your asthma?[4]

BB: Well, I-I've noticed a difference in breathing a little bit since I'm not exposed to their dander.

JM: Yeah. [*sighs*]

BB: But, um, *the dust* is here! It's like I'm exposed to dust every day.

JM: This house is great! *It goes on and on.*

[*Light pours in as Beverly opens the window shutters*]

BB: Well, this was what grant money helped do, help make.[5] This was an apartment.

JM: [*chuckles*] Let's hear it for grant money.

BB: This was Jackie's apartment. And so to make an apartment into a studio takes a lot! You know, you need horizontal space. You don't need space to... [*pushes furniture around*]

JM: [*sighs*] That's right. Yeah, but more and more, I like living—

BB: The loft area is a storage area for right now, and I'm gonna change that. But it takes time to do that and also make work. So since I need to make work, I have to put that on hold.

JM: Yep.

BB: But getting the light in here is just so wonderful.

JM: It sure is. The *space* in here is incredible. *The height...*

BB: Well, this was the deck that I had enclosed in glass, so that I can use this as a...

[*Beverly opens the door to the sun-room, which is filled with hanging planters and faces the verdant backyard*]

JM: Yeah, I've loved this ever since I first saw it, but I didn't know it was a deck.

BB: It was originally a deck, and I enclosed it in glass for the plants. And so I come out in the mornings and sit here. If I don't go outside, I'll sit here and eat. I used to have drawings [stored] on this table, and I brought them inside now, because I was afraid of mold.[6]

JM: Mm-hmm, yeah.

BB: But at least I can sit and look at my plants and stuff without being exposed to the humidity outside. This morning was an exception. I could actually *go out,* about 7:30, outside. And as it began to get a little warmer, I couldn't do that. But I can be in here, and... it's really *very* nice. At night especially. It really is.

[*Judy pivots the camera to face the large, wall-mounted thermostat. It reads just shy of 80 degrees Fahrenheit. To its right, Beverly leans in the sun-room doorway, admiring the view of her garden out the windows*]

JM: Can we talk just a little, about—?

BB: Yes!

JM:—about Mary Lou?

BB: Sure!

[*They exit the sun-room, and head back down the hallway*]

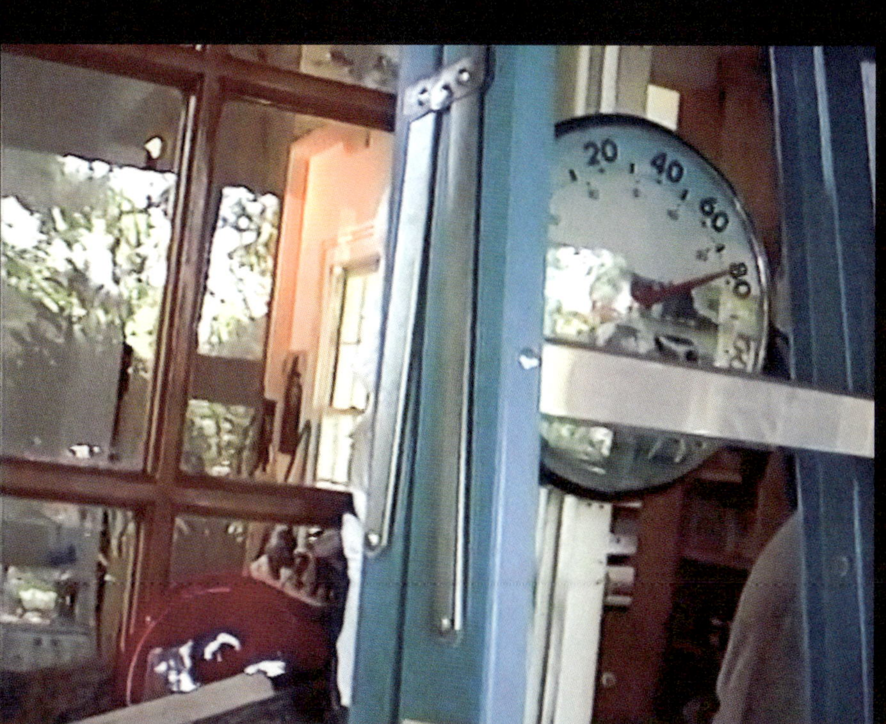
20 40 60 80

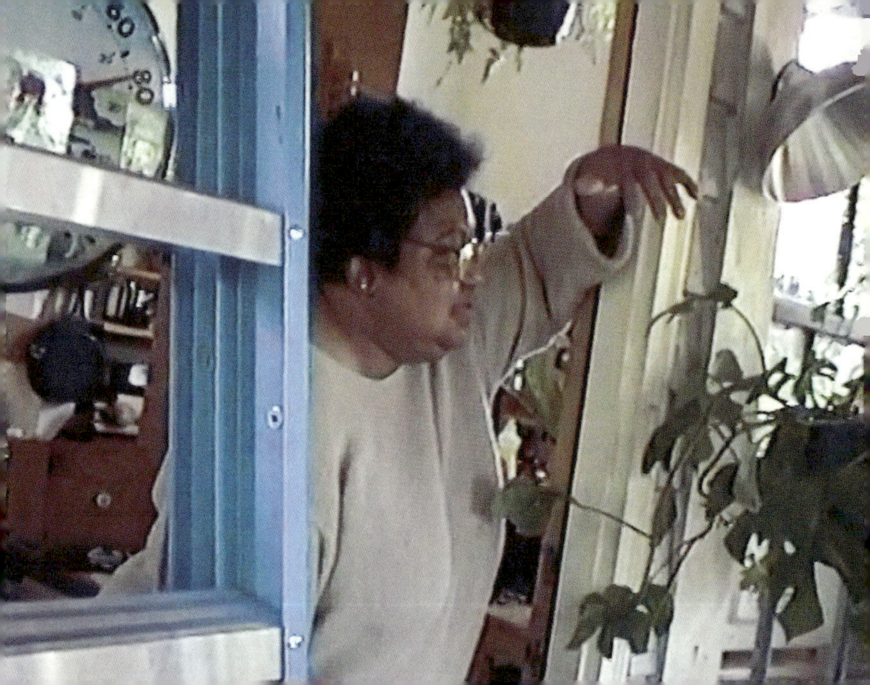

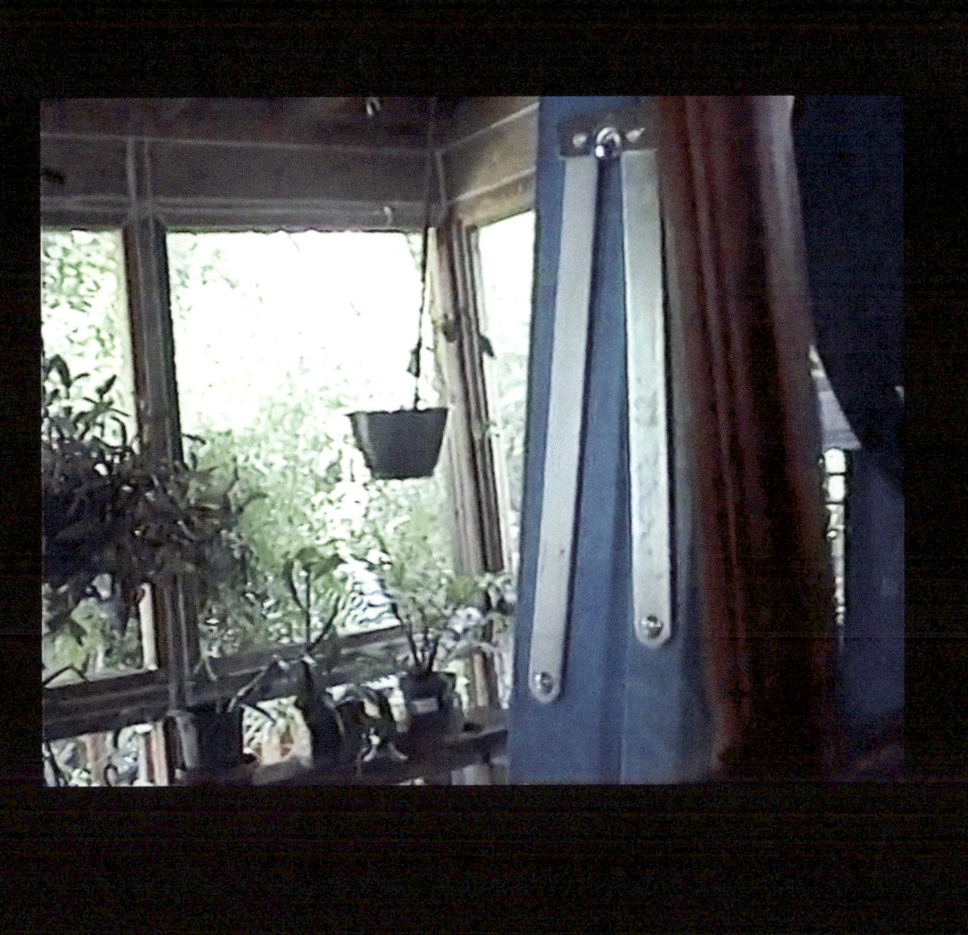

JM: The reason is that, for instance, when I was over in Augusta, a couple weeks ago... It was a bunch of people, I think they were art teachers. I don't know what they were. But, of course, they were all just *flipped* over those photos, and every question was about her.

BB: Ah, jeez. I had put the [photos of Mary Lou] that I took away, you know, to show you. And I can certainly gather them up. But we can talk about that, even if I can't.

[*Beverly ducks into a room off the hallway, and shuffles through a pile of photographs as she speaks*]

JM: Okay, I'd love to see just any of them, you know? But, uh... I mean, you know, it-it's... You're speechless in the face of somebody like her.

BB: Yes, you are!

BB: Oh, I'll gather them. I'll gather them up 'cause they're all in a bunch! It's 'cause I was saving them for you.

JM: This-this book that I'm supposed to be working on—[7]

[*Beverly emerges from the room with some large photographs in her hand*]

BB: That's me! That's Lucy Lippard!

JM: Oh! Oh yes.

BB: Lucy, I was showing Lucy some stuff. [*laughs*]

[*Beverly places the photographs of Lucy against the windowsill—amongst toy cars, paper shack cutouts, blue glass bottles, and rocks—then starts to walk down the hallway. Judy follows behind her*]

We can come in here and-and talk about Mary Lou because... I have a bunch of them! I was saving them just to show you. [*rummages through more piles in the hallway*] But I wanted to talk to you about her because, um, I didn't know...

[*Beverly trails off in thought as she walks through the doorway back to the studio*]

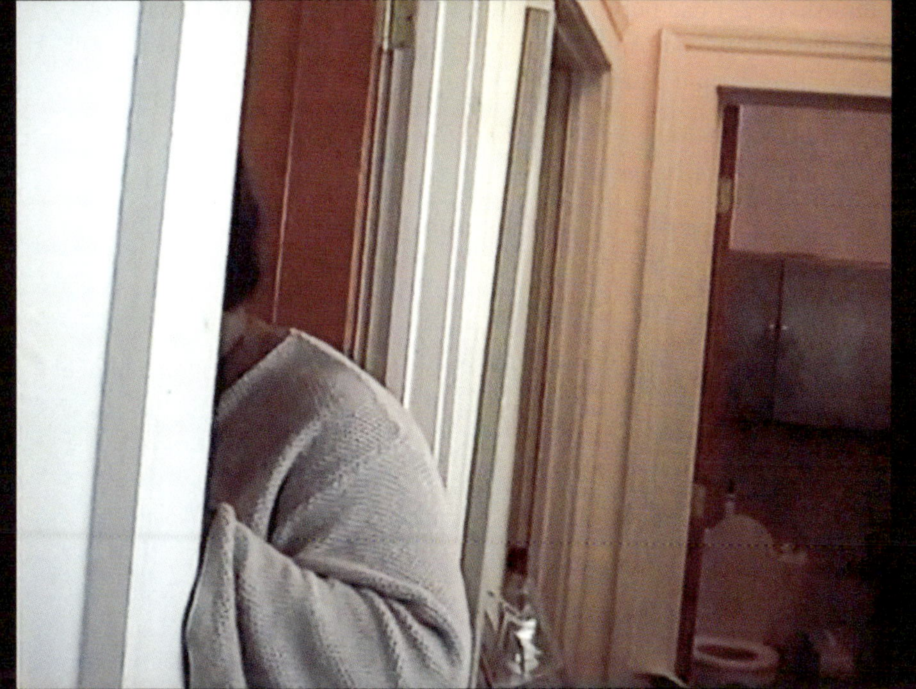

Scene 7

The Chair

01:00:10–01:25:19

Back in the studio, both artists get settled into their chairs and remain seated for the majority of the scene. The camera is mostly stationary on a tripod, freeing Judy up for a lengthy conversation with Beverly about Mary Lou Furcron. Beverly sits in a leather chair, facing the camera. Tall shelves packed with books fill the frame behind her.

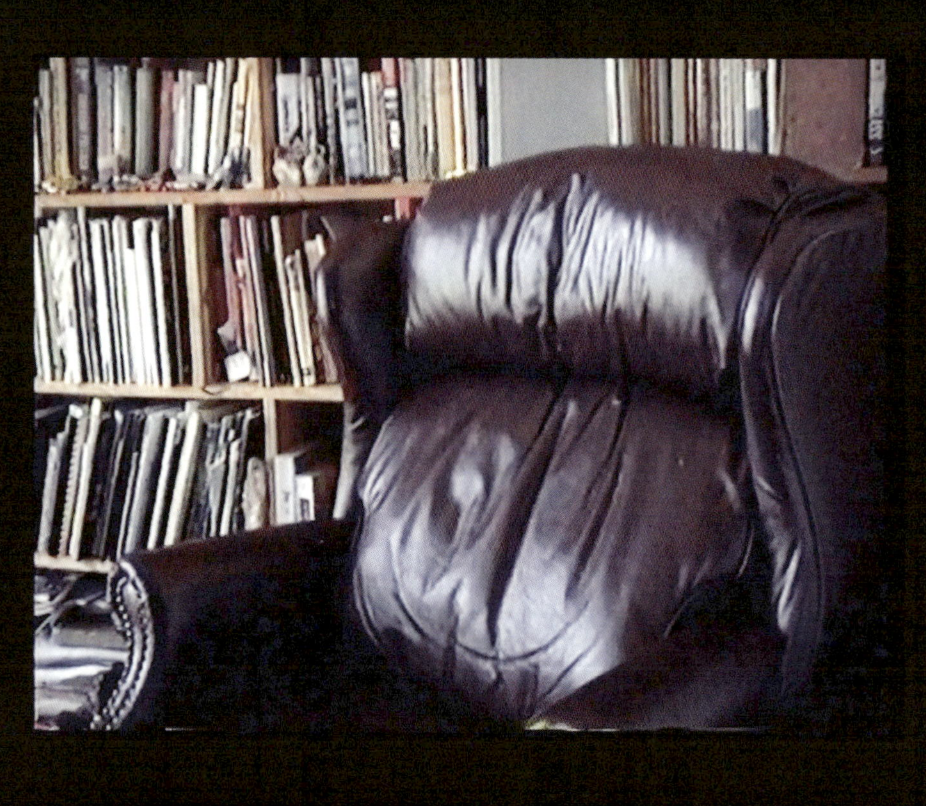

Beverly Buchanan: Which chair would you like to sit in? Would you like to sit in *my* chair? [*smiles*]

Judy McWillie: No, you sit in your chair!

BB: This is a *wonderful* chair.

JM: [*laughs*] You sit in your chair. You'll look great on video in your chair.

BB: [*playfully*] This is a nice chair, it's a comfortable chair.

JM: Yeah, but this is–this is good for me 'cause it wheels around and I can get different shots.

[*Judy spins in the chair, pointing the camera toward the bookshelves. Out of the frame, Beverly rearranges objects to access the room's large, wooden window shutters*]

BB: I'm gonna take these down and open [the window shutters], 'cause I usually open them. This chicken [sculpture] was outside.[1] It's gonna go back outside. It was on a post, and I took it off. But all of these [shutters] open during the day. I get ill if I don't have a certain amount of light. Even if it's artificial. It makes me sick if I don't have it.

JM: Mm-hmm, mm-hmm.

[*The window shutters now open, Beverly takes a seat in her leather chair, facing Judy*]

BB: Mary Lou was quite something. It was... I was not *prepared* for this kind of person... I wasn't prepared because the two guys who had told me about her—Andy Hines is still around.[2] His partner, the wrestler, I don't know, retired or something, and Andy bought him out.

JM: They live around there?

BB: Andy's wife is a CPA in, uh, in Lexington, and Andy has that little antique shop that's on the right there.

JM: Yeah, okay.

BB: Okay. Well, it's like if you're gonna go to Goodness Grows, you just keep driving, you know? Well, I was on my way to Washington, Georgia, and I'd been there many times, headed towards downtown Washington, you know? And I wanted to photograph this house that had blue—white house with blue trim. *Everything* was blue trim! All the trim on that house was blue! That's not unusual in the South, but I just, something about, I want to know! And one day I wanna stop and-and hand them these photos and say, "Tell me, uh, why did you, um...?"[3]

And so I stopped in [to the antique shop] and I told them where I was going. They teased me. They said, "No! You wanna go look and see this-this lady that built her house out of twigs!" I said, "Oh, come on! You're *always* doing this. You're making up something to get me interested in it, and then you just go *hoo, hoo, hoo.*" "Noooo, we mean it. Just go on up there and turn towards Elberton." So, I took 'em up. I thought, "Okay, I'll-I'll try this."

I was not *prepared for her*, and so I couldn't find the house. Couldn't find it and came back to the monument company, and asked these men in there if they knew who this person was.[4] They said, "Yeaahh, she's probably out there most days sweeping her yard."[5] I said, "Well, um, uhhh... does she... have a dog?" [*raises eyebrows and smiles*] They said, "No." I was scared right that minute! [*laughs*] I thought, "Uh oh, she doesn't have a dog, I'm scared now!" And so they told me where to find her. And then pulling up, I was not *prepared*, from the vegetation, to pull up in front of that. [*wags finger*]

JM: Which you couldn't see from the road.

BB: If I had had a clutch, my foot would have come off the clutch, you know? I really just sat. I turned, just like, "What?" So I didn't even see *her* over on the side. [*clears throat*] I'd never seen any—[*shakes head*] The *impact* of that was—Even if I had ever seen anything [like] that same structure, the *emotional impact of that* was something I had not ever seen or felt. And I-I was just... I couldn't talk. And so I turned off the engine and just sat there and looked at [Mary Lou Furcron's home] and just went, *Oooh myyy loooord.*

And then I became aware of a presence. [*motions with hand, clears throat*] And looked over and saw her. And she kinda glanced up at me, and then slowly bent, from the bending position, got upright. And I thought, "GET OUT OF THE TRUCK! GO OVER SAY SOMETHING TO THIS PERSON! SAY SOMETHING TO THIS WOMAN!"

JM: Was she working on the beans, tying the, uh?

BB: Yeah, she was working on, mm-hmm. [*nodding*]

JM: [*sighs*] When she bent over, I never saw anybody like that.

BB: That's right! It was—

JM: She didn't bend her knees! She—

BB: No! *From the waist!*

JM: A perfect right angle!

BB: That's right! That's right! And I wasn't prepared. It was like, I was immediately... *reverent*! I mean, something just said, [*lowers voice*] "Waalk slooowly. Waalk," you know? And, uh, her conversations with me were... I mean, it was like you wanted to do *exactly* what she said to do. I tried to put it in perspective in terms of, who does this person remind me of? And I couldn't come up with a *single* name. I couldn't come up with anybody! [*laughs*] Except maybe my grandmother. Except that my grandmother was-was *warm* and-and I knew loved me, and came to me with a sense of LOVE! And this person was like, so self-contained! It didn't matter if I was there or not. She had things to do. She was gonna do them whether I stood there or not! It didn't matter.

JM: "*That's the way that is.*"[6]

BB: "*That's the way that is.*"

JM: "*That's the way that is.*"

BB: That's right! And our subsequent conversations were, um, my asking permission, and her—We finally got to a stage when she, like, I knew she wasn't gonna listen to me, you know, my asking her, "You need for me to bring anything for you back from Athens?" And when she said, "Bring me some stockings. I don't want any silk stockings." And so I broke my neck getting back to Athens to try to find them. I thought, "Oh my lord, she meant cotton stockings!" So I ran around all over town, talking to people about where can I find... [*gestures with hands emphatically*] And so finally one of the older ladies downtown said, "When she tells you not silk, she meant she didn't want nylon." I said, "Oh, thank you so much."

I ended up, of course, calling Sears catalog store in Chicago. I found some downtown [in Athens], but that was the last place I found them. The next group I had to order from Sears, but they had them downtown! I went back with, like, ten pairs or something like that. And then she wanted to try to pay me for them. She said, "Go in there and get some money." And I said, "Uh, no, I can't do that." Okay. There was this silence. I'm used to that silence, that "I heard what you said, but then you didn't hear what I said" kinda thing!

JM: Yeah!

BB: She'd give me about five seconds, so I would then change the subject, you know? She would then come back to it and say, "Go in there in the jar, and get that money." And I said, "Ms. Furcron, I-I can't do that. I—this is a gift for you." And she had to slowly look at me, and I would just not change my expression. [*laughs*] Finally, I just said, "That-that's it. That's a gift for you. Just, I want you to have it, and that's it."

JM: Did she ever talk to you about...? Apparently, her family moved to Philadelphia lock, stock, and barrel, at some point when she was a young woman.

BB: Oooh yeah.

JM: And [they] brought her.

BB: She didn't talk to me about that.

JM: All she ever said, if I got it right, is that—

BB: Oh, you got it right! You got it *all* on there! I saw that! [on the video recording]

JM: You know how she went to work in a factory?

BB: Yes!

JM: Okay. And-and then they fired her, you know, because she was "too slow."

BB: Yes! "Too slow!"

JM: And when-when they said to her, uh, you know, "You're fired." She goes, "*But, that's the way I work*."

BB: Yes. That was familiar to me. That, to me, was a Southernism. You know why? One of Patricia's relatives, who's a sweet old white lady down in Macon. [*laughs*] Ella [Martin] used to work at—it's not Roberta—it's down there between Macon and uh... Juliette! At the cotton mill that was in Juliette. Patti's relative, Ella, used to work there. And a bunch of us went up in that mill one time, and-and I got, I had an asthma attack. [*touches chest*] But we took these old spools and stuff with all these no trespassing signs in Juliette. And we went inside, and I tried to push one of those heavy carts that was iron, an iron and wood cart. [*motions pushing with hands*] And I had a hard time! And I was a stronger person then!

I told Ella that I had gotten a spool. When Ella saw it, she asked where I got it. She said, "I used to work in there." And I said, "Ella, really?" I thought she was one of the spinners. She said, "I pushed a cart." And I said, "Ella, I went in that building. The only carts I saw—ha ha ha—were these big, heavy iron—" She said "Yeah!" I said, "Ella, you couldn't have." She said, "I was no bigger than a pencil! The men all did it, and I didn't have a job. And that was the only job I could do. And they told me that I'd have to keep up with the men." I said, "Ella, *I* had a hard time pushing that big cart. How could you?" She said, "I pushed it." She pushed it, and she got sick! But she pushed it! Okay?

JM: [*sighs*]

BB: And she said they fired her from doing it. [*waves arm in the air*] They moved her from doing that. She said, "Because I was too slow!" [*throws hand forward emphatically*] "I was too slow," she said, "But I got it done." And I thought, "*That's the way she works.*" So when I heard that on your video, when [Mary Lou] said, "That's the way I work," I thought about Ella. I thought, "This is not a Black/white thing here! This is a cultural thing. This is a "*That's the way I work!*"

JM: It's also like, a Zen thing. I mean, like, she—

BB: Well, but "That's the way I work" and "That's the way it is"!

JM: "*That's the way that is.*"

BB: It's like the little Southern girls up in New York City who are making biscuits for these fancy restaurants, and you've eaten four. [*laughs*] And they're about to close, and you want another one. [*shifts to impersonation*] "I'm so sorry. You'll have to come back tomorrow. Lizzy is not making any more biscuits because *that's the way Lizzy works!*" [*groans*] So I-I was just right on that, but I'll tell you something. Mr. Sanders and Lucille [Sanders], and...

JM: He passed last year.

BB: Yeah... Well, one time I went back when [Mary Lou] first got in the nursing home. [Mr. Sanders and Lucille] were telling me the same things that I already knew about the family. Only, [Lucille] told me about the cow, that she was waiting for the cow to come back to that shed. They said, "You know she has a son?" I said, "What?"

JM: [*gasps*] What?!

BB: Do you want to keep this running? [*laughs*]

JM: God, I didn't know that!

BB: [*clears throat*] I sat down for that. I was at their house, standing up. [*chuckles*] I sat down on the front porch.

JM: 'Cause I always asked her if she had any children. She said, "*Nooo ma'am.*"

BB: They said, "Her son came down," from either Baltimore or New York, [where] he lives. He heard she was in a nursing home. Wait a minute. [*holds out hand, smiling*] Aaand, she wouldn't acknowledge him. As her son. *That's her son.*

JM: Something happened when she was—

BB: Yes! And see, what I thought was, when I saw your video, I thought, "She got raped up there. She had a baby." That's what happened! That's what-that's what, that's why she had to stop! That's why she had to come back!

JM: And that's why she lived alone.

BB: And she hated to come back! That's why she—

JM: Completely. Alone.

BB: That's right! When they told me that, I said, "Oh my god." [*brings hand to forehead*] "If I go to see her, I'm not gonna mention it at all." [Her son] went to the nursing home to see her, and he said, "I can—" He wanted her to come live with him!

JM: Had he ever come and visited her when she lived in the house?

BB: I don't know.

JM: But she wouldn't, you said she wouldn't claim him?

BB: No, she wouldn't claim him. But *he is her son.*

JM: Oh my god.

BB: They can prove it. He wanted her to come back with him. He wanted to take care of her. I think he *did* see the house. I think he did.

JM: Did the Sanders know him before he came down?

BB: I don't know. They didn't tell me that.

JM: I wonder how he found out.

BB: But we can certainly ask Lucille 'cause, you know? [*nods*]

JM: I would like to go talk to Lucille some time.

BB: But he wanted her to go back with him.

JM: Oh, that's beautiful.

BB: He said, "I can–I can afford it." I think he even called her "Mother." She would not acknowledge him as her son AT ALL. And I-I just, my brain went, when I saw the video, I went, "*That's it*. That's what happened to her."

JM: That's it. Yeah. It was very clear, that she had had something *really horrible*—

BB: Something terrible—

JM: —happen.

BB: That's what happened to her. But *she had the baby*. She had him. And she left him *up there*. She didn't bring him back *down here*. It would have been a disgrace!

JM: God, god. And all of her relatives left him up there, stayed up there.

BB: Yes! It would have been a disgrace! It would have been a disgrace! Yes!

JM: But god, she went off and lived alone.

BB: Yes, she did.

JM: And—

BB: He wanted to take care of her. He wanted to. He really did.

JM: Oh, I'm so glad. That's amazing.

BB: She *did not* want it. She would have nothing to do with it. But he saw her in the nursing home! When she got out of the hospital, and went to the nursing home, he came down. He came down. Now, who alerted him—

[*There's a jump cut in the video that abruptly interrupts the conversation. The video resumes with Beverly still seated in the same spot, still facing the camera, and the conversation continues*]

JM: What she did was, uh, Mary Lou, when it was cold like that, would *stay up all day*. I mean, excuse me—

BB: Stay up all *night*.

JM: Stay up all night and sleep all day.

BB: Yeah.

JM: And she had like, uh, layers and layers and layers of cardboard, that she put across those doors.

BB: Yes. [*nods*]

JM: And one day I went out there. I knew that she could take care of herself, but I thought, "God, it's two degrees. I don't know what she's doing."

BB: Yeah! It's freezing!

JM: And so she said, "*Go on now. I can't open the door*," which is 'cause she left it [covered in cardboard], but [that] she's alright. And she had that, uh, fifty-five-gallon drum filled up with wood, and-and that was her heat. And, uh, her whole thing was that she *stayed up all night* when it was cold. God... [*sighs*]

BB: And then slept during the day, so it wasn't as cold as night.

JM: Well she, she had a good relationship with the Sanders.

BB: Yes she did. She absolutely did. One day, when I went out there, she had had a little fire. And I have photos. The photos that I have of her, that back of the house had caught on fire. And Mr. Sanders said he was putting a new pipe in for her stove. And the stove was right near where she was gonna sleep on the floor. So that was gonna be some heat for her. And I thought, "Good." [*places hand on heart*]

But little smoke, little, uh, blue smoke, was coming out. [*motions hand in the air*] Something was starting to catch on fire, and so that was the day that I went out. That was the day that I took her the stockings, and she wanted to pay me. And Mr. Sanders was laughing 'cause she and I were having this little banter about paying me for it, and he was just... [*chuckles*] And she wanted to pay him. She offered him money for helping to put the stove. So he said, "I can't." He said, "Ms. Furcron, I'm not gonna take your money."

JM: Mm-hmm.

BB: When I saw that, I thought, "Well, then I have to get the same attitude, you know." [*hollers*] Because, this woman is just AN IRON HORSE! [*laughs and shakes fist*] But she said the same things to me that she said to you on that [video], about the family. This one lady that I met, who's gotten money from the humanities [department] to research that county, has met people, has met some of Mary Lou's relatives.

JM: Oh boy.

BB: Has talked to them. And I can never remember her name, but I know her when I see her! I said to her, "Please call me and come by to see me, so we can get together with *you*." [*points to Judy*] And then she can tell *you* the stuff that she's told me. That this is Mary Lou's *second* house. Her first house *burned*. She said, "I have lots of Mary Lou stories you won't believe." I said, "I bet I will!" [*laughs*]

JM: Oh my god, that's great!

BB: Yes! But this is the second house, and her first house BURNED TO THE GROUND. Or, it's not burned to the ground. Burned pretty substantially. And so she started the second one.

JM: So she *built*—

BB: The one that we know.

JM: —the one that we know.

BB: YES MA'AM!

JM: Okay, so the first one was probably the smokehouse kitchen.

BB: It probably was. It burned. And she, you know, she—

JM: Man!

BB: Some-somehow it got set on fire.

JM: Because I thought, I mean, she didn't wanna say she built it. She said, "*It was just an old smokehouse kitchen*."

BB: Uh-huh.

JM: But, *my god*.

BB: So some remnants of that may have survived the original, the other fire, you know?

JM: Oh man. Well, she said she had relatives around there.

BB: Oh yeah, she told me that too, and she does have, apparently! 'Cause from what this lady has been able to find out. And I was so glad to hear that. I kept saying, "Put this on tape." I said, "What you–what you want to tell me, just get a tape recorder and say it into the tape recorder, even if you tell me later! And take notes on who these people are who are telling you this!" [*gestures emphatically*]

JM: Yeah.

BB: She said, "I think you're right." But she said, "Having seen [your] photos has helped make me determined to go out and find out more." I thought, "Well GOOD!"

JM: You bet.

BB: Oooh Judy.

JM: You know, I wanna go see her. She's still in that-that nursing home.

BB: Yeah, yeah. And Lucille said she looks good. She said, "Looks better than me and you." [*laughs*] And I said, "Yeah, I bet she does."

JM: Well, she must be eighty-five by now.

BB: You know, she's in good health, and *we're the ones* that are out here, wheezing and struggling.

JM: Where, which house is the Sanders house? It's on farther down that—?

BB: Just that next house, on the left. It's a big two-story... [*raises arms up*]

JM: Yeah.

BB: Yeah, that's it!

JM: Yeah, that's it.

JM: Well, she—

BB: [*sighs*]

JM: I always felt like something bad happened to her when she was up there.

BB: It did!

JM: But now, she kept talking about—Let me ask you about this! God almighty. Did you see that *circle of stones*?

BB: [*wide-eyed*] Yes, I-I don't know. I don't remember seeing that when I was out there. Unless it freaked me out so much.

JM: Right, yeah. Listen, this is weird. Uh, before the pulpwood company came in and flattened everything. So there's no even sign of the—

BB: No! There's no—

JM: Uh, okay, Beverly. The only thing that was not overgrown with pine saplings, *that darn stone circle was still up there*! It was the highest point on that land. It was up there. *Nothing grew inside that thing*!

[*Laughing, Beverly removes her glasses, and places her head in her hand*]

This is like a year and a half ago. Nothing grew in it! And everything else was saplings. And the saplings grew around the house, so it protected it from the wind.

BB: Right.

JM: And as recently as a year and a half ago, whenever it was I was there, the last time. Beverly, *nothing* in that house was disturbed. Everything in there was *exactly* as she left it, and had been standing there for six years! All the bleach bottles. The bed, with the headboard. The furniture.

[*Beverly chuckles in her chair*]

The-the can of nails. It was like *nothing had been touched*!

BB: But I thought—Well, now, I need to ask Jean Westmacott if they actually got the other—

JM: I think they got that three, uh, legged stool or something.

BB: But is that *all*? Because I thought that she said, "We have the furniture."[7]

JM: Well, then maybe she went back before they completely flattened—

BB: I hope they did 'cause the same day you called me, I called Jean Westmacott. I immediately called her. Left a message, and she called me back. And I said, "I think you gotta go do something *now*. Because, um—"

JM: They had plowed all around it, you know. Except they left the saplings and the house, and you could see it there like, like a little spot, you know, out in the middle of that field.

BB: I-I didn't ask Jean. I saw her at the show, but I didn't get a chance to talk to her. I meant to ask her if they—But she said, "We got the furniture."

JM: Good. Okay.

BB: And-and one of the wonderful things in your video that [you] showed was, you remember the *older* hoe, not the new hoe, the *old* hoe?[8]

JM: Yes... Yes!

BB: The chopping hoe. I have that!

JM: Oh, that's wonderful.

BB: Willie Ed [Sanders] gave that to me. I-I was out there—

JM: And the brooms.

BB: The last time I was out there—

JM: *The brooms were still there. Laying on the ground.*

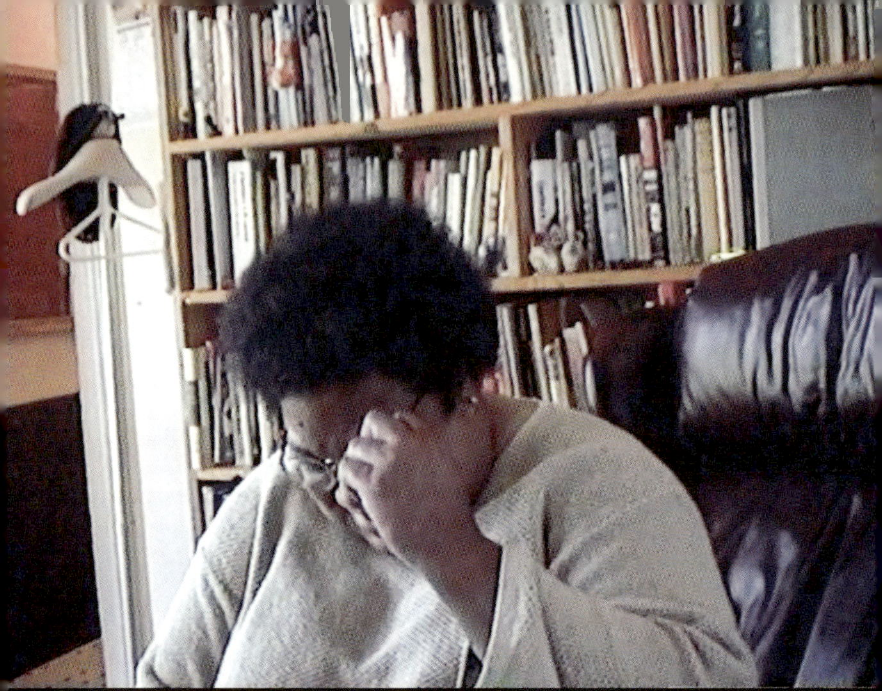

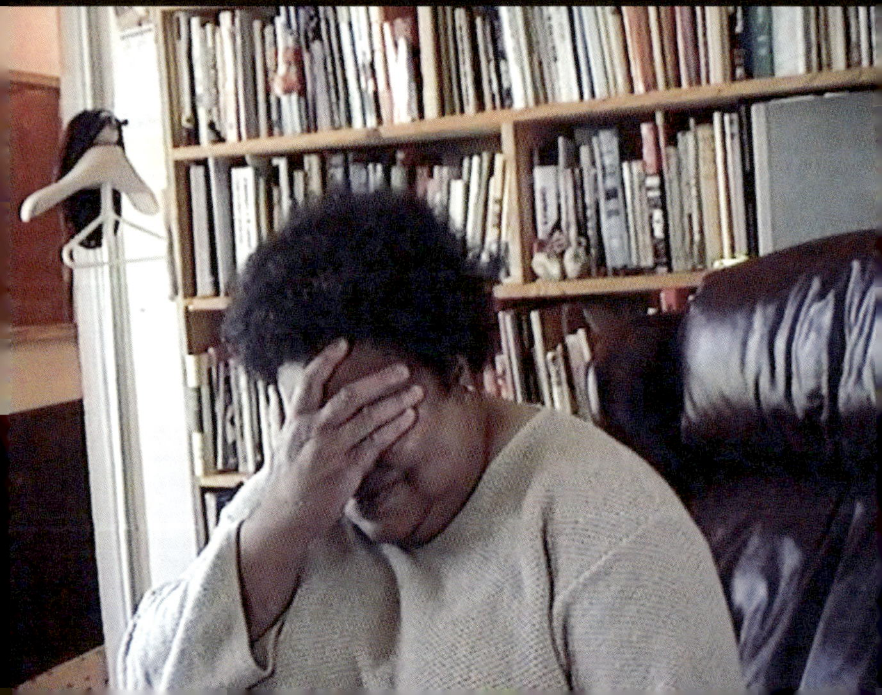

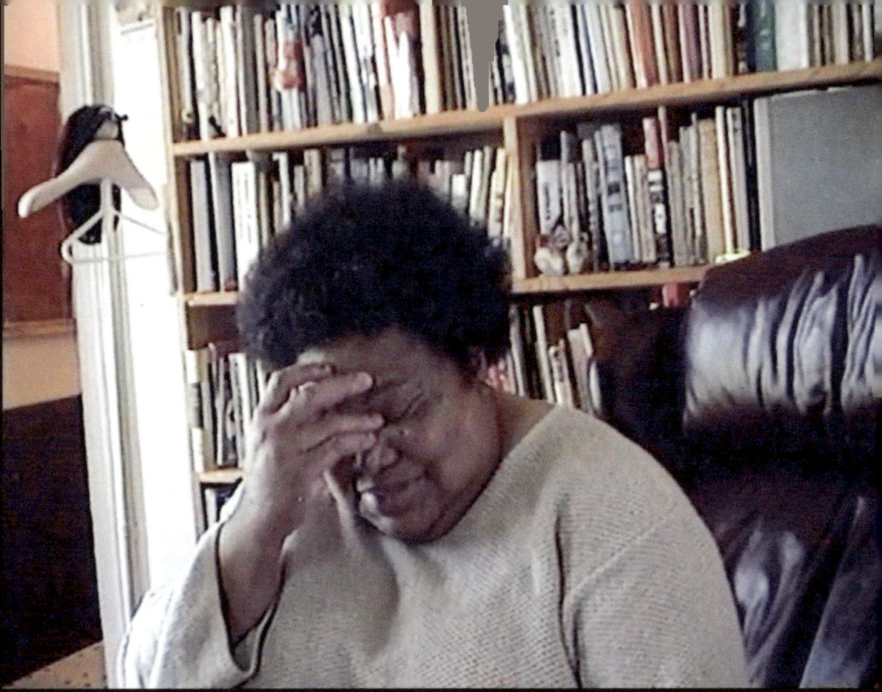

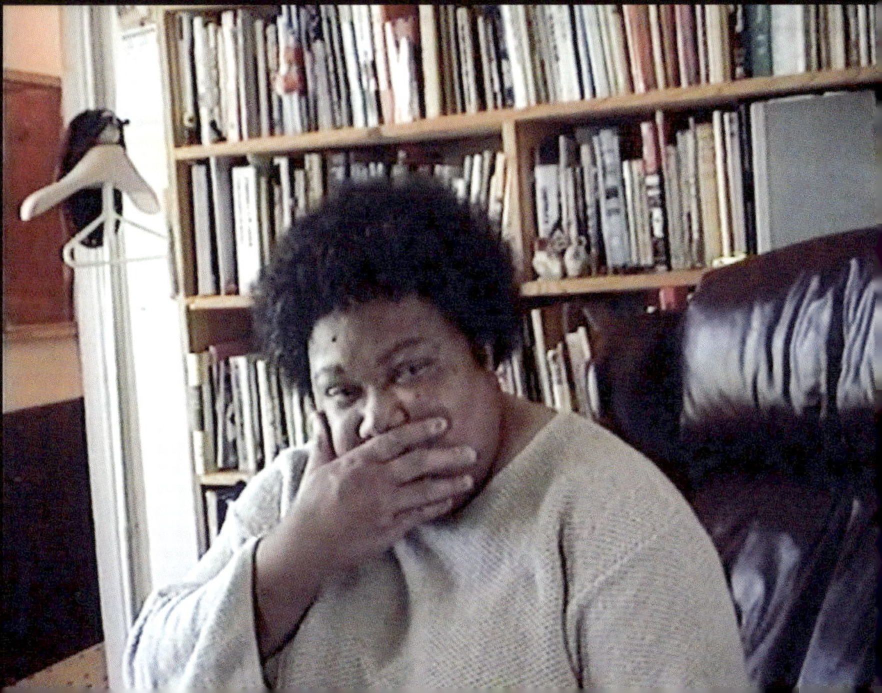

BB: Ah, geez. [*sighs, brings hand to face*]

JM: I mean, *the work* that woman put into keeping that place.

BB: Yeah, yeah.

JM: It was a—

BB: I have the hoe. I thought, "I got to show this to Judy," because [Jean and Richard] wanna have an exhibit of all the Mary Lou stuff that *they* have. And I said, "I have the hoe. Her old hoe." 'Cause I said [to Willie Ed], "I wanna photograph it, and I'll bring it back." He said, "Don't worry about it." And I thought about it. I thought, that's *incredible*. It's like if I had taken it back, it would have gotten plowed over or something!

JM: That's right. That's right.

BB: And it's fine if somebody would take it! But it's just since nobody ever took it, it would just be *nothing*! It would be under the ground, you know?!

JM: Her ladder was there. Grey Gundaker was visiting when we saw that. And we started out across that plowed field.

BB: [*sighs*] Gosh, yeah.

JM: We made it about halfway. It was mud all the way up above our knees. It was like quicksand, and so we couldn't get it.

BB: No, no.

JM: We couldn't–we couldn't get all the way out there. And then within, I guess, six weeks, it was gone.

BB: Gone.

JM: Flat.

BB: [*sighs*] Yeah, yeah.

JM: Well, I'm so glad to know that there are relatives there and that somebody's—

BB: Yeah, I am too, 'cause it was like... Oh, this woman is just researching, is just—She said, "I have various stories you wouldn't believe." I said, "Yes, I would believe them. I really would!" [*laughs*] But it's really incredible. I talked about being up North, and I thought, "Ah, that's it!" When I came back one day and said to Patricia, "She had a son. She has a son." "Woaaah!" I said, "Oh yeah, Lucille told me that they—"

JM: Mm-hmm. Mm-hmm. She-she had the baby, and she left it there.

BB: That's right. That's right.

JM: She kept saying, "*My father's door was down this way. My father's door. My sister's door.*" 'Cause apparently that's where they all lived, when they were still in [the] South.

BB: Right.

JM: And she, she really had a fixation on *exactly* where each house was.

BB: Yes, she did. Yes, she did.

JM: And of course, the hard stones were still there.

BB: You remember that little wall of stones that you had the video on? [*points to the ground*]

JM: Yeah.

BB: I asked Mr. Sanders what that was one time 'cause, you know, I just, I love rocks!

JM: Right, right.

BB: He said, "That was the wall of the old school." I said, "Excuse me?" He said there was a school. [*shifts voice to low pitch*] "We had a school here."

JM: So that's what that *circle* was.

BB: "We had a school here." I said, "A schoolhouse?" And then I started talking about my grandmother's house, you know?

JM: Yeah!

BB: I said, "You know, my grandmother had an old school. I have photographs of her old one-room schoolhouse." And that was *before* the Rosenwald School, so I have photos of what later became a Rosenwald school. But my grandmother's [school] house was not a Rosenwald school.[9] It was just a log, you know? [*gestures a triangular roof with hands*] And it's still standing! It was used as a, uh, as a barn.

JM: Yeah.

BB: And so I said, "I can't believe it's a school." He said, "Yeah. We went to school. It was *our* school." I said, "Who went to school?" He said, "Well, *I* went to school here." I said, "Okay. There was a schoolhouse here." And that's why the board of ed used to own it. The board of ed used to own the land.

JM: Where she—?

BB: And see, that's why I never felt that anything was gonna really happen *bad* to her.

JM: She didn't own—

BB: 'Cause the board of ed *owned the land*!

JM: Yeah. At first, I thought she owned it. Then I heard she rented it, or people just let—

BB: When you asked her if they [the Furcron family] owned it, and she said they owned it, but she didn't, they didn't own it. The board of ed owned it.

JM: I tell you, nobody messed with her.

BB: No they didn't. No.

JM: And-and Oglethorpe County—

BB: No, *nobody* did. [*nods*]

JM: Ever. And, uh, now the shoes. Oh god, I don't remember if this is on the tape or not, but she had a lot of things about shoes.

BB: I'll tell you what Mr. Sanders told me about the shoes. 'Cause I was so intrigued by all those-those shoes. [*gestures a vertical wall with hands*]

JM: Yes, mm-hmm.

BB: I asked about the shoes. *He said*, "She didn't want them shoes." I said, "What?" He said, "She didn't want 'em." I said, "What? I thought that people brought her shoes, and she would wear them." He said, "No."

JM: Uh-uh.

BB: Said, "She just put them there, and she's gonna end up throwing them in that shed in the back."

JM: Remember that one shed where she had all the coats people brought her?

BB: Well, that's what she did! He told me that! I-I said, "Let me see this. Not that I don't believe you, but—" [*laughs*]

JM: She said that she would *never* put on somebody else's shoes.[10]

BB: That's right! That's right!

JM: Uh-uh.

BB: He told me that. He said, "People bring her things, and when they get out of sight, she'll take them and throw them *all* in that shed." [*chuckles*] I thought, "Oh my lord, the clothes and shoes." [*points at Judy emphatically*] And hats!

JM: She must have built the shed for it!

BB: Can you imagine how people must have brought her?

JM: You know what? That-that day of the tape, I didn't get this on tape, but she was up *on top* of one of those sheds, nailing the tin down.

BB: Yeah! 'Cause I would ask how she climbed up to do things, and he said, "We helped her. We would help her put roofing stuff on top." He said, "Well, if you see nails, it's where *we* nailed stuff in. Where you don't see nails is what she did."

JM: She put rocks up there.

BB: Yeah. I thought to myself, "You stubborn, stubborn woman. [*shakes head*] I know well that you give people a hard time!" [*laughs*] But I was really tickled about it 'cause I just thought, you know, she wants it done her way, and as she said, "That's the way it is. *That's the way that is.*" [*smiles*]

JM: God...

BB: And I was just convulsed! When I saw people looking at the photographs of the shoes [in my exhibition], and they thought, "Isn't that wonderful that people just gave her these shoes?" And I wouldn't say it, but I would just start to laugh. [*laughs, brings hand to face*] I thought, "You don't know." She didn't wanna wear other people's—

JM: Oh god, and the coats. You know, the thing that used to just take my breath away was that sweater.

BB: That was her.

JM: That was really about eight sweaters.

BB: Yes it was.

JM: And *every* hole was—

BB: And her shoes, the shoes, the things that she put together for shoes, as a shoe!

JM: But that garment, that sweater garment with those colored threads around those holes, you know, sewing one over another.

BB: It was a wonder. It was a wonder. [*nods*]

JM: Yeah.

BB: A work of art.

JM: A miracle.

BB: A miracle! Yeah, a miracle!

JM: Man... But, you know, this book that we're working on is supposed to be specifically about, uh, homeground.[12] Kinda like the way you *care for your surroundings*, uh, reflecting what you believe in.

BB: The bamboo that's on the shack that I'm now working on... [*points toward other room*] The bamboo is from the fishing pole of an old Black man and his wife whose house I photographed, 'cause it was bulldozed. [*gestures a collapsed structure with hands*] That Prudence showed me. And so I have *his* cap, and I've incorporated his fishing pole into that [sculpture]. And I-I'm starting to do that now, to incorporate people's belongings that I *found* into things like that.

There's an old Black lady who Prudence found one day, um, with a swept yard. She was sweeping her yard, and Prudence asked her if she could come back and take some pictures of it. She said "Yeah." And so I said, "Please—" She'll take me with her, but we gotta do it soon! Because it's like, you know, last week I had bronchitis.

JM: Yeah, yeah.

BB: And you know, it's like you could be here today, and not here *tomorrow*. Or it could be bulldo[zed], with all the stuff with the Olympics happening.[11] With all roads and land being sold so fast, it could NOT BE THERE NEXT WEEK.

JM: That's right.

BB: Okay. So I wanna try to find those Mary Lou photos.

[*Beverly gets up from her chair while talking and exits the room. Judy stays put, facing the now empty chair. Beverly shouts from the hallway as they continue conversing*]

BB: If I don't hand them to you today while I've got 'em... But I had them all laid out for you, and it's just pitiful! [I don't know] where they all are?!

JM: But, the thing is...

[*Judy opens the* House and Home: Spirits of the South *catalog and holds it up to the camera. The spread features one of Beverly's photographs of a structure built by Mary Lou Furcron. Though it's grainy, there's a clear impression of its asymmetrical assembly using scrap tin and lumber, bearing likeness to Beverly's shack sculptures throughout the house. A ladder pieced together from branches leans against the architecture*]

BB: You know, the tape is so wonderful!

JM: The thing is you *found her place after* you'd made all these things.

BB: Yeah. That-that's amazing, I think. Yeah. I don't know if it's amazing or not... I don't know what to call it.

JM: I know that's the way it works, but I don't know how to get at that. Maybe that's the kinda thing you shouldn't talk about.

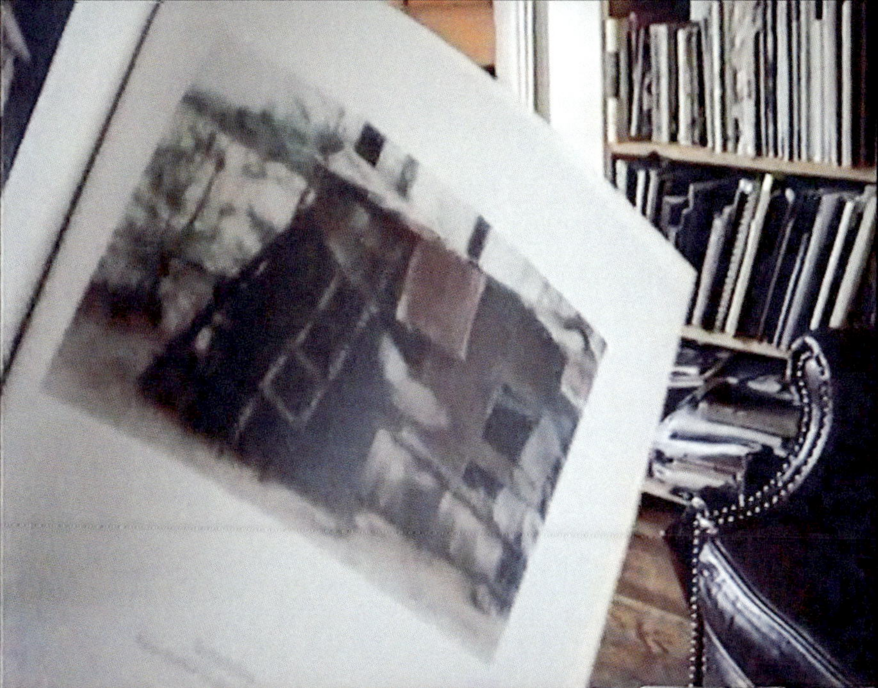

Scene 8
The Hand

01:25:20–01:27:58

While Beverly searches for her photographs of Mary Lou Furcron in a different room, Judy remains in the studio with the camera. She films a group of Beverly's four-by-six-inch photographs, placing them one by one onto a pile. Viewed from above against the dark, matte leather of Beverly's chair seat, Judy's hand moves in and out of the frame. As she slowly adds photographs to the top of the pile, she pauses on each individual image.

[*Shouting from separate rooms*]

Judy McWillie: Nah, I'm okay! But if you're real hungry, you know, we could—

Beverly Buchanan: I ate already!

JM: Nah, I'm fine.

[*Judy shifts her voice to narrate for the camera, which faces a photograph of a collapsed barn in a rural setting*]

This is Oconee County.

BB: 'Cause Judy, that's what's happening all around! It's not just Black people, it's white people too!

JM: Yeah, *real fast*.

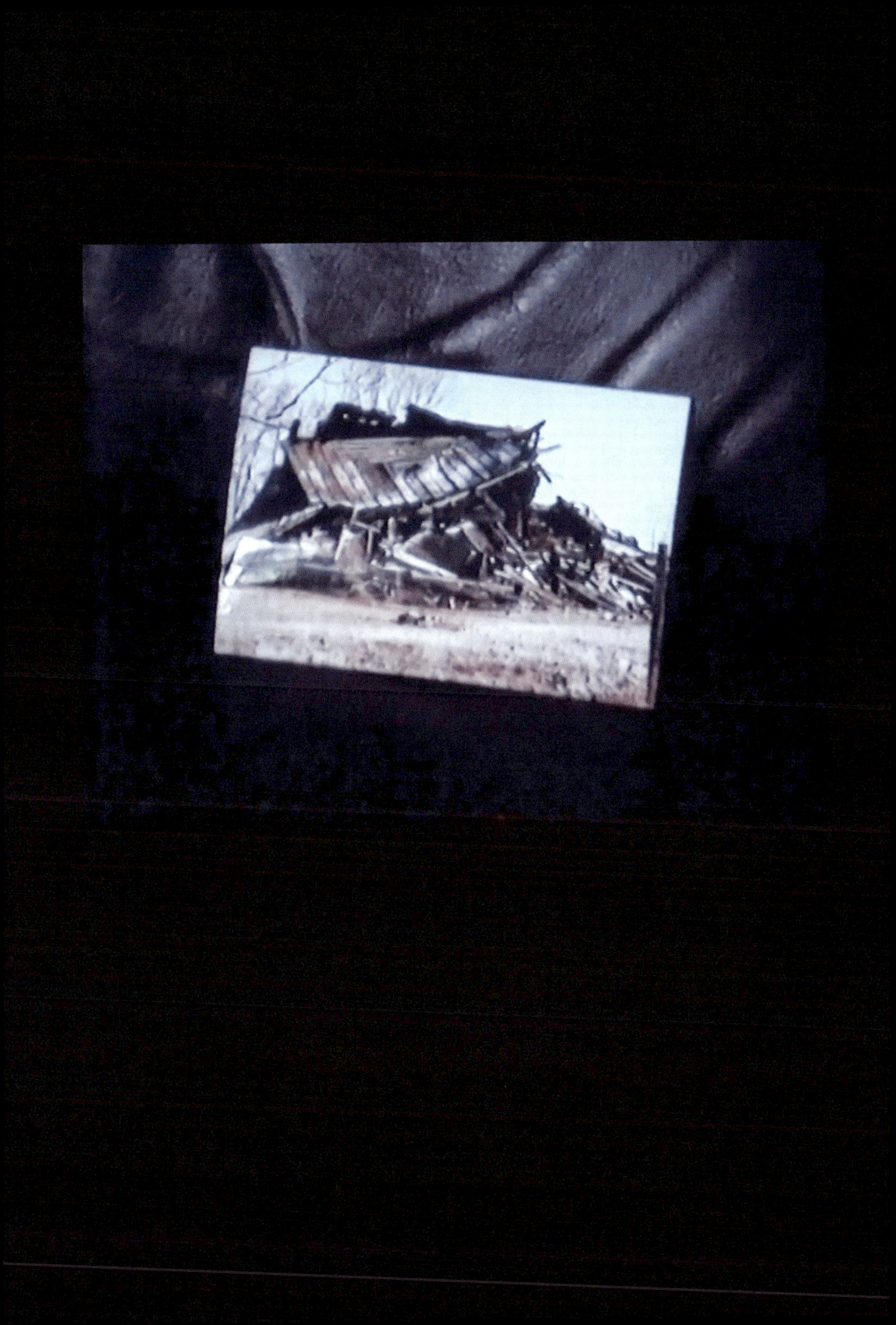

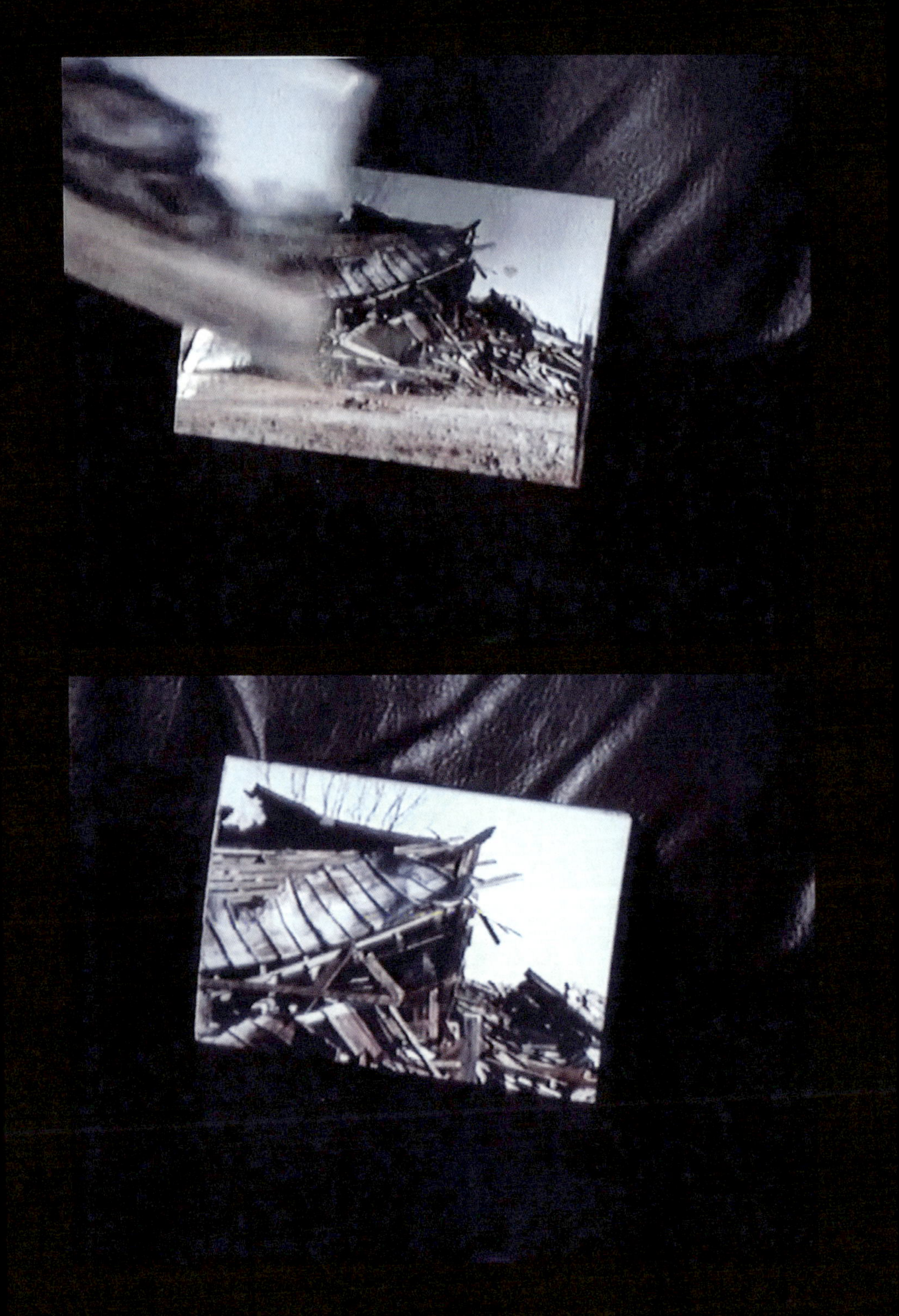

[*Judy places a second photograph onto the chair seat. The photograph depicts the collapsed barn from a further distance and slightly different angle*]

BB: They're losing their...

JM: I don't understand the... [*places a third photograph onto the pile*] You think it's all the Olympics? Or you think people are just *dying* soon?

BB: I think it's a combination of both of them.

JM: Mm-hmm.

[*There's a break in the dialogue. Judy pauses on a photograph, a closely cropped detail of the barn's split beams. She then places another photograph on top, showing a different angle of the same collapsed structure. And another*]

BB: This is what happens when you put Mary Lou Furcron photos in a special place!

JM: Yeah. Anytime you put something in a special place, you lose it, I tell you. [*gasps*] Oh, my god. Look at the foundation!

[*Judy carefully places a photograph of stacked stones on top of the growing pile*]

Is this–is this stone wall the foundation of one of these houses?

BB: I have to look at it and tell you.

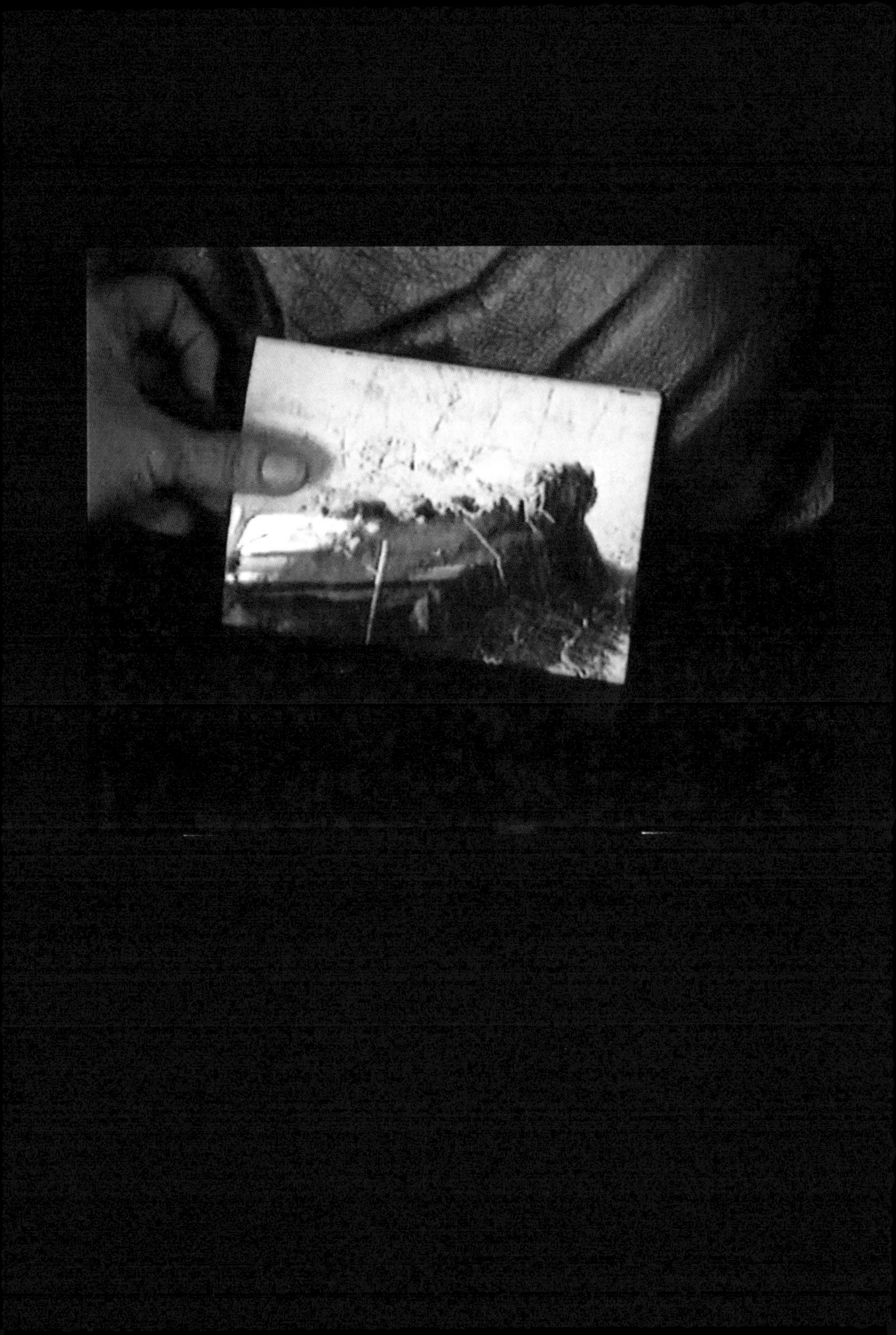

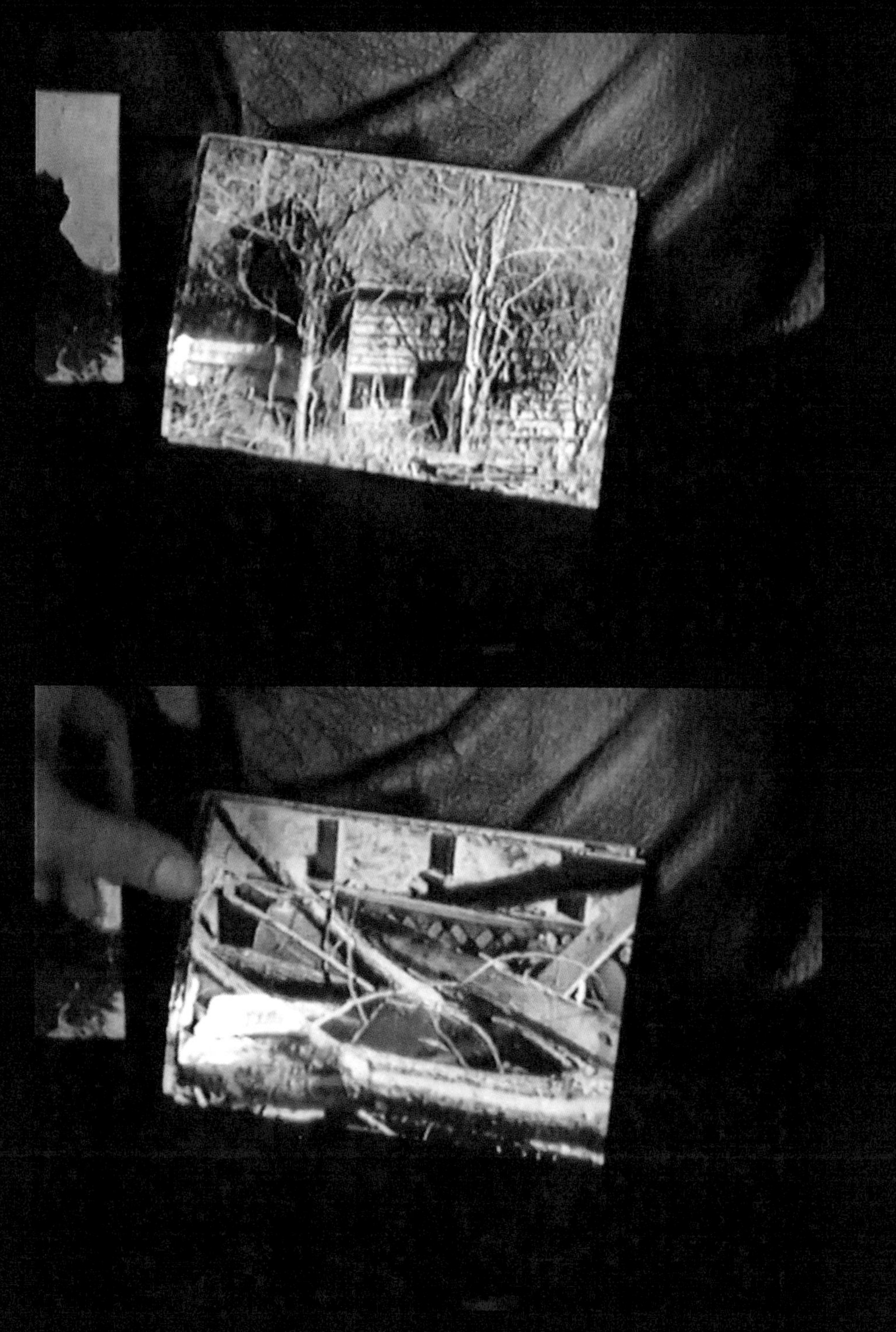

JM: [*temporarily sets the photo aside*] Okay.

[*The dialogue pauses again. Judy continues to place Beverly's photographs, one by one, onto the seat of the chair. One photograph shows a shack structure hidden behind trees, seemingly abandoned. Others detail jagged and broken elements of the collapsed barn*]

BB: I got stuff moved around. I didn't want Roger to be able to-to see them, so I-I moved them when Roger was here.

JM: [*sighs*] Yeah.

BB: That's what happens when you do that. [*groans*] When you move stuff!

[*Their conversation pauses again. Meanwhile, Judy continues to add photographs to the pile. This batch depicts one of Beverly's drawings of shacks, made with colorful, expressive lines*]

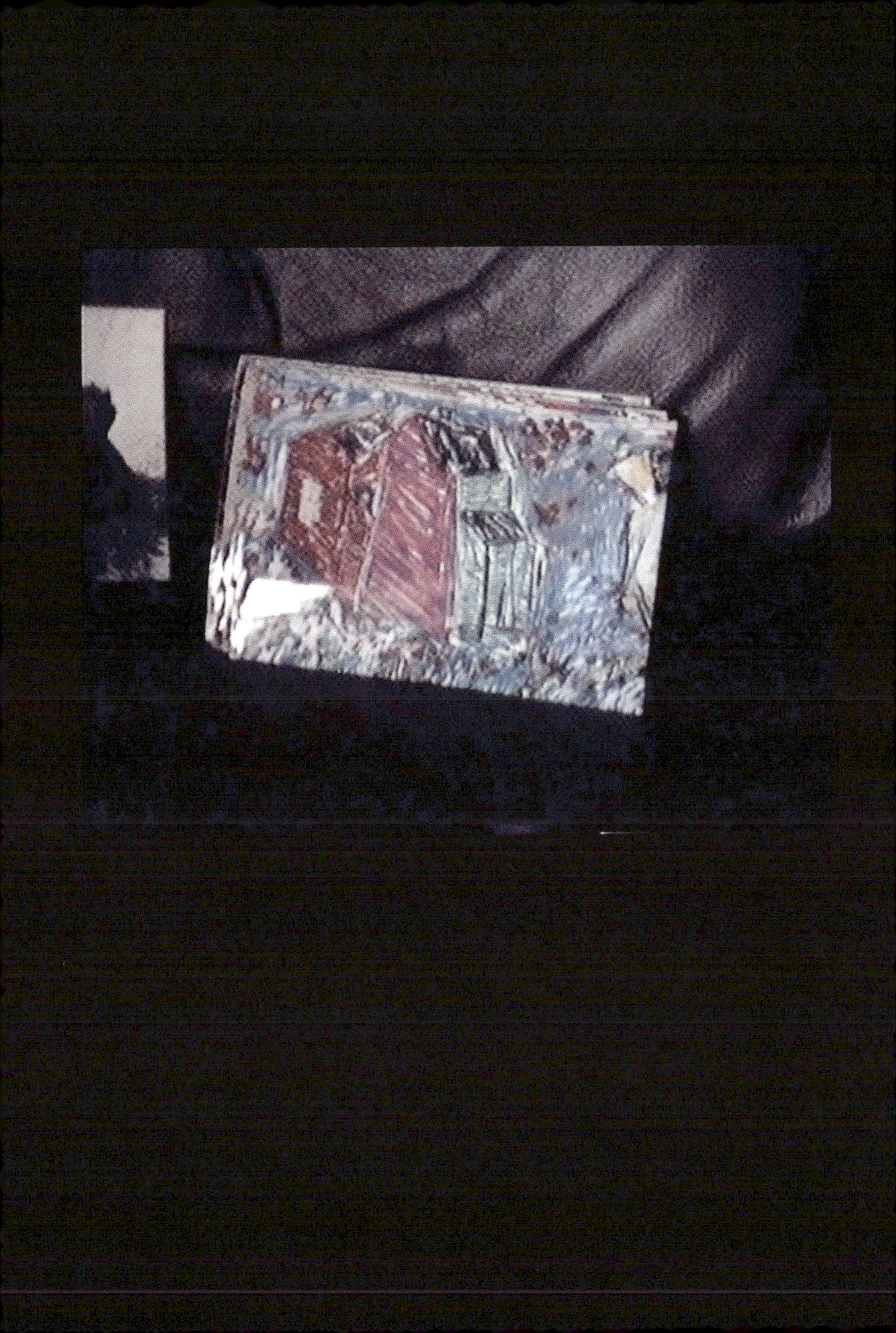

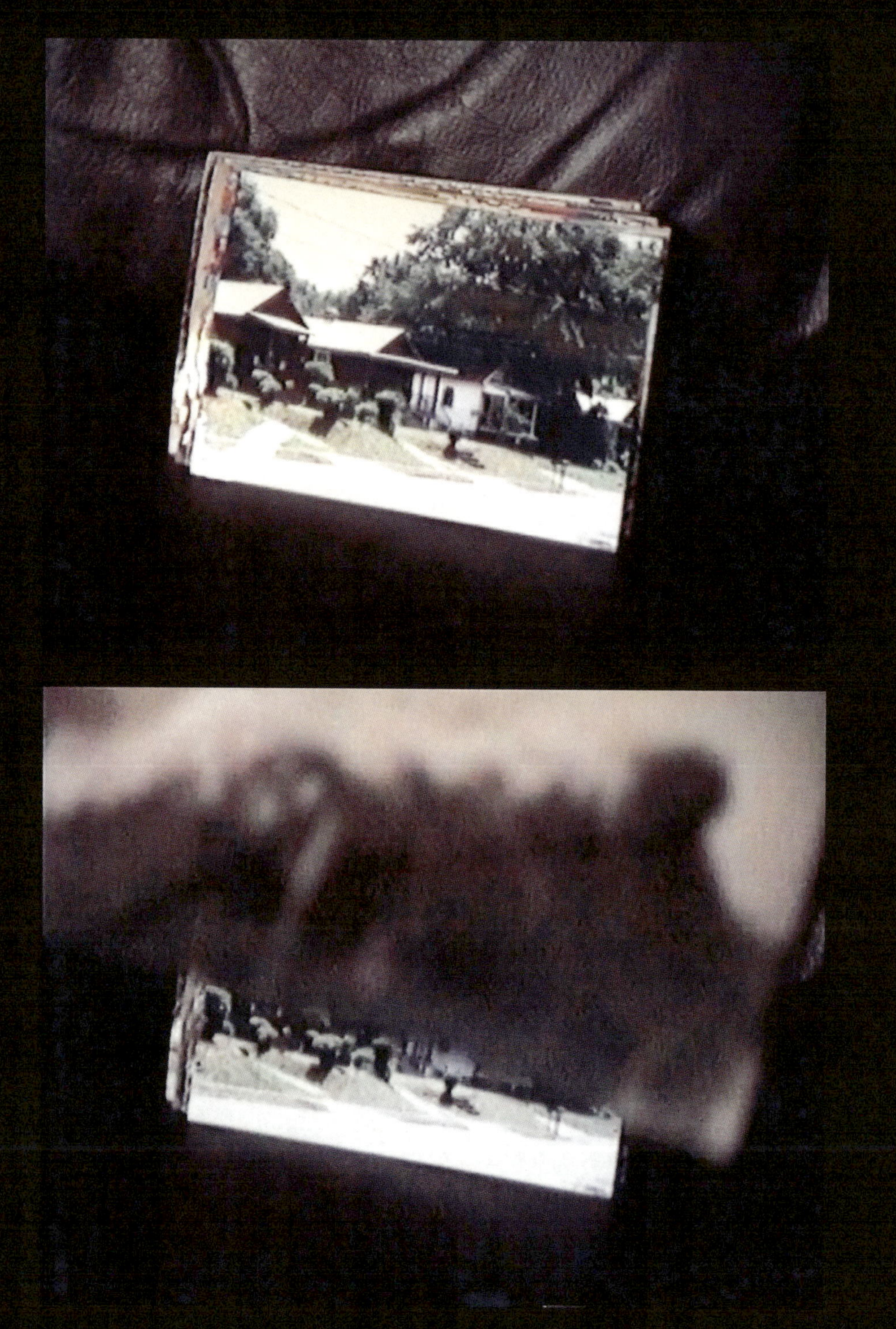

[*Beverly reenters the room*]

BB: I have another place to look, too. You can look at anything. Let me get by you a minute to...

[*Judy places a photograph depicting a row of shotgun shacks on an urban, neighborhood street*][1]

JM: God...

BB: When Roger was here, I didn't want Roger to hook onto, um—

[*Judy shows Beverly the photograph that'd she'd set aside*]

JM: Is this a–is this a foundation? Is that what this is?

BB: Yes! Behind that house! And see, Prudence and I decided this must have been an old slave somethin'.

JM: Yeah.

BB: We did! We really did! And the old smokehouse was still there, out there. I think one of those photos might show an intact smokehouse.

JM: Oh god, well you know, *they built it*! *They built it*!

BB: Yes!

JM: God...

BB: Yes, they did. But *their garden*, people remember their garden!

[Beverly walks to another area of the studio. Judy removes the photographs, and the camera continues to record the leather chair seat]

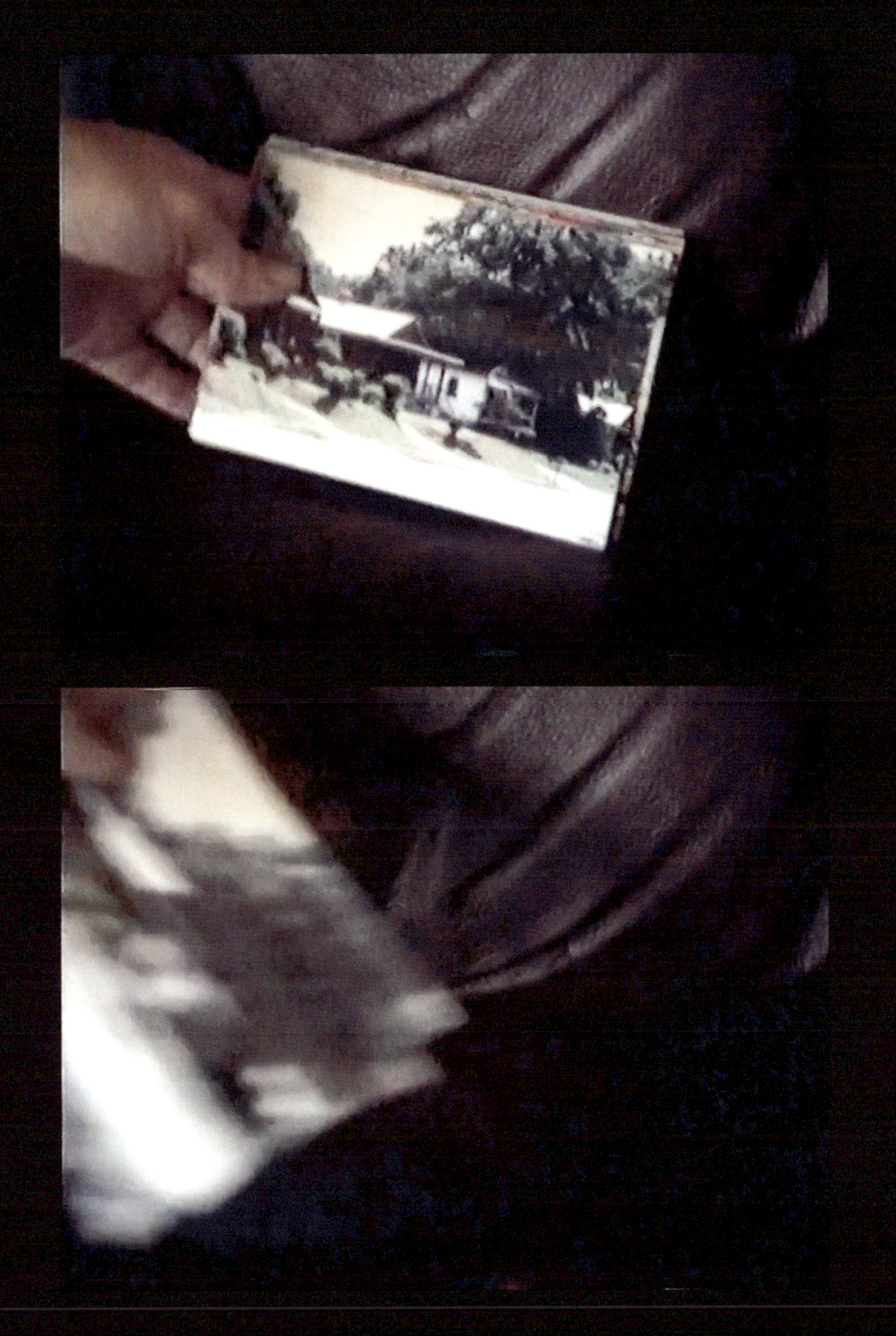

Scene 9

The Flat File

01:27:59–01:44:54

Beverly rounds the corner of the studio, and sets up a chair in front of her large flat file storage drawers. Judy follows, and arranges her camera on a tripod off to the side. She records Beverly in profile, rummaging through the flat file drawers looking for the photographs of Mary Lou Furcron. As Beverly searches, she speaks to the drawers, addressing Mary Lou directly. In the process of searching, she finds other photographs that she shows Judy, alternately holding them up for the camera, handing the photographs to Judy, or placing them on the floor. Their conversation jumps around in relation to what emerges from the flat file.

Judy McWillie: You know there's always a kind of ironic thing, about when stuff like this is destroyed because... Most people look at it and just see poverty.

Beverly Buchanan: Yeah, yeah...

[*Seated, Beverly opens a flat file drawer*]

JM: And one of the things I loved about Renée Stout—The first day she was in town, we went to see the *House and Home* show, and went immediately to the Mary Lou Furcron stuff. The first thing Renée said was, "You know, this isn't poverty."

BB: No! [*looks up from the flat file drawer*]

JM: Bingo.

BB: That's right. [*nods*]

JM: And so, when I was calling around, trying to figure out if there's any way to save Mary Lou's house, I thought, "Well, what are you gonna do? Get a helicopter and lift it, and put it in a backyard somewhere?"

BB: That's right. That's right.

JM: And turn it into a museum?

BB: No. No. [*shakes head*]

JM: And there seemed to be something *obscene* about that.

BB: No, you can't do that! That's like, "No."

JM: Yeah, that's right.

BB: That's right. No, it's not poverty.

JM: Unh-uh, it isn't. God almighty. But it's those, it's *those details*, you know? It's *the stacked stones*.

BB: And Judy, there's stuff around like that. It's *disappearing*! It's like, Prudence was sick this past week.

JM: What's disappearing is the, is the... the *fervent touch*.

BB: Yeah, well I mean, *finding them* is disappearing.

JM: And, you know, I know this sounds awful—

[*Beverly pulls out a photograph from the flat file drawer, leans over, and hands it to Judy*]

BB: This is a shot of the *Blue* [*Station*] *Stones* down in Florida. It's just a small shot.

JM: Oh yeah. One day, I wanna visit that!

BB: I wanna go back!

JM: Where is it exactly?

BB: Well, I have an address. If you get on the Metrorail system, you have to go by the Earlington Heights Station. It's the station right after, or before, Betye Saar's piece. Two stations down from the [Louise] Nevelson piece.[1] [*smiles*]

JM: Okay, gotcha. [*chuckles*] Alright, I'll find it.

[*Judy holds the photograph of* Blue Station Stones *in front of the camera, obscuring the view of Beverly. Though the photograph is out of focus on video, there's an impression of trees*]

BB: But what I mean by disappearing is that, um, by the time... If we see it one day, it may not be there next week, is what I'm saying.

JM: There's still *a lot* in Mississippi.

BB: Is there?

JM: Yeah. But-but Mississippi is still... Oh man!

BB: Is there still, are there bottle trees?

JM: Yeah.

BB: 'Cause, see, Patricia doesn't look for stuff like that. I wanna see a *real* bottle tree, 'cause my blue bottle tree out here is just a *symbolic* tree.[2] [*points to the backyard, shakes head*]

JM: I'll tell you, a good bottle tree is in Brent, Alabama.

BB: Really?! That's where Bill's from! [*smiles*] Bill, the museum director, is from near there. You're kidding!

JM: What!? Bill Eiland's from Brent?

BB: He's from nearby.

JM: He has to go see Reverend George Kornegay!

BB: He probably knows him.

JM: [*emphatically*] His yard is *amazing*. Not only has he got beautiful bottle trees, some of them are painted silver. They're beautiful.

BB: Oh, I'd love to see that! [*smiles*] About how many hours away is that? Not too far?

JM: It's three hours maybe, at the most.

BB: That's not bad. [*closes one flat file drawer, opens another*] You know, [the photos of Mary Lou are] gonna appear when you get out of here, I know it.

JM: You can't stop it, you can't stop it. There's another dimension to this work that you've done, with these shacks. And that is that it's almost, Beverly, like when you made these, and you put them in the gallery, it was almost like it was *permission*, for people to love them.

BB: Yes. [*laughs*] Good for you.

JM: Who *didn't know* whether to love them or not.

BB: Good for you. I discovered that! When young Black kids would talk— My first show at Heath Gallery, with the paper ones, the response was, "I-I told my daddy about these, and he said, [*shifts to impersonate man's voice*] 'Oh, why she wanna do something, dragging old stuff up!?'"[3]

JM: But-but it took the—

BB: THEN, they took a photo of it and showed it. No. THEN, they went home and their attitude was like, "When was this old barn built?" One of the guys said to me, "I started asking questions one at a time. I'd wait. I'd ask *one question* at breakfast, *one* at lunch, and *one* at supper. A different question about the barn. And then it got to be, by the next morning, Daddy had me by the hand, taking me out there, showing me something."

JM: See?

BB: He said, "That's the difference! If you hadn't *let me see this*, I wouldn't have had *the sense* to ask Daddy!"

JM: Yes! It took the *art* to make that permissible.

BB: That's what that young man said to me. I'll never forget it. He was from South Carolina. I said, "That made my whole year, your saying that."

JM: And you know something? I'll tell you what else. Writing about it wouldn't have accomplished that.

BB: I think maybe not, 'cause a lot of people don't read and write. You can't imagine how many people can't read.

JM: I *know* it wouldn't have. But not just 'cause they don't read and write. But when you read about something, it makes it even more... I don't know. It cuts something off. In other words, it would have taken *the physical object* for that process to happen.

BB: Yeah, I think so. I think you're right. I think it gave them permission because that's been the response, for so many of them to say to me, you know?[4]

JM: Yeah. I had a hard—I *still* have a hard time—[with] Michael Harris, about the, um, visionaries and the, you know, the artists. 'Cause he says, "Oh, it's just like primitivism and modernism."[5]

BB: Uh, no! It's not! [*opens another drawer of the flat file*]

JM: No! It's like–it's like *Sam Chatmon, Mississippi John Hurt*.

BB: Yeah! That's right. [*smiles, nods*]

JM: You know, *Robert Johnson, Bukka White, Gus Cannon*.

BB: That's right, yes, yeah.

JM: You know, *that's what it is*! You know, it's the first ones.

[*Beverly removes a stack of large color photographs from the flat file and places them on the floor*]

BB: These are photos of the house that they're gonna tear down over here, that this Black man owns. [*points toward the backyard*] But I'm just throwing them down because I wanna get to...

JM: Yeah, yeah.

[*Judy turns the camera toward the photographs Beverly has placed on the floor. The photograph on top shows two wooden buildings in a wooded area. The trees are bare, and the front porch in the foreground is flooded with light*]

BB: Mary Lou's gonna come out at me when you leave, I know this. And I said to Patricia, "I'm gonna give all these to Judy McWillie."

JM: That's right. [*laughs*] I sure would like to see them.

[*Judy tilts the camera back to eye level, facing Beverly. Beverly leans over an open flat file drawer. As she digs through the contents, searching, she pushes layers of photographs and prints into a vertical cascade*]

BB: And it's like, Roger came. I did not want Roger to see them. I really didn't. So they've been put somewhere.

JM: Well, let me ask you this.

BB: Ask me. I'll find 'em.

JM: Uh, are you willing to publish any of them in the book?

BB: Absolutely! Yes, ma'am. You can publish *anything* you want to. That's what I'm trying to tell you!

JM: That's wonderful! Wonderful!

BB: I'm not always so clear, I'm sorry. You can publish anything. That's why I'm trying to find 'em!

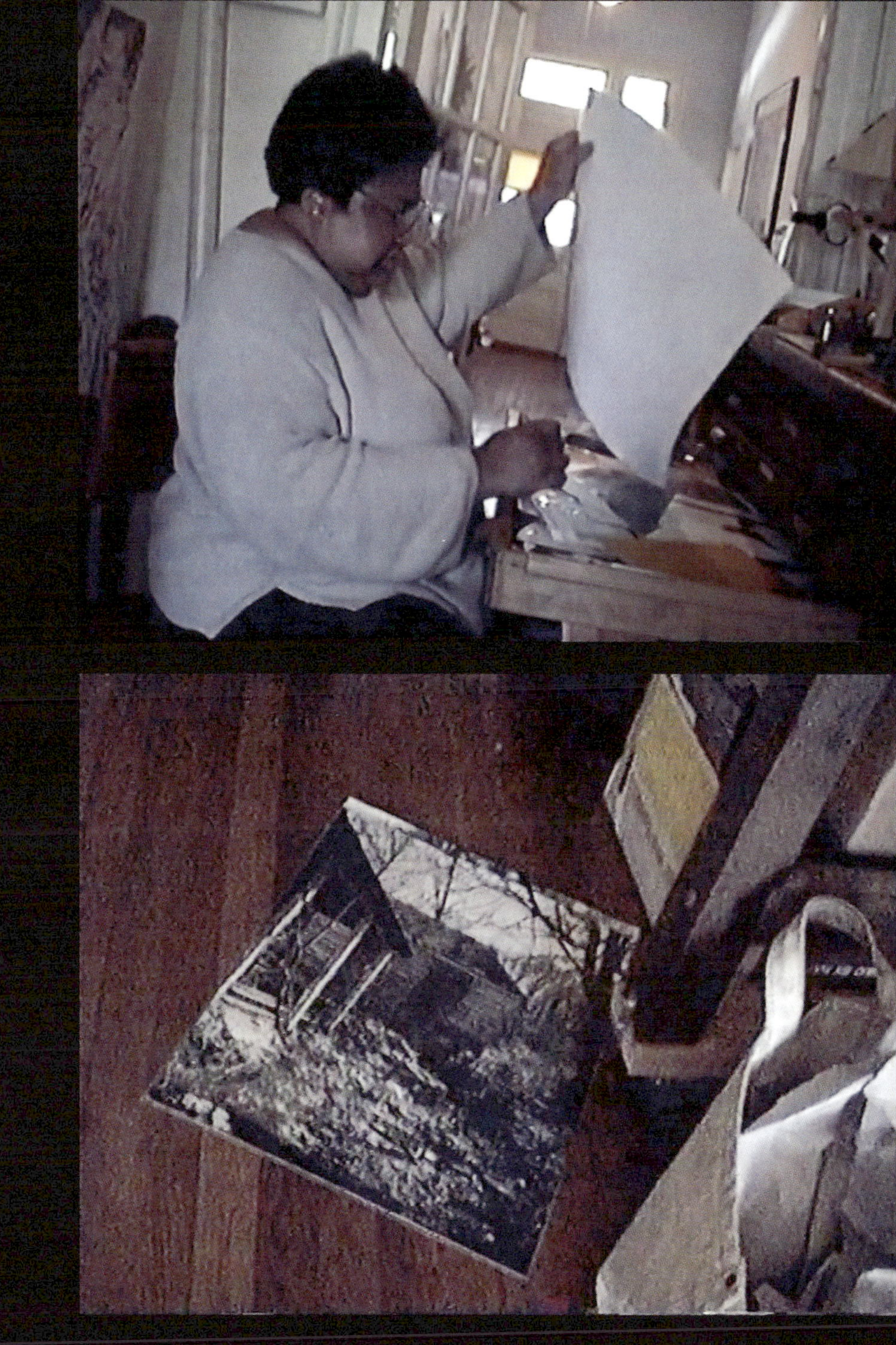

JM: This book... See, I gotta have you in this book because of that—

BB: You don't have to have me in the book.

JM: Yes, I do! Because of that thing that we were just talking about. I mean, the thing's not *complete.*

BB: [*playfully speaks in baby voice*] I don't have to be in the book.

JM: Yes! It's not complete until that gets in there. 'Til this, *this quantum leap here*, gets in there.

[*Out of the frame from behind the camera, Judy points at one of Beverly's shack sculptures, arranged up high on a shelf. Beverly looks upward, nodding*]

BB: [*points up*] That particular shack Alice Walker saw when she came over, when I lived in Forest Heights. And she walked up to it, embraced it, and said, "I grew up in something that looked just like this." And I had never seen Alice Walker's family home in Eatonton.[6] And I was very impressed, touched by that. I really was.

JM: Well, again, it was permission.

[*Beverly picks up a postcard from the drawer, and studies the back of it*]

BB: This woman I met at the Morris Museum, Melinda Moore Lampkin. "East Lansing, Michigan. *African Ancestor.*" This is her work. This is what she made, and her card is here. [*holds the postcard up to the camera, showing a stylized bust of a Black femme collaged from flat colors and found patterns*]

JM: Oh great.

BB: But see, I'm saying that people from *all over the United States* have come to the shows, and the response has just been so amazing! [*continues rummaging through the flat file drawer*] Mary Lou, I know you're hiding in here somewhere! I'mma find you!

JM: Wait a minute, I'll get me a divining rod. I bet I can feel where those things are. Something tells me they are...

BB: I bet you could! [*pulls out a large color photograph, showing a road, a white* *stump, and trees*] This was down in Wadmalaw Island. And I took a photo of this lady's mailbox, that did *not* come out. Hoo-hoo-hoo. Her white stump came out! [*smiles*] But her mailbox did not come out! That still floors me to this day. That her mailbox did not come out, in that photo. [*places hand on forehead*]

JM: What was it?

BB: Just, it was a white mailbox with her name and her house number on it. It was not meant for me to take that. [*places the photograph back in the drawer, continues to sift through layers of photographs and papers*] Mary Lou, I know you're in here! *I know you are*. You're just being… [*closes the flat file drawer, opens another*]

JM: You know, I feel like they're over near that tall window back there, in the kitchen.

BB: Really?

JM: I don't know why.

BB: I don't know why either. I never put anything… [*laughs*] But see, hiding stuff from Roger, I certainly could have!

JM: Maybe you put 'em up high somewhere?

BB: But they're *stacked*! They're a bunch of them, 'cause there's *so many*. They're a bunch of them.

JM: [*reassuringly*] Oh, when they turn up—

BB: [*pretends to cry*] I can't believe this!

JM: —give me a call, you know.

BB: I can't believe it, I can't believe it. [*mock cries*] I didn't want Roger to see them. Isn't that funny? It was like, I liked him, but he was not, I *did not* want him to see them.

JM: I tell you, the one I really adore is the—hah, I love all of them—but the one in particular, where she's sitting on the porch and the smoke's coming out. Man, it's got smoke coming out.

BB: Yeah! Well, that was when it was caught on fire!

JM: No!

BB: That was the fire they were putting out, yes!

JM: You mean that was a fire?! It wasn't a—?

BB: No, it was a fire! That was a fire!

[*Laughter*]

JM: All this time I've been trying to figure out where that pipe that made that smoke could have been, because it wasn't in the—

BB: In the back, in the back. It was the fire! That was the day that I went up there, and the place was—I thought, "Oh god, am I gonna have to help put out this fire?" But [Willie Ed Sanders] had it, they had it under control! [*laughs*] But I was scared to death. [*shakes head*]

JM: [*chuckles*] God, that's a relief.

BB: Oh, I was scared out of my mind. I thought, "Oh, lord, I'mma watch this building go up in..."

JM: Hey, Beverly, is this one of your paintings here? Starting?

[*Beverly turns around from the flat file, as Judy pivots the camera to a large painting, maybe five feet tall, leaned against the wall just behind Beverly. The painting is abstract, with expressionistic colorful lines in hatched marks*]

BB: Yeah. No, it was from '85, and I had it in that room, and I took it down. I get tired of looking at them. I'm tired of them.

JM: Oh, I know, I know.

BB: [*continuing to rummage through the drawer*] I can't believe it, I know they're here.

JM: The only way to, I think, to keep from getting tired of your house, is to have it so complicated that you can't... [*laughs*]

BB: Yeah, I think you're right. I hate to say that, but I think you're right. Have it so complicated that you—

JM: I threw everything out of my house. I thought I wanted to live in this *blankness*.

BB: You know, it's like, it gets to be too much after a while.

JM: Hell no. No blankness.

BB: Mary Lou, you're hiding. I know you're hiding. I'll find you! [*closes flat file drawer, opens another*] 'Cause you, you know, I put you away so that the guy wouldn't see you, but you're hiding. [*raises eyebrows*]

JM: I'm just gonna look in there, just...

BB: Oh, help yourself, I don't care!

JM: Maybe they're right here, on this pile? That's probably what—

BB: I don't know! I don't know. I can't believe this... Well, that means you have to come right back.

JM: [*from a distance*] Yeah, I will.

BB: You know what I mean? That means you have to come right back over here.

[*The conversation pauses. Judy seems to have left the room. Meanwhile the camera remains stationary on the tripod, facing Beverly in profile as she continues searching the flat file drawer. For about a minute, there's no dialogue. The hum of the fish tank trickling in the foyer is once again audible, punctuated by the sounds of rustling photographs and papers*]

JM: You know, one time I lost my—

BB: That means you have to come right back over here because, that means that, like, tonight I can start—I'll take *everything* out of here, to look for it.

JM: I will. You know, I lost my iron one time, and I had put it in my refrigerator. [*laughs*]

BB: [*nods*] But knowing me, hiding stuff from Roger, it's like, 'cause he was all, he was walking around looking at stuff, and I didn't want him to *really* see... So I *know* that she's here.

JM: Are they, maybe they're in Patti's room?

BB: No, I wouldn't do that. Because that's a separate area.

[*The video fades to black abruptly, then resumes with Beverly still seated at the flat file, searching the drawers*]

JM: So, I called a few people, you know, and told them that [Mary Lou's] house was going. But there was something about, "No you can't. You can't stop it."

BB: [*forlorn*] Yeah, I know.

JM: And plus, god, there would have been something almost, almost *morbid* about moving it from her.

BB: See, it's like there's so many... [*picks up a four-by-six-inch color photograph from the drawer*] This is a photo [of] that house that was [on the way] going to Jefferson. There were all these Black people that lived in this house, and it was just before, um, Arcade.

JM: Oh yeah! All the way to... Absolutely, absolutely, yeah.

BB: [*holds the photograph up to the camera, showing the front porch of a shack, pictured from a distance, with a road and foliage in the foreground*] This is it! And I could never stop and photograph it! 'Cause there was always somebody around! And so this is called, I call it a "ride-by shooting."

[*Beverly, wide-eyed and smiling, hands the photograph to Judy, whose arm reaches out into the frame*]

JM: [*laughs*] Yeah, got a bunch of those myself.

BB: I've shot a lot of photos like that. Ride-by shooting. And that [house] doesn't exist anymore. [*places the photograph back in the drawer*] But I have

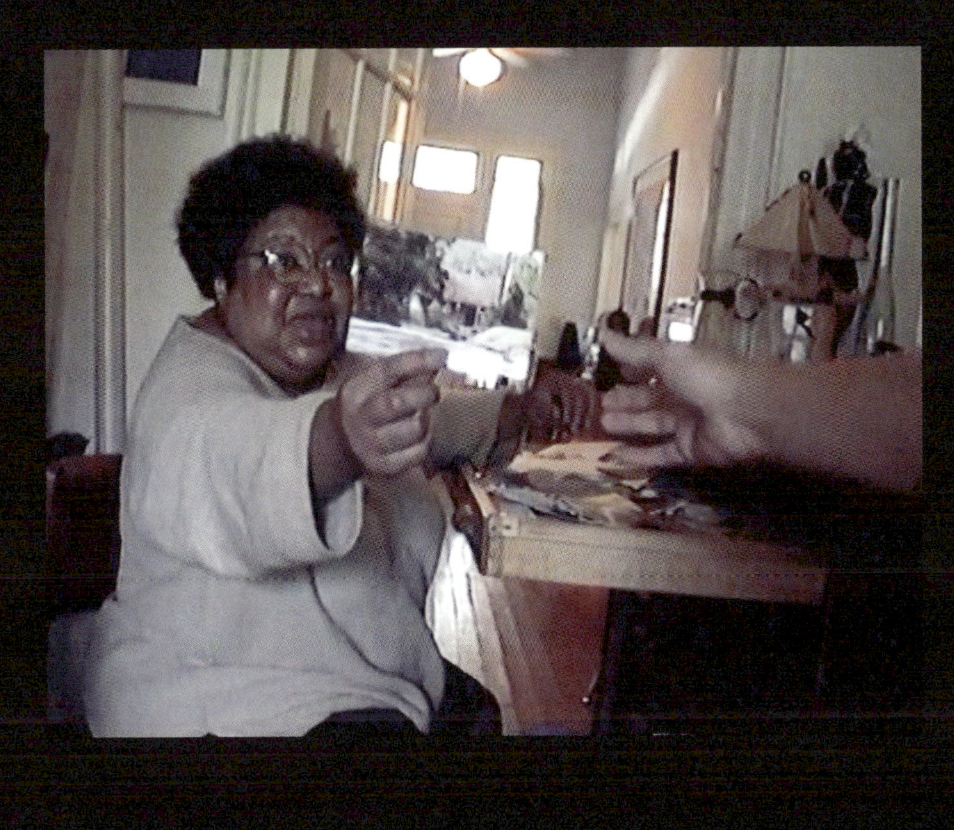

a lot of photos of places that have burned to the ground and don't exist anymore, but *used to exist* when I first came to Athens.

JM: You know the singer Precious Bryant?

BB: Yeah, yeah.

JM: Now, she lives in a *mind-boggling* house.

BB: *Really*?

JM: And I went to see her in it, and I can't remember where it was. It was central Georgia. I think it was near Macon, but I'll ask Art Rosenbaum.

BB: Wow...

JM: Anyway, Beverly, I mean, that thing—

BB: I met Art for the first time at my show, and I loved him! I said, "Oh, I love your work!" And I started talking to him about his work. [*continues shuffling through the drawer*] I'm gonna find you, Mary Lou.

JM: Uh-huh, uh-huh. Yeah, he would know where Precious lives. And it was one of those houses up on stilts.

BB: The mind-boggling, up on stilts, yeah. [*nods*]

JM: That didn't even have a front door, so she only stayed there in the summer.

BB: Right.

JM: But I mean, it didn't have a door. It was just an open—

BB: So in wintertime, you couldn't close the door!

JM: Uh-huh. And it was just an open, big open room.

BB: I'm gonna find this. I'm determined. See, I should have had all this done before you got here.

JM: She's amazing. You know what she did? Her husband beat her up. She shot the mother!

BB: [*laughs, opens another drawer*] When I got to Macon, they were telling me about this wonderful woman, churchgoing. She was just real sweet, and her husband went out every night, they said. He used to come in early in the morning, and she'd go on to work and fix him breakfast. And one morning he came in, she's sitting on the couch. He opened the door and saw her and said, "Hey, sweetheart!" And as he walked in the front door and said that, she reached down in the couch and got this big gun. And I don't think he even had time to say, "Wait a minute." Boom! Put him away. You know, she never went to jail.

JM: No, no. Precious didn't either.

BB: I learned that in Macon. What scared me in Macon is that these women would shoot these men, and not spend time in jail. That used to just blow me away! [*places hand on forehead*] Oh my god.

JM: I don't think Precious even had to answer any questions.

BB: Uh-huh, uh-huh. That used to frighten me in Macon. Frighten me! Because I thought, "If somebody thinks I'm out there running around with their husband, I am in deep trouble." [*groans*] Like this one young man who taught me how to drive a school bus. He took me out to his house. I met his wife, and I said to him, "Your wife doesn't really like me." "Yeah, she does!" I said, "I don't mean, she doesn't *dislike* me so much. It's just that, she doesn't really want me around you." You know? [*chuckles*] And I was right.

JM: [*chuckles*] Mannn. Hell hath no fury.

BB: And I'm scared! I said, "This is Macon. Women don't seem to go to jail here." In other parts of the state, they may, but they don't seem to go to jail here. [*laughs*] That scares me, man.

JM: Very few people go to jail in Macon.

[*Laughter*]

BB: Well, yeah! You know, it's like, Macon's a real special place. And I don't really want some woman to shoot me. I said, "If she kills me outright, that's one thing, but I don't wanna linger. I can't afford rehabilitation."

[*Laughter*]

JM: Macon had a club that I always wanted to go into, and I was too scared. It was called the Tomcat Club. And the sign in the front was a circle, just with two triangles on top. [*laughs*] It was great! The Tomcat Club... If I'd been there on a weekday, I'da gone in, but I was there on a Saturday. God...

BB: I'm gonna find Mary Lou. I can't believe it.

JM: You'll find her. She'll turn up.

BB: I'm gonna look for her. You're right she'll turn up! I'm gonna find her. *I put her* in a special place, Judy. They're all stacked, they're all together. I know what they look like! They're all together stacked up. [*closes the drawer, opens another*]

JM: I probably need to go out and see the Sanders to, uh—

BB: Yeah, see Lucille.

JM: Yeah, that's right. Have you seen her since [Willie Ed] died?

BB: Yeah, I took her some money at Christmas, and, uh, I haven't been back since. But I'm gonna go. I called her 'cause I was scared about her not having, um, any wood.

JM: That's right, 'cause [Willie Ed] would have—

BB: But, I haven't been back out there. I need to go. It just hurts. I just, I can't look at the spot where [Mary Lou's] house used to be.

JM: I need to go see the Flemings. Fox and Juanita Fleming.

BB: Hm, I don't know who they are?

JM: Fox and Juanita Fleming. They live, I don't know the name of the road, but they live nearby. And I *think* that they're in Richard's book.

BB: Do you know that I've never met him? I've never met him! I'm gonna kill Jean. I said, "Jean..." [*laughs*]

JM: You never met Richard Westmacott?!

BB: No!

JM: Oh, for god's sake!

BB: 'Cause I've known Jean, you know?

JM: Well, anyway, Fox Fleming knows where all the old graveyards are in the woods out there.

BB: Ooooh. [*closes the drawer, bends down to open the bottom drawer*]

JM: And I've never gone with him to see them, but, I mean... There's still *a lot* in Oglethorpe County.

BB: Is there?

JM: Yeah, there really is. There's this one highway [where] there's a funky antique store. It's on the way, just before you get to Lexington. And you can't miss it. It's this huge, like, block house. It was an antique store. Then there's a little highway off to the left. That whole strip in there is, the mother lode. Gorgeous stuff.

BB: Wow. I've not paid attention to that.

JM: Well, one day we should get in the car, you know?

BB: Yeah, one day, get in the truck! So we can throw things in the truck!

JM: Yeah, yeah, the truck. [*chuckles*]

[*Beverly has taken out an envelope of photographs, and is looking through them*]

BB: I've got to find, I'mma find Mary Lou. 'Cause I've-I've put them away. I've hidden them. Hiding them from Roger. [*bends back down to the bottom drawer*]

JM: Boy, every time I put something where it's supposed to be, I lose it.

BB: I want you to have them and use whatever you want to use. I don't care. I really don't. Mary Lou, where are you? *I know* you're here, *somewhere*. I SAVED you!

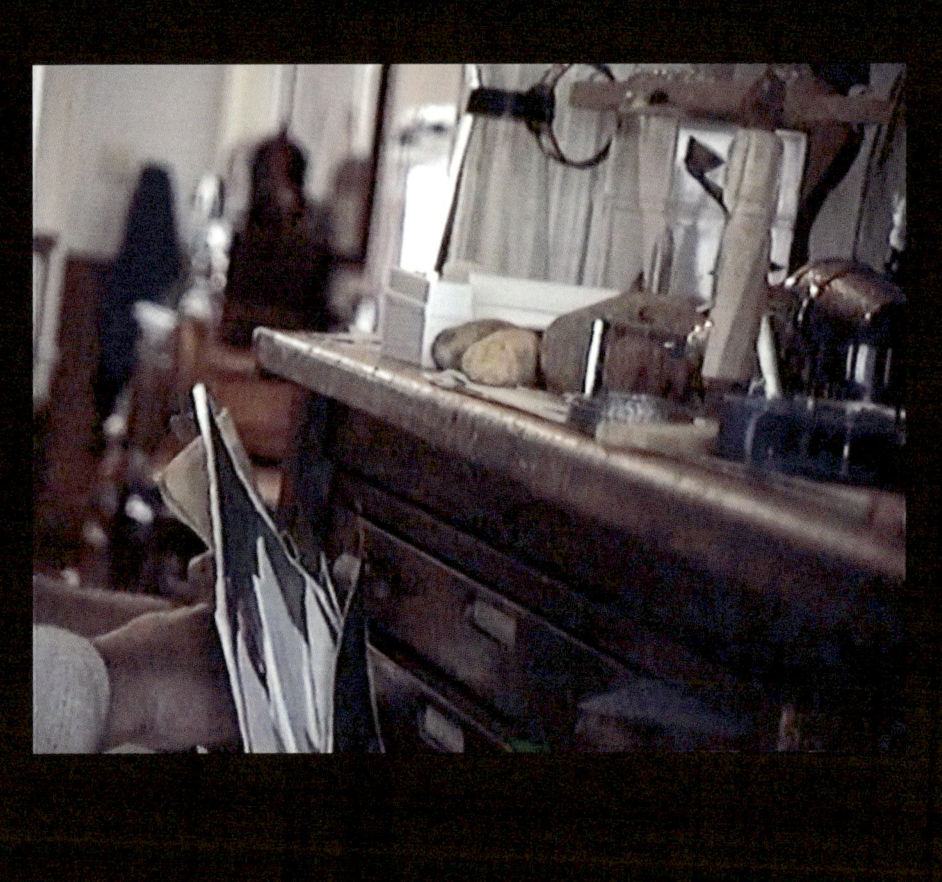

JM: Well, Grey is anxious to get this book done, and I'm trying to get enough time to do it right, and it's—

[*Beverly rises from her chair suddenly, and begins to walk away from the flat file*]

BB: We will find them before the day is over...

JM: Okay. [*chuckles*]

Scene 10

The End

01:44:55–02:01:08

Fatigue sets in, bringing out different tones in Beverly and Judy's exchange. Like the whirlwind of brain fog, Beverly and Judy revisit the same rooms and piles of photographs, reanimating their stories of Mary Lou Furcron with new insights. The video, too, feels dreamlike, broken up with sudden jump cuts as it tracks Beverly and Judy moving throughout the house, the camera twisting and turning from its tripod mount as Judy carries it along. Beverly's voice trails in and out as she continues searching for the photographs, and heads to the kitchen to tend to her health. Meanwhile, Judy focuses her attention on different sculptures and artworks scattered about, mostly on the floor. When Beverly gives up searching, she returns to sit in her leather chair, a large sheet of fresh drawing paper behind her. Once seated, the fatigue gives way to flowing and tender conversation.

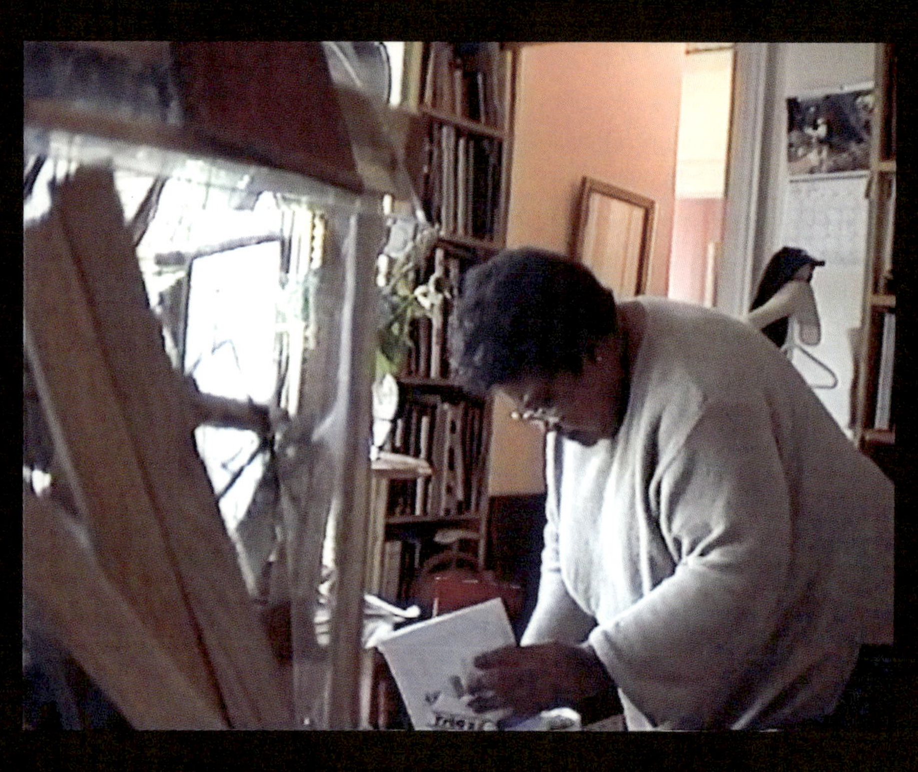

Beverly Buchanan: I can't believe it. All this saving and...

Judy McWillie: It's okay. Just sit down for a while, and it'll come to you.

[*Beverly walks to the main seating area of her studio, where the plexiglass shack sits on its workstation, near her coffee table, chair, and library*]

BB: [*sighs*]

JM: They'll show up. They will. [*facing the plexiglass shack sculpture*] Well these shacks... See, when I look at Christenberry's shacks, to me they were *always* Hans Hofmann paintings, 'cause he—

BB: Well, I like them. They're just different from what I'm doing, and I—

JM: I mean, I do too. I really like them.

BB: They're just different.

[*Beverly leans over the coffee table, covered in piles of photographs, rummaging through them as she speaks*]

JM: But I know that, uh, looking at Mary Lou's sheds, it was a case of...

BB: Yes. It was a case of astonishment at first sight. I could not believe I was seeing that.

JM: Seeing it in the art first, and then going out and finding it.

BB: Could *not* believe it. It was like... There were no words. There weren't words. And I came back that day and made the shack that Patti owns, with the sticks. In honor of her. I came back *that day* and made that.[1] It was like I couldn't, I couldn't write about it.

JM: Unh-uh.

BB: Words weren't... It's like, I can't do words here.

JM: Well, words even do damage. That's what's so difficult about trying to do anything connected with Mary Lou. I mean, other than a transcript, I don't know. I think of maybe transcribing that tape and having what she said...

BB: The video is *so wonderful*, Judy. It's so wonderful! It's so wonderful!

[*Judy jostles the camera as Beverly rummages through piles*]

JM: Well, I think I'm gonna get it transcribed, and publish it.

BB: It's so wonderful! But *your eye* is just perfect. You focused on exactly what I would have. You went to the rocks, and... [*points out the window toward the garden*]

JM: *Those rocks, man*. Now that I know that was *the schoolhouse*, that blows my mind the schoolhouse was there!

[*Beverly begins searching for the photographs in the bookshelf*]

BB: Yeah, it was a schoolhouse. That's what she said.

JM: And the board of education owned the place where she was.

[*Beverly walks out of the studio to the hallway, leaving the frame. The camera remains stationary, facing the bookshelves and the doorway. On the left, a vase of blue hydrangea flowers and a clamp light frame the foreground*]

What a poignant story about her son.

BB: Isn't that incredible?

JM: Boy, I bet somebody knows how to get in touch with him.

[*The scene abruptly fades to black, then reopens as Judy pans the floor with her camera. She steadies the camera to focus on a cast cement stone sculpture sitting on the wooden floor, surrounded by cardboard boxes*]

JM: .... are everywhere!

BB: What little stone?

JM: Right there! [*laughs*] You know, your *Blue Stones* out in the garden had the birdseed.

BB: Oh, I have stones everywhere. I love stones!

JM: Yeah... [*cracks up with laughter*]

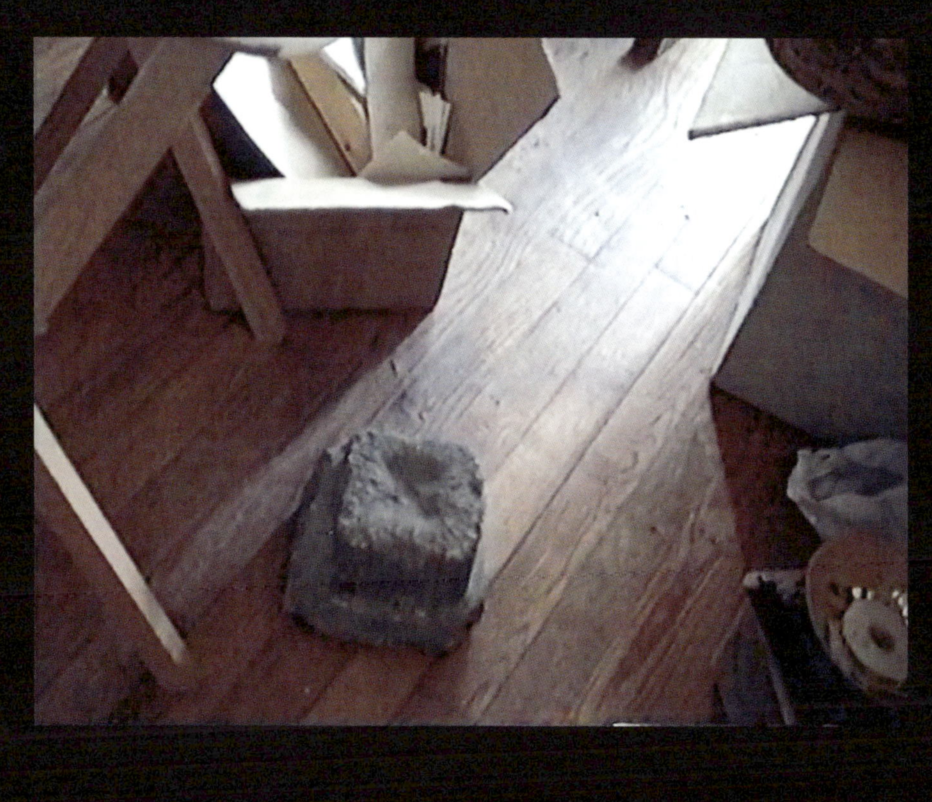

BB: Haven't you noticed? There are rocks everywhere!

[*Laughter*]

JM: Yeah, there are! I even like the one in the front yard with the bricks.

BB: There are rocks *everywhere*!

[*Judy continues to record the cement sculpture on the floor. Beverly's volume is trailing, she seems to be walking away*]

JM: Yeah I gotta get a picture of those bricks—

BB: *Everywhere.*

JM: —before I go.

BB: [*shouting from distance*] The only reason I'm reminding you about when to eat is 'cause, being diabetic, I'm aware of people having to eat. If you're alright, that's okay!

JM: My sugar's okay today. Some days it isn't, but this day it's okay.

BB: I'm just in the habit of asking people, so I don't mean any harm.

JM: Mm-hmm. I had hypoglycemia for about a year, and I'd, like, *pass out* or something if I didn't eat. But I'm okay now.

[*Judy moves throughout the studio panning the camera to record the details of Beverly's workspace, pausing on her drawing, zooming out the window to the bottle tree again. Beverly is still in another room. She's speaking, but the recording is inaudible, just a faint trace of her voice's rhythm in the distance. The image suddenly goes black. The video resumes as Judy records a close up shot of another sculpture by Beverly, a wooden figurative bust whose hair and features are composed from diagonal, angular pieces of scrap wood*]

JM: Oh the other thing about Reverend Kornegay, who's in Brent, is that he made a house that looks so much like the Blue Light Recreation Center.[2] You wouldn't believe it. Anyway, Armell Stroud told me that the Blue Light Recreation Center, no wall in there is at a right angle. And that that's something that his father is really proud of, the fact that he could cut wood at all these strange, oblique angles and put them together in architecture. So when he looked at Kornegay's, he went, "*Yeah, but those are all right angles.*" He says, "My father's house, there's not a right angle in the house." You know, he was *so proud* of it. God...

BB: That's what Cathy Fox said about the first shack show at David Heath. She said, "None of these structures are at a right angle."

JM: That's right.

BB: And people were just bent out of shape about that.

[*Judy pans the camera to face Beverly, who stands in the kitchen drinking a glass of water.*]

JM: Hey, when was that first shack show?

BB: I think it was '85 or '86, something like that.

JM: Okay, yeah. God, [the shacks are] everywhere! [*laughs*]

BB: [*looks up, smiles*] Um, Mallory Lopp made that for me.

JM: That's great. [*chuckles*]

BB: That's "Bev's" everything. "Bev's market. Bev's art. Bev's burgers. Bev's..." [*grins ear to ear, and takes a sip of water*]

JM: Did you make the little one out in the back, with the crooked door? Or did somebody give it to you? Straight back.

BB: That's orange? [*points to the garden*]

JM: Uh, where the dove house is, yeah.

BB: That was at the *Spectacles* show at the High Museum.[3]

JM: I remember that!

BB: And the chair that's inside, and the fireplace. So that was there for five years, and the only person interested in it at one time was... John Whelan. And so, nobody seemed to want to buy it, so I had to bring it back here. Luckily, I had this house then because, where could it have gone over in Forest Heights?

JM: That's right. That's right. Don't you *love* this house? I just love it. Everything about it.

BB: *Yes.* Pat Lasch did all this stuff on the windows. [*places the glass of water down, and starts walking*]

JM: Man.

BB: I heard that Tom [Cerbu] got married again.

JM: See, I didn't know him that well.

BB: Oh, well, Pat went around telling people that I was her best friend, and that was not true. [*giggles*] I didn't even know him!

JM: You don't wanna get shot again!

[*Laughter*]

BB: [*sighs*] Oh, Judy...

JM: You know what? They're gonna turn up.

BB: You're just gonna have to let me find...

JM: They're gonna turn up.

[*There's a cut in the video, and the scene fades to black. When it reopens, Judy is zooming in on a colorful, small assemblage sculpture on the floor, tucked under a desk. As the image comes into focus, so do the found objects that comprise the sculpture, including toy cars, miniature hats, and tinsel*]

JM: Well, they'll come out when they want to.

BB: [*groans*]

JM: I'll be back, as soon as you find them.

BB: It's hysterical!

JM: There's some reason not to look at 'em right now.

[*Judy pans the camera across the studio, recording the plexiglass sculpture for the last time. In a pile of objects on a nearby table, a box with printed text reads "Medi Guard." A flower vase displays a bouquet of blue, yellow, and white flowers*]

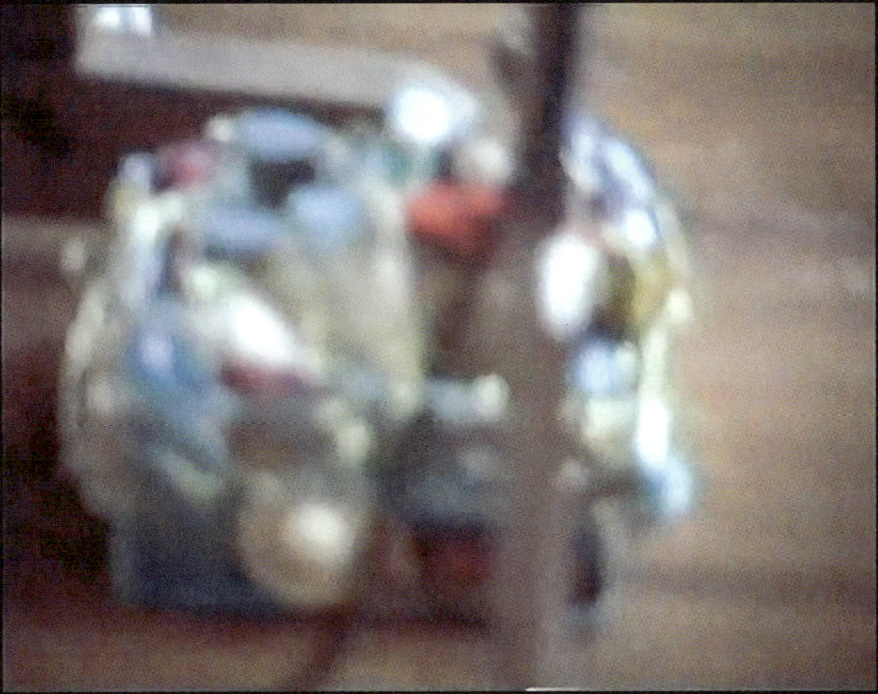

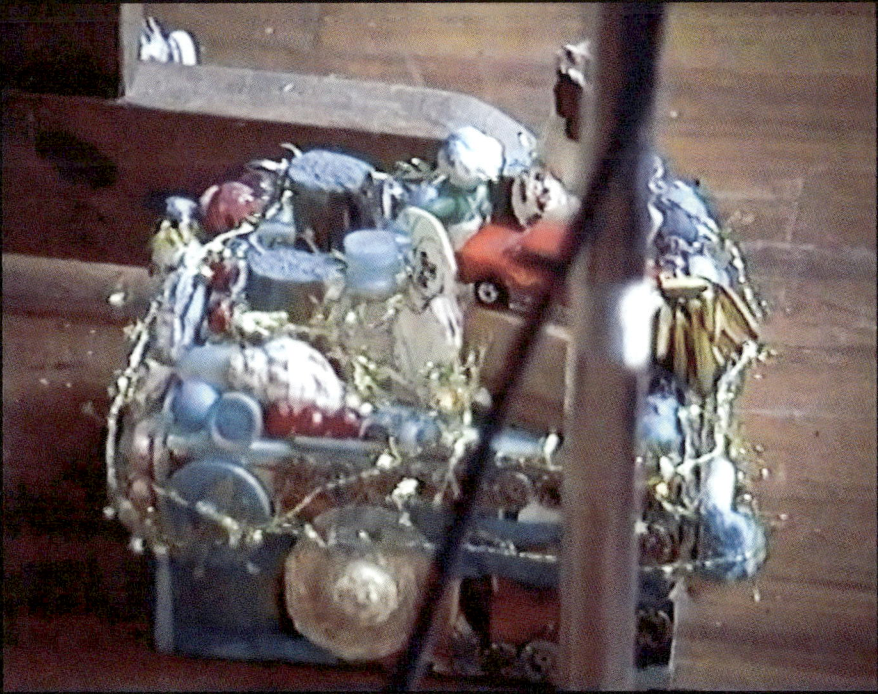

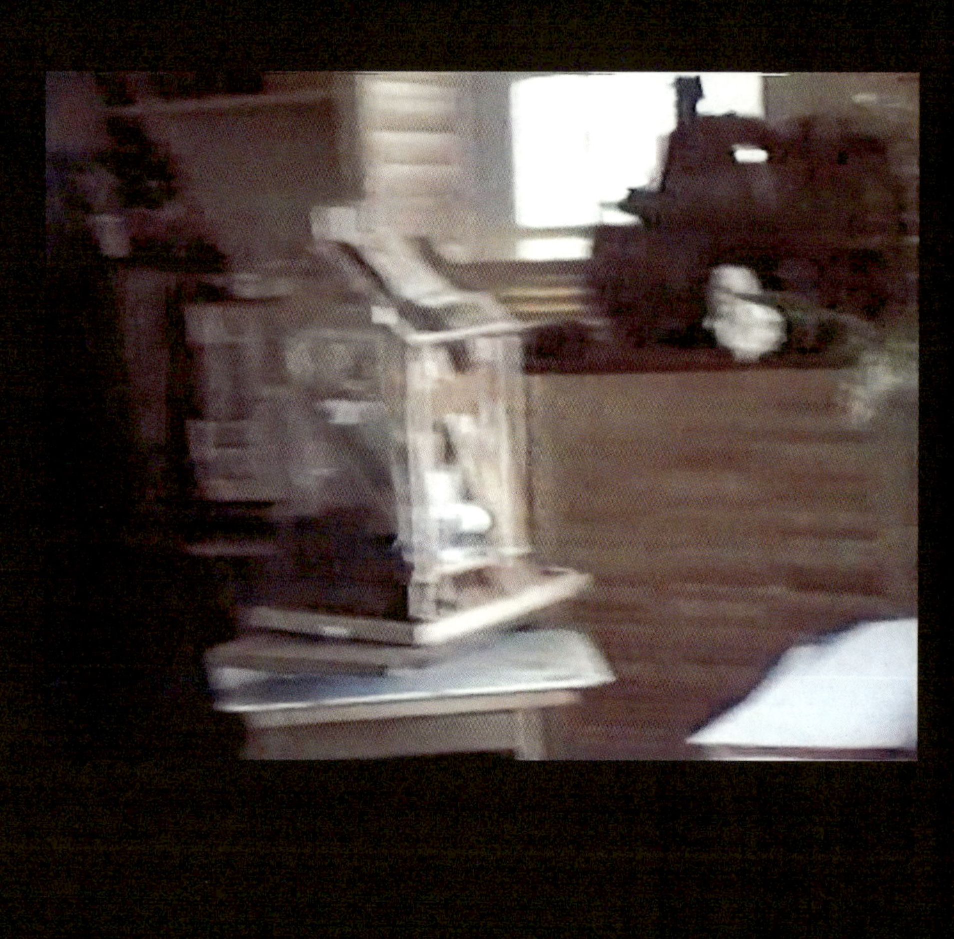

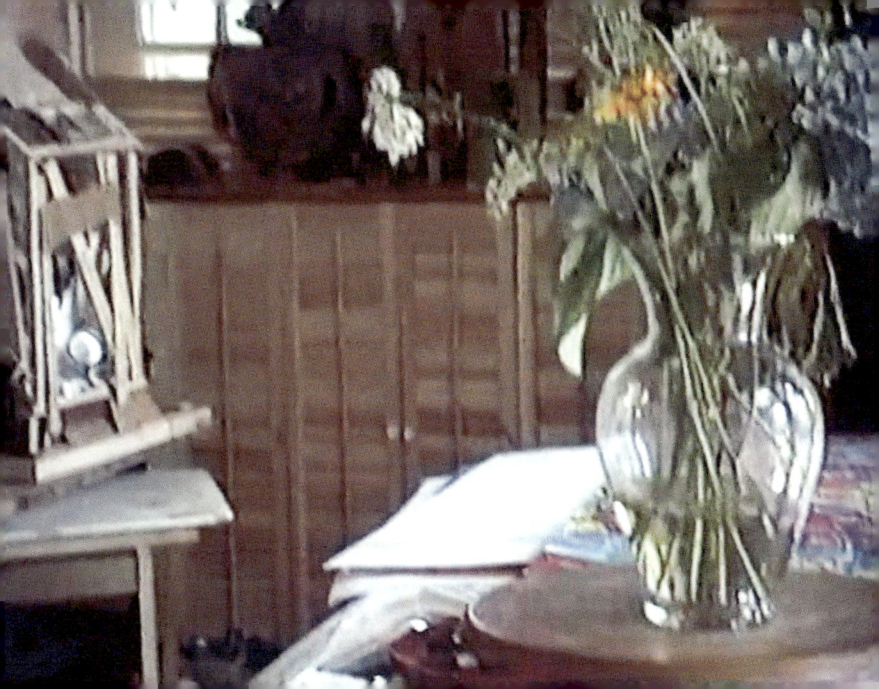

[*Beverly takes a seat in her leather chair, and looks off into the distance. Resting, her tone shifts from the frantic energy of searching to a contemplative and tender calm*]

JM: I swear to god, writing about her is the hardest damn thing. I don't think I can even do it. I've been trying for years. There's just something about it that, it's not... It's visual. It's not–it's not—

BB: [*nods*] Your video is so poetic, and so wonderful. It really... *It really is*.

JM: See, I wanna publish *your* photographs of *her*.

BB: *It really is*... You're welcome. You're welcome. She's, she's just, I don't know. She asked me, um, what my name was. "I'm Bev." And Lucille and I talked about this, that she knows somebody whose name is Beverly. So that's why Lucille thought that she might not forget the name, 'cause she could make an association. She asked me how old I was and whether I was married, if I was married. [*smiles*] Told her how old I was, and I said that I was not married. She said, "I never married either." [*turns to face Judy*] So, it's like we have this thing in common.

JM: Oh yes! [She was] defiant about that.

BB: She asked me where I lived, and I told her Athens. But after that, we didn't talk about *me* after that. Usually, I wanted to know if she needed something. She said she liked bananas. I remember that. Liked bananas.

JM: Yes! Isn't that true? She always wanted bananas and apples.

BB: Well, because bananas have potassium. So you just saw me take two potassium pills. If I ate more fruit, I wouldn't have to do that.

JM: She *loved* bananas, I remember.

BB: And, uh, Patricia had not seen the house, so I said, "Let's go out and see Mary Lou." So I stopped and got her some... something like tangerines. Tangelos or something. Took a big sack of them, and I left them one day. And the *next day* I went out to see if she had gotten them, or two days later. And, they were still where I left them, and I had this feeling of *dread*.

JM: Mm-hmm.

BB: So as I pulled up, one of Lucille's grandkids came on a little motorbike thing down there. And I said, "What happened? Where is she?" Said, "She had—she was in the hospital–she was in the hospital–she's in the hospital." [*sighs, rubs knee*]

JM: That was the stroke?

BB: Yeah. And, uh, so I picked up the sack and said, "Here, take this home, 'cause they've been sitting here overnight," you know?

JM: Well, you know, when she had that stroke—see, first they cut down the woods to the east of her.

BB: Yeah, yeah. I-I kinda remember that.

JM: And, she had that stroke, like, almost *as soon*—

BB: As they did that.

JM: Well, no. *Then* they cut down the woods between her and the highway, so she was gonna be *exposed*.[4]

BB: Right.

JM: And by god, Beverly, she had that stroke within a week.

BB: Yeah. That would have done it for me, because I just remember the last time... I took a photo of the last time I was out there, and it's *so lonely looking*.[5] It's not like any other photos of it I ever took. It's like it *knew* that it was—

JM: I know, I know. Well, one of [those photographs] was in the show, with the saplings up around it.

BB: Yeah! It looks like, "This is it."

JM: It was terrible, I mean—

BB: I looked at it and thought, "Somehow I don't think I'm gonna see you again." I *did*, twice, after that, but it was like, NEVER AGAIN would I... You know?

JM: That was it, when she was gone.

BB: Yeah. It *showed*. It was like, whoooaa. [*sighs, looks downward*] God...

JM: Well, that woman... is, now, forever.

BB: Yeah... [*looks up at Judy, nods*]

JM: But the last thing, I've-I gotta go see her in the nursing home because—

BB: I couldn't bring myself to do it 'cause I just—

JM: I haven't either, in all these years.

BB: I really couldn't, man, I just—

JM: But, like, if she's doing the garden!

BB: Yeah! [*cracks a huge laugh, removes glasses*]

JM: See, I mean, it's a triumphant thing. So I gotta go see her, and get a picture of her, because it's not *all* sad.

BB: Of her garden, yeah!

JM: SHE OUTLASTED THE HOUSE!!!

BB: YES THAT'S RIGHT!!!

[*Laughter*]

JM: SHE OUTLASTED THE HOUSE! [*cracks up*]

BB: Yeah, yeah. That's amazing! *Most houses outlast people.*

JM: Yes! Outlasted the friggin' house!

BB: Of course. So when Lucille said, "She's in better shape than me and you," I believed her. I go, "Yes she is!"

JM: Oh yeah. She was in great shape anyway. She told me she was seventy-four, and that's when she was climbing up on those roofs, getting that, uh—Hey, listen, did you by any chance, do you ever watch TV? That woman that did that film *Triumph of the Will*, that Leni Riefenstahl?

BB: Yes. I have always liked her. I mean, I know people don't like her, associated with the Nazis.

JM: And she's ninety-four. Her lover—

BB: But her film! When she focused in on Jesse Owens's face, for the Olympic film thing. There's nothing that's like that! It captured *everything*, all the emotions that he was feeling.

JM: Yeah, yeah.

BB: And one of the German guys had given a suggestion to Jesse Owens about his running, "a little advice on your running," something, and that's when Jesse beat 'em. Beat 'em all.

JM: You know something. Didn't he look contemporary? There were clips of it the other night.

BB: Yes! Yeah, yeah, yeah.

JM: Jesse Owens looked like he was contemporary, right now! And all those other guys, those Nazis and everything, they felt distant.

BB: Yes, they did!

JM: They felt *old*.

BB: She captured that! I thought, "Good for you!" I'm surprised they didn't have her killed for that, you know?! [*laughs*] But what a wonderful film.

JM: She scuba dives!

BB: I don't have the book that she did on the Maasai. And it's still in print. I would love to have that.

JM: Uh-huh. I love it too.

BB: She was an extraordinary photographer.

JM: I don't agree with the criticisms of it, that she, uh, glorified the body, and all that stuff. Those are some of the greatest photographs! They are incredible.

BB: Yes! I would love to have the book! I really would. A wonderful photographer.

JM: But this woman, now Beverly, she's skin diving at ninety-two. She's got a lover forty years younger than she is.

BB: Oh god. [*removes glasses to rub eyes and laugh*]

JM: She's still, she's about ninety-five now. Anyway, there was this great three-hour thing on her the other night on Channel 8. I got a tape of it. I should make you a copy of that. It's pretty interesting.

BB: I didn't see all of it. I saw little clips of it, and then I fell asleep.

[*points toward the right, out of the frame*] One of my relatives is that old lady that's on the photo right there on the wall. That's Aunt Lucy. I'm in the process of trying to find out exactly who she was. That photograph was in my grandmother's house up in the attic. I was a grown woman when I found it up in the attic, and brought it outside. There was a little family gathering.

[*Judy pivots the camera to the small, black-and-white photograph on the wall in the distance. As she zooms in, it shows a grainy portrait that looks to be a white woman, dressed in period clothing from an earlier era*]

JM: God, what?

BB: And I sat it against the tree and photographed it. And I said, "I found this picture of this old white lady upstairs."

[*Judy rotates the camera back to face Beverly*]

And everybody got quiet for a second, and then everybody burst into laughter. And my Uncle Oliver, my mother's brother, said, "That's Aunt Lucy." And he said to one of the young ladies there, "She looks like an old white lady, don't she?" And everybody laughed. No one ever told me who she was until I went "up-country," as they say, and was walking with one of my roommates from New York. And one of my cousins said, "Lucy's house used to be over in there," so I knew I was on her property.

JM: Mm-hmm.

BB: They were scared that I would fall into a well. "She had two wells, one in the front of the house, one in the back. Take this stick." So they gave me a stick to punch the ground in as I walked ahead of 'em. [*mimes the motion*] And by golly, the stick went down into one of those wells.

[*Laughter*]

And I picked up a rock... I could see the hole where the well had been. I picked up a stone, and I threw it. And I've yet to hear that stone hit the bottom!

[*Laughter*]

And I turned around and came back towards the house. One of my cousins said that she had a son named Cash. So in calling some people in North Carolina this past—I did it before Roger came 'cause I wanted to find out who that might be. 'Cause I'm gonna go to Duke, and half of Harnett County will probably show up. So, I was telling Roger about it, and I said, "This lady who was my mother's friend and knew my grandmother, and I thought might have known who that was, but she didn't know. There's an old lady who was ninety-two who might know." I said, "Lillian didn't know that I had asthma."

[*turns to face Judy*] And a lot of people in my family, on both sides, died from asthma. Lot of people. And, um, my grandmother had asthma, but not when I knew her. And she cured herself, and I had the good sense to ask somebody about it.[6] And they said, "The Indians cured her. She smoked rabbit tobacco." She never had asthma a day in her life when I knew her, as my grandma. [*shakes head*]

JM: Mm-hmm.

BB: Um, Lillian has asthma. Lillian somehow didn't know that *I* had asthma. I said, "Lillian, at Irene [McKay's] funeral, I couldn't come out of the back bedroom to talk to you, to greet you, because I-I was having asthma problems." She said, "I didn't know that!" I said, "You thought I was just being stuck up!" She said, "I didn't know *what* was wrong!"

[*shifts to a somber tone*] Lillian said, "Well, I used to be on prednisone." I said, "Lillian, I can't get off prednisone."[7] She said, "Well, I took myself off 'cause I've had two hip replacements, and it—" I said, "It makes your bones soft, and you know, if I don't get off it..." She said, "Well, one of our cousins, an old man up in the mountains, up in the hills, he told me, 'Well, *we all have it*. Try not to get cold.'" And I thought she meant "catch a cold."

JM: Mm-hmm, mm-hmm.

BB: No. She meant... And I thought, you know, that's interesting 'cause at night I sleep in a gown and something over it, *'cause I get cold*. I mean, it's like, "Try not to get cold, and take three swallows. Go to the..." She was very careful about asking me about alcohol. I said, "Well, yeah, I can have a little drink, Lil."

JM: [*chuckles*]

BB: She said, "Well, then go to the–go to the liquor store, and get you something called Rock and Rye. Take one swallow three times a day of that." [*raises eyebrows*] "Okay Gram." It took me about a week before I began to pursue this.

JM: [*chuckles*]

BB: So one day, I tried to find it. Drove all over Athens. Couldn't find it. Finally went to this store on Alps, and they had *one bottle*. They usually had more. It took me about four days to try. I thought, "Let me try this," because you really don't know. With all these old remedies, you have to not take your medicines and stuff, and so I'm not gonna do that.

JM: That's right, yeah.

BB: You know, it's like if somebody tells you to smoke rabbit tobacco, then you can't take something else with that. It's like they didn't have all this synthetic stuff when they...

JM: Mm-hmm. Mm-hmm.

BB: Okay. I started taking one swallow of that stuff three times a day for about three days. Exactly a week after I talked to her. No, about a month, I guess, after I talked to Lillian, *I had cut my prednisone dosage in half.*

JM: Oh, absolutely.

BB: *In half*!

JM: Doc Harris saved my life.[8]

BB: And what happened is, I got bronchitis, so I had to come back up on the prednisone, but I'm going back down on it now. *I was amazed*. It was like, this can't be true. [*laughs*] This can't be true.

[*As the video abruptly comes to an end, there's a fragment of Judy's voice mid-speech, and the image of Beverly laughing fades to black*]

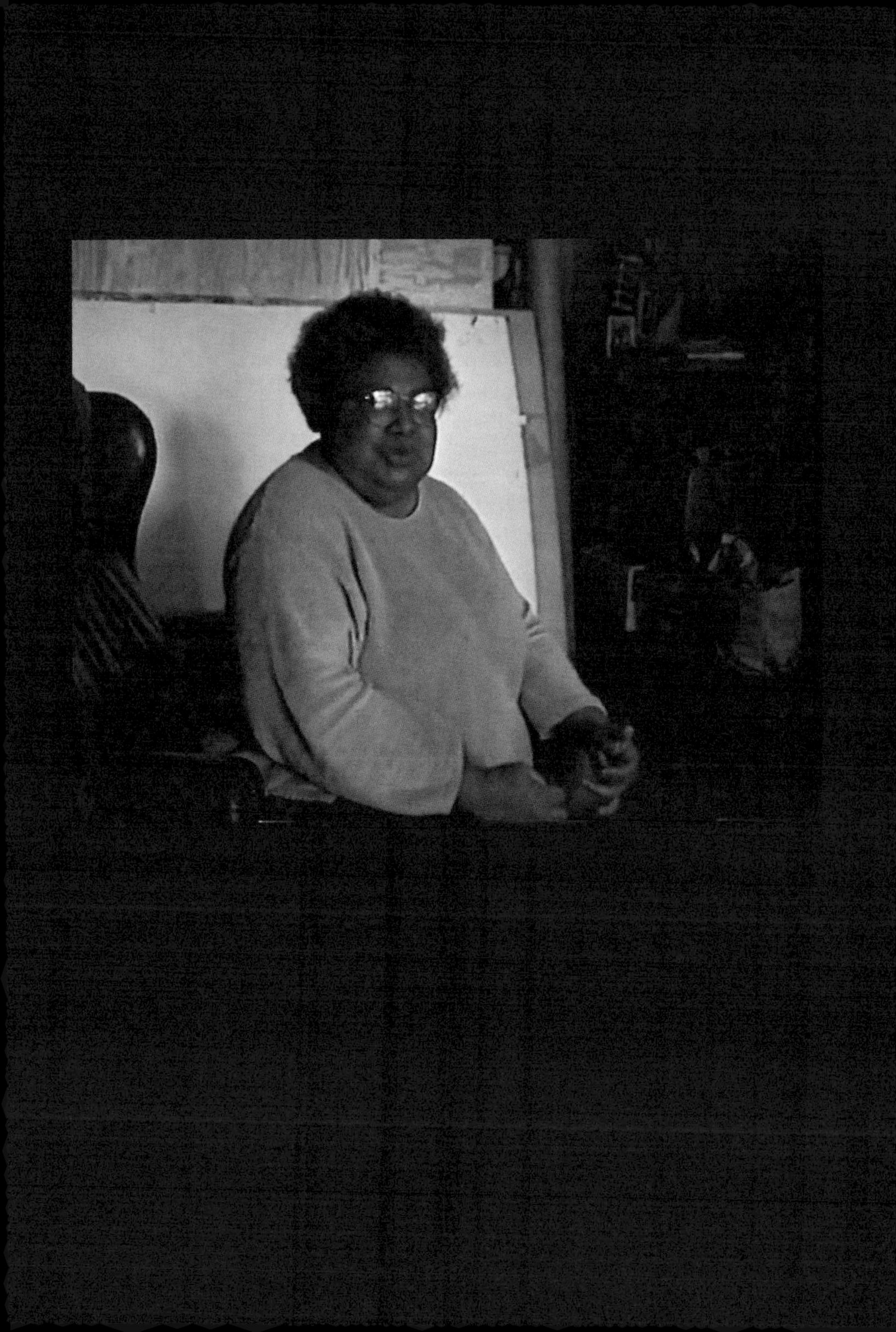

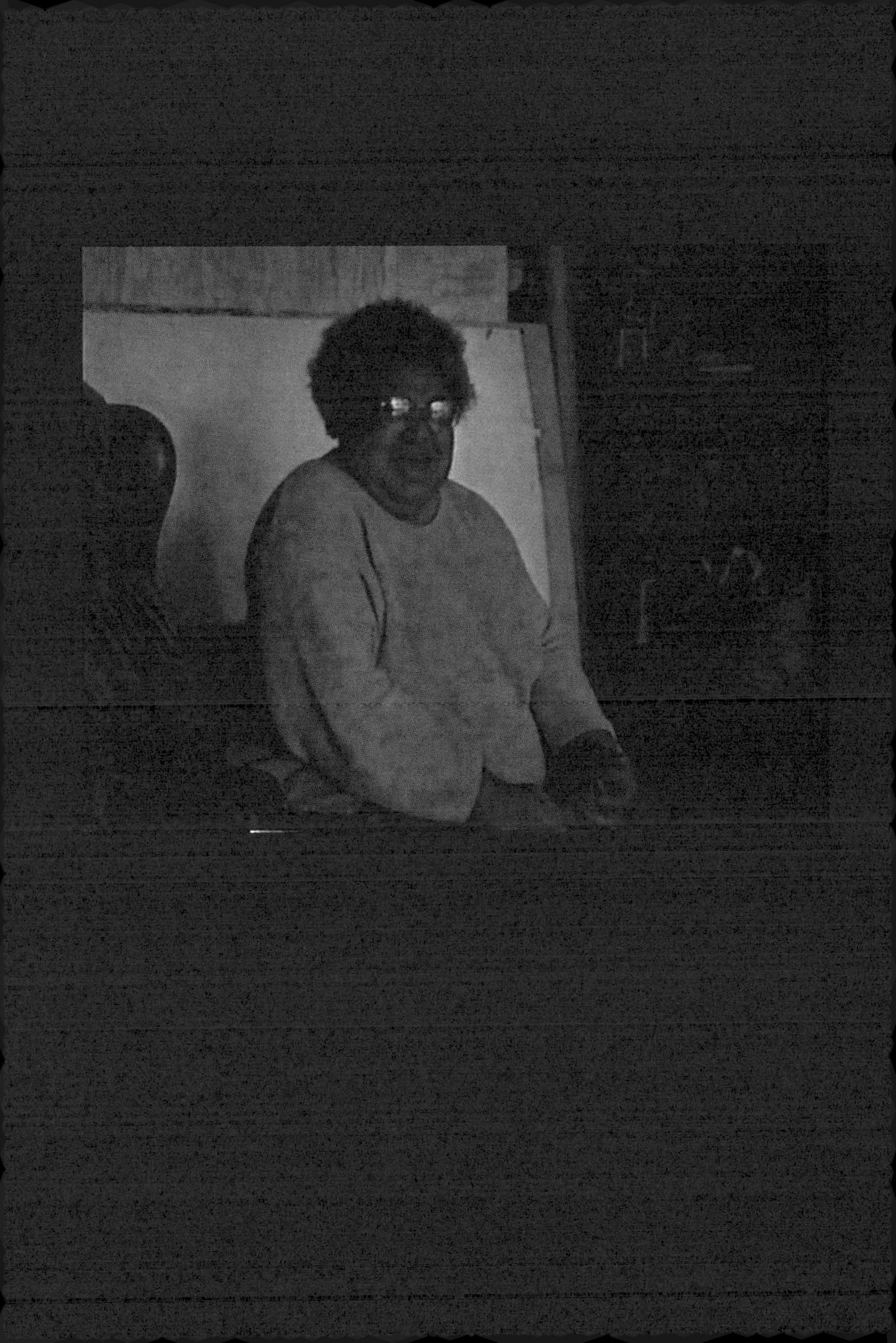

Tribute to Mary Lou Furcon

Artworks and texts by Beverly Buchanan

In her works honoring Mary Lou Furcron, Beverly Buchanan worked iteratively across a range of media. The selection presented here focuses on the artist's documents and documentation, with "tribute" as a central theme. Buchanan created two sculptures titled *Tribute to Mary Lou Furcron*: the first on the day she met Furcron in 1989, and the second twenty years later, shortly after Furcron's passing. Buchanan's informal documentation of these sculptures opens and closes this section, tracing Furcron's enduring impact across two decades.

Excerpts from Buchanan's twenty-five-page artist's book *MARY LOU FURCRON'S HOUSE & GARDEN* illustrate the nonlinear chronology of her process. On the book's inner cover, Buchanan wrote "copyright 1989," which references the year she photographed the images in the book. Buchanan took these photographs when Furcron was still living on her land and tending proudly to her gardens. The book's preface, however, is dated 1994. Buchanan wrote the text after Furcron moved to a nursing home following a stroke in the summer of 1989.

The photographs of Furcron's land shown here correspond to specific images described by Buchanan and McWillie in their 1995 recorded dialogue. Spreads from *MARY LOU FURCRON'S HOUSE & GARDEN* depict Furcron's hand-built home, its stone foundation, the donated shoes that Furcron refused to wear, and her neatly maintained garden and swept yard. Two photographs that Buchanan took after Furcron's stroke document the land in Furcron's absence. These images and the accompanying captions echo Buchanan's recollection to McWillie: "I took a photo of the last time I was out there, and it's so lonely looking. It's not like any other photos of it I ever took."

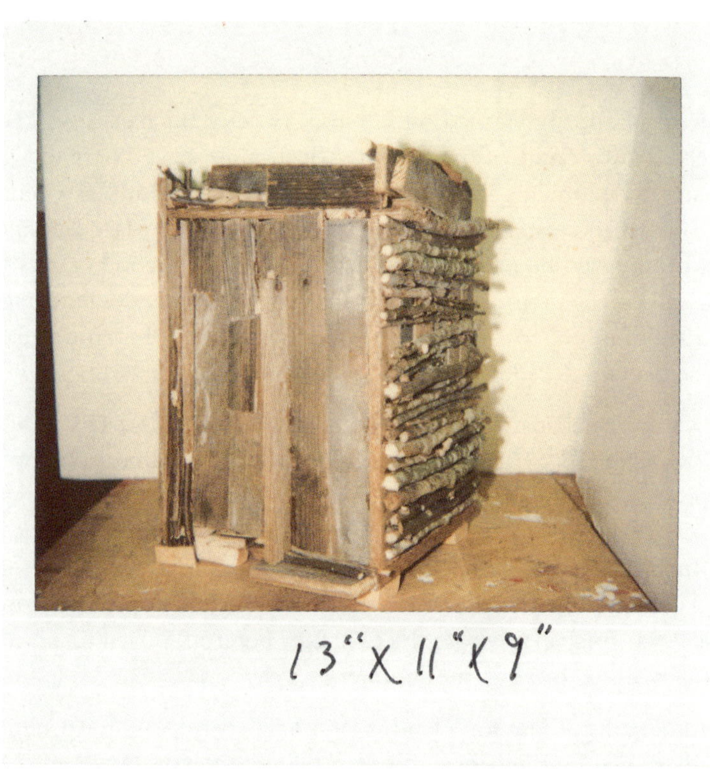

Beverly Buchanan, Documentation of *Tribute to Mary Lou Furcron*, 1989. Color Polaroid photograph, 4.2 × 3.5 in. Beverly Buchanan Papers, 1912–2017, bulk 1970s–1990s, Archives of American Art, Smithsonian Institution.

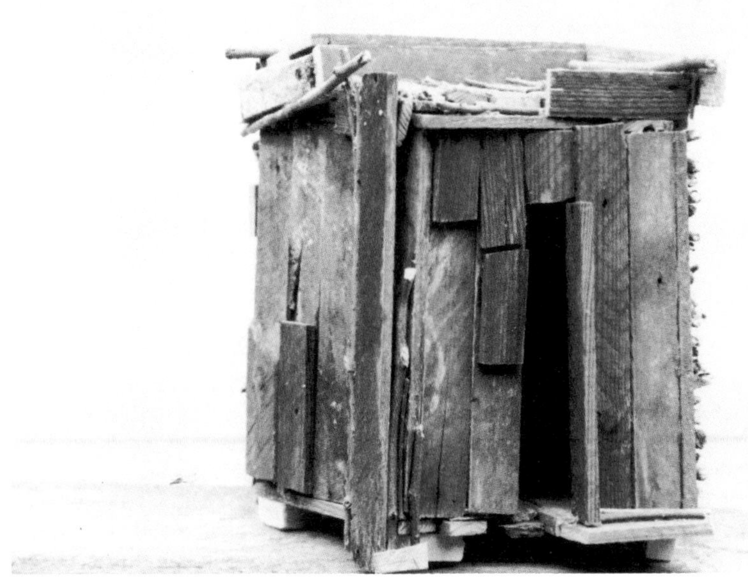

Beverly Buchanan, Documentation of *Tribute to Mary Lou Furcron*, 1989. Black-and-white photograph, 4 x 6 in. Beverly Buchanan Papers, 1912–2017, bulk 1970s–1990s, Archives of American Art, Smithsonian Institution.

SCULPTURE FOR MS. MARY LOU FURCRON

I was headed to Washington, Georgia, to photograph a house with blue trim because I had painted one of the shacks and had added blue trim because it felt right. Stopping off at a junk haunt on the way, I heard about an old lady who lived in a house made of sticks and twigs and that she had made her house by herself. These two good old Georgia white boys liked to tease me so I thought they kind of made it up but they were insistent that I see this so I headed toward Elberton. I drove all the way to Elberton, turned around, headed back, looking into the woods and suddenly, what I thought might be a giant animal shelter, caught my eye and I left the road and slowly drove in.

The first sight of the house was like a bolt of lightning had hit me and I could only sit and stare. Then I noticed her in part of her garden. Getting out cautiously, I said something like, "How are you today?" and told her that I just came by to see her house because I heard that she had built it. She wasn't hostile, but reserved: I am familiar with the reserve of old black women who live alone with no visible means of protection. I was scared to death. Before I could ask anything about the house, she said, "Help me with this."

A pile of twigs and sticks lay at her feet and next to them, a log of some kind. Pointing to the log, I said I would take it for her. I'll never forget her look when she said, "You can take that by yourself?" I said proudly, "NO PROBLEM." How could she know that I was a strong woman sculptor used to lifting large boulders and rocks and that my shoulders could move a car if I wanted to and so --- I bent down, properly, to tackle this object, to discover that I could not move it at all. Trying again, and mindful of her eye, I was heartsick to find out that this was impossible. I prayed. How to get God's attention was first, then the object could slowly be put upright. What now, SPORT? Somehow I got it level with my hip and side and locking my knees together in a triangle shape I said from my gurgling throat, "WHERE DO YOU WANT IT?" I let it drop in front of the house which seemed like a mile away. I was grateful to be able to be upright again. She was already in the nursing home when I learned that it usually took two men to carry one of those logs. I asked permission to photograph the house and her.

Before leaving, I asked if she wanted anything from Athens. "Yes, cotton stockings. Not silk ones." I said, "OK" this time instead of "No problem." She then informed me that the last person who told her that had never come back with the stockings. I was to find out why. She said to get them from SEARS. My Grandmother wore cotton stockings, but that was a long time ago. I tried everywhere. I even stopped people on the street. I called SEARS in Chicago. I prayed. I FOUND them. In Athens. Downtown. I took them out to her the same day I heard that my Mother had died. Ms. Furcron and her guardian were installing a new stove pipe. They had put out what had been a small fire whose smoke I captured in a photograph taken while she berated me for not taking the money for the stockings.

 Beverly Buchanan, Athens, GA, 8 July 1995

This woman was proud of her gardens and whether you were there for long or not, she had things to do around there and you felt intrusive. She had asked how old I was and if I was married. She said that she had never married.

I miss her more than she knows. Her house LOOKS abandoned, as her yard and gardens show. Apparently one time she "got loose" and walked for ten miles toward home. I can hardly make it up a small hill. I made this structure the day I met her.

It is a tribute to her.

Beverly Buchanan
Athens, GA

SCULPTURE FOR MS. MARY LOU FURCRON

I was headed to Washington, Georgia, to photograph a house with blue trim because I had painted one of the shacks and had added blue trim because it felt right. Stopping off at a junk haunt on the way, I heard about an old lady who lived in a house made of sticks and twigs and that she had made her house by herself. These two good old Georgia white boys liked to tease me so I thought they kind of made it up but they were insistent that I see this so I headed toward Elberton. I drove all the way to Elberton, turned around, headed back, looking into the woods and suddenly, what I thought might be a giant animal shelter, caught my eye and I left the road and slowly drove in.

The first sight of the house was like a bolt of lightening had hit me and I could only sit and stare. Then I noticed her in part of her garden. Getting out cautiously, I said something like, "How are you today?" and told her that I just came by to see her house because I heard that she had built it. She wasn't hostile, but reserved: I am familiar with the reserve of old black women who live alone with no visible means of protection. I was scared to death. Before I could ask anything about the house, she said, "Help me with this."

1

Beverly Buchanan, *SCULPTURE FOR MS. MARY LOU FURCRON*, c. 1989–94. Typewritten text on paper, 3 pages total, 11 × 8.5 in. Beverly Buchanan Papers, 1912–2017, bulk 1970s–1990s, Archives of American Art, Smithsonian Institution.

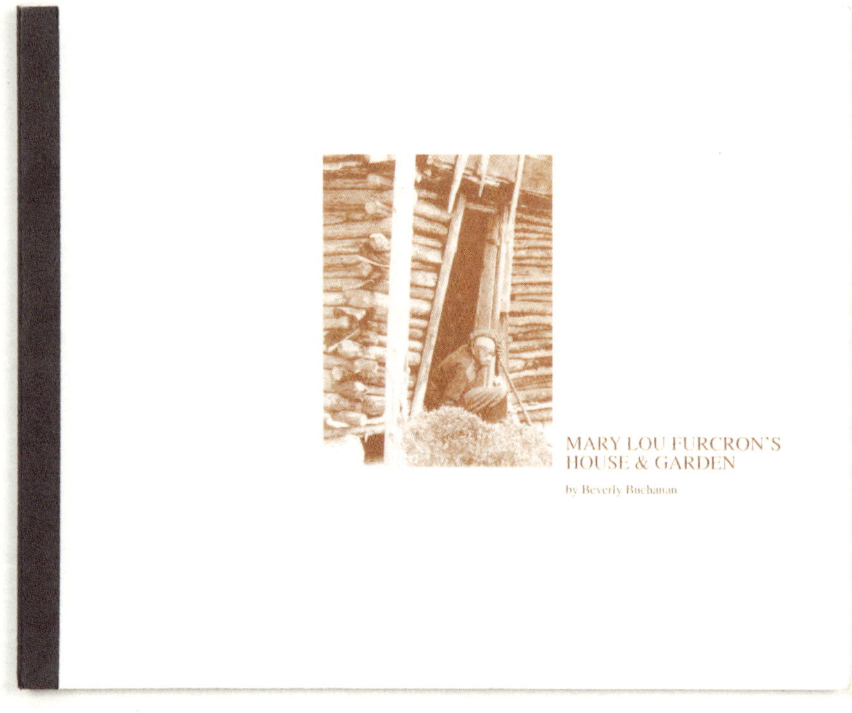

Beverly Buchanan, Selected pages from *MARY LOU FURCRON'S HOUSE & GARDEN*, 1994 (with photographs from 1989). Bound artist's book with color reproductions, 25 pages total, 8.5 × 10.75 in. Courtesy of Prudence Lopp.

PREFACE

Mary Lou Furcron single-handely built her house and garden. Buchanan met her in the late eighties. She writes about her encounters with this valiant women:

"The first sight of the house was like a bolt of lightning had hit me and I could only sit and stare. Then, I noticed her in part of her garden. Getting out cautiously, I said, something like, "How are you today?," and said that I just came by to see her house because I heard that she had built it.

She wasn't hostile, but reserved. I was familiar with the reserve of old Black women who live alone with no visible means of protection. I was scared to death. Before I could ask anything about the house, she said, "Help me with this!" A pile of twigs and sticks lay at her feet and next to them, a log of some kind. Pointing to the log, I said I would take it for her. I'll never forget her look when she said, "You can't take that by yourself?" I said proudly, "No problem!" How could she know that I was a strong woman sculptor used to lifting large boulders and rocks and that my shoulders could move a car if I wanted to and. . .so I bent down, properly to tackle this object to discover that I could not move it at all. Trying again, and mindful of her eye, I was heartsick to find out that this was impossible. I prayed. How to get God's attention was first, then I prayed that the object could slowly be put upright. What now, Sport? Somehow I got it level with my hip and side and locking my knees together in a triangular shape, I said from my gurgling throat, "Where do you want it?" I let it drop in front of the house which seemed like a mile away. I was grateful to be able to stand upright again.

She was already in a nursing home when I learned that it took two men, usually, to carry one of those logs.

Ms. Furcron was proud of her gardens and whether you were there for long or not, she had things to do around there and you felt intrusive. She had asked how old I was, and if I was married. She said that she had never married.

I miss her more than she knows. Her house looks abandoned as her yard and gardens show. Apparently one time she "got loose" from the nursing home and walked ten miles toward her home. I can hardly make it up a small hill.

Beverly Buchanan, 1994

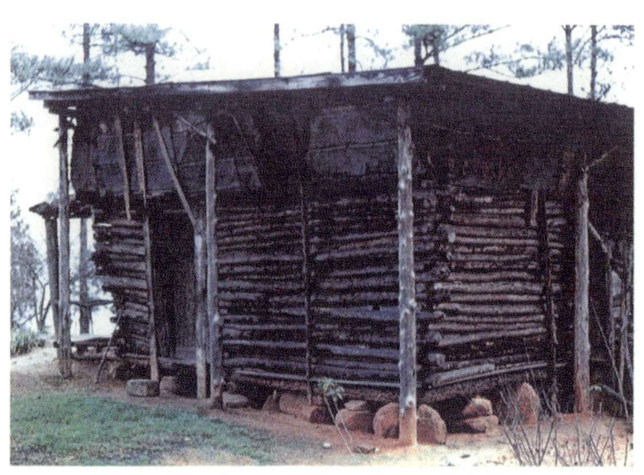

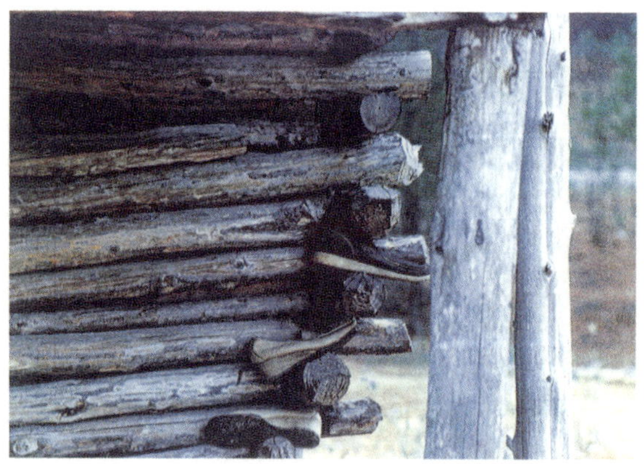

Beverly Buchanan, Selected pages from *MARY LOU FURCRON'S HOUSE & GARDEN*, 1994 (with photographs from 1989). Bound artist's book with color reproductions, 25 pages total, 8.5 × 10.75 in. Courtesy of Prudence Lopp.

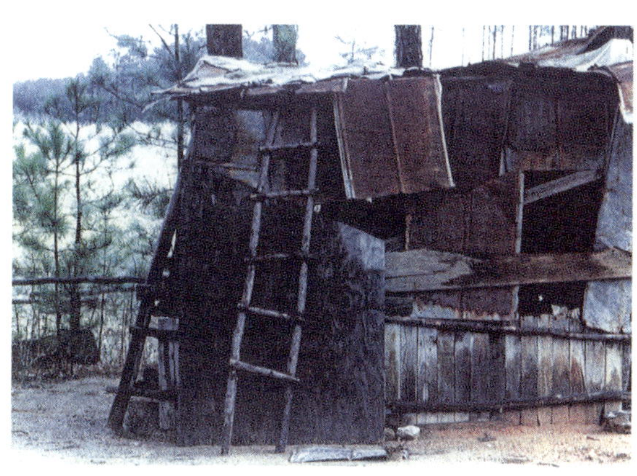

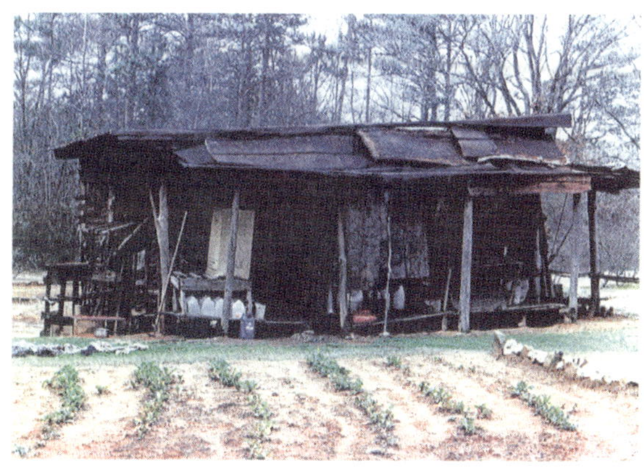

Beverly Buchanan, Selected pages from *MARY LOU FURCRON'S HOUSE & GARDEN*, 1994 (with photographs from 1989). Bound artist's book with color reproductions, 25 pages total, 8.5 × 10.75 in. Courtesy of Prudence Lopp.

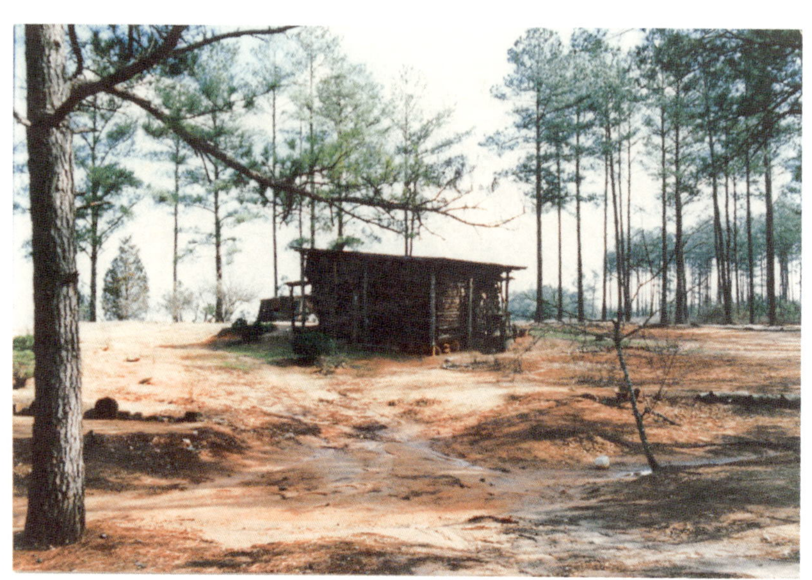

The LAST TIME
I SAW MS. FURCRON'S HOME.

Beverly Buchanan, *The Last Time I Saw Ms. Furcron's Home*, 1989. Front and back of color photograph, ink, 4 × 6 in. Courtesy of Prudence Lopp.

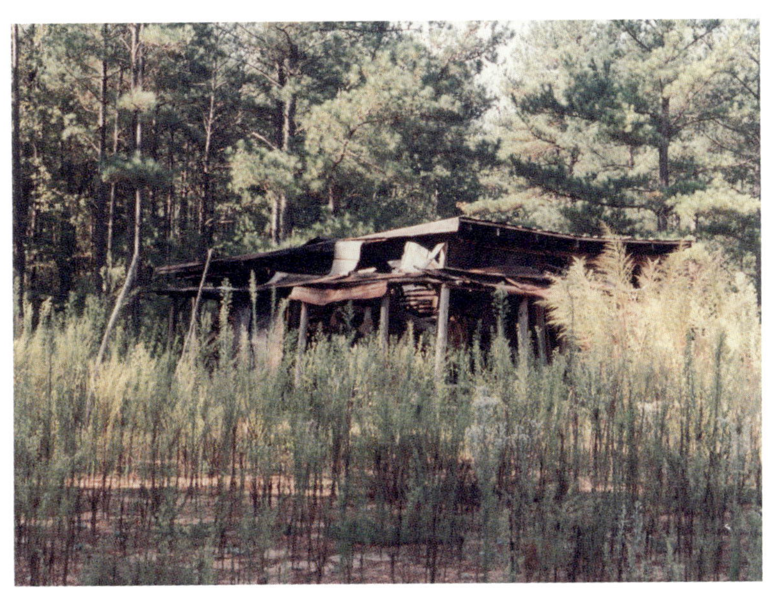

#0043/16-"FURCRON HOUSE WITHOUT HER- WEEDS"

Beverly Buchanan, *FURCRON HOUSE WITHOUT HER – WEEDS*, c. 1990–94. Front and back of color photograph, ink, 5 × 7 in. Beverly Buchanan Papers, 1912–2017, bulk 1970s–1990s. Archives of American Art, Smithsonian Institution.

MY YARD

Some parts are not to be believed. I've accepted the fact that I inherited my green thumb from my Mother. I am, I guess, a RENTER versus a CROPPER though my output of tomatoes wasn't spectacular nor was my crop of Tahitian squash or tahitian beans. Seed pact labels sounded so exotic and artistic with imagined ripe, swollen, off-beat squash and who-knows-what-beans. The squash took over the backyard with green spotted, huge leaves that, alone, would look great in hanging pots on the deck next to and with the trailing Bougainvillea, Swamp Hibiscus blooms, Banana trees, Mistletoe Ficus (with real berries), and an assortment of "experiments". The squash, finally, after numerous weeks with yellow fruitless blooms, emerged as exotic or obscene, elongated delicacies tasting like sweet potatoes. My "shape up or ship-out" philosophy worked this year; everything produced. It's sad to think of Mary Lou Furcron's yard, as immense as it was, with fruit trees and strawberries, weed-angry without her. Almost NONE of the green items are fit for human consumption. One can't throw a piece of ham in a pot and "simmer" the Ficus leaves. The beans, though, are different. They're cute and edible. They're just so--------------SPARCE!

MY YARD---

There's also the scarecrow with painted wood hair and fluorescent fingertips. She was to scare the deer from the tomatoes. It didn't work. Next time, I'll plant enough for the DEER FAMILY. Then, of course the rabbit—old cotton tail. Where's Peter? Wheelbarrow is under an oak tree. No car up on blocks because it (a classic German convertible) is getting a tune-up in a Japanese car hospital. All I need is some low country South Carolina ornamental grass, and moss, and rose bushes from Edisto Gardens and Santee river tree stumps, Okra and rice in a pot on the stove with pork cooking real slow and a Palmetto and—Cracklin Bread—and a Rooster, Sweet Potatoe pie------------------

Beverly Buchanan, Athens, Georgia, 1990

MY YARD

Some parts are not to be believed. I've accepted the fact that I inherited my green thumb from my Mother. I am, I guess, a RENTER versus a CROPPER though my output of tomatoes wasn't spectacular nor was my crop of Tahitian squash or tahitian beans. Seed pact labels sounded so exotic and artistic with imagined ripe,swollen, off-beat squash and who-knows-what- beans. The squash took over the backyard with green spotted, huge leaves that, alone, would look great in hanging pots on the deck next to and with the trailing Bougainvillea, Swamp Hibiscus blooms, Banana trees, Mistletoe Ficus(with real berries), and an assortment of "experiments". The squash, finally, after numerous weeks with yellow fruitless blooms, emerged as exotic or obscene, elongated delicacies tasting like sweet potatoes. My "shape up or ship-out " philosophy worked this year;everything produced. It's sad to think of Mary Lou Furcron's yard, as immense as it was, with fruit trees and strawberries, weed-angry without her. Almost NONE of the green items are fit for human consumption. One can't throw a piece of ham in a pot and "simmer" the Ficus leaves. The beans,though, are different. They"re cute and edible. They're just so--------------SPARCE!

Beverly Buchanan, *MY YARD*, 1990. Photocopy, 2 pages total, 11 × 8.5 in. Beverly Buchanan Papers, 1912–2017, bulk 1970s–1990s, Archives of American Art, Smithsonian Institution.

I've noticed an attraction to "enclosed" black women. It might have started with Mary Lou Furcron (Now 100 yrs. plus) the latest is a lady who lives at the end of my old neighborhood on Boulevard here in Athens. She was energetically cutting her grass with a power mower. She looked in my (I thought) discreet direction as the shutter went "click". I froze! Then there is Mom May over on Martin Luther King, Jr. Drive (80 years), driving her car past her saddlebag house's porch filled with glorius blooming plants.

Families or individuals often seem trapped or permanently "settled" in their present locations. This, I think, is part of my attraction to the "Isolation of Surviving Structures and Inhabitants of Present-Day Southern Landscapes in Georgia". Isn't that a great title?
Forget it - I have enough degrees.

-Beverly Buchanan

Beverly Buchanan, Untitled, c. 2000–03. Printed text on paper, 11 × 8.5 in. Beverly Buchanan Papers, 1912–2017, bulk 1970s–1990s, Archives of American Art, Smithsonian Institution.

I've noticed an attraction to "enclosed" black women. It might have started with Mary Lou Furcron (Now 100 yrs. plus) the latest is a lady who lives at the end of my old neighborhood on Boulevard here in Athens. She was energetically cutting her grass with a power mower. She looked in my (I thought) discreet direction as the shutter went "click". I froze! Then there is Mom May over on Martin Luther King, Jr. Drive (80 years), driving her car past her saddlebag house's porch filled with glorious blooming plants.

Families or individuals often seem trapped or permanently "settled" in their present locations. This, I think, is part of my attraction to the "Isolation of Surviving Structures and Inhabitants of Present-Day Southern Landscapes in Georgia". Isn't that a great title?

Forget it – I have enough degrees.

Beverly Buchanan

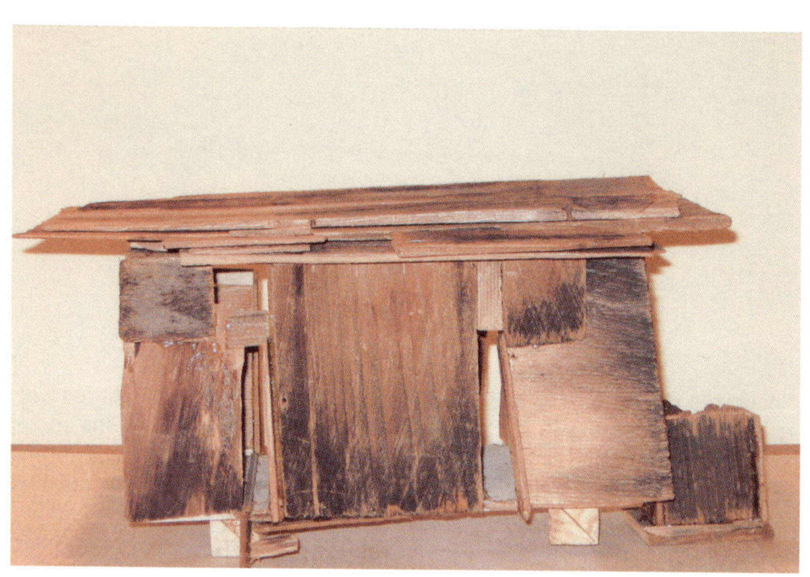

5) Tribute to Mary Lou Furcron (2009)

Beverly Buchanan, Documentation of *Tribute to Mary Lou Furcron*, 2009. Front and back of color photograph from photo album, 4 × 6 in. Beverly Buchanan Papers, 1912–2017, bulk 1970s–1990s, Archives of American Art, Smithsonian Institution.

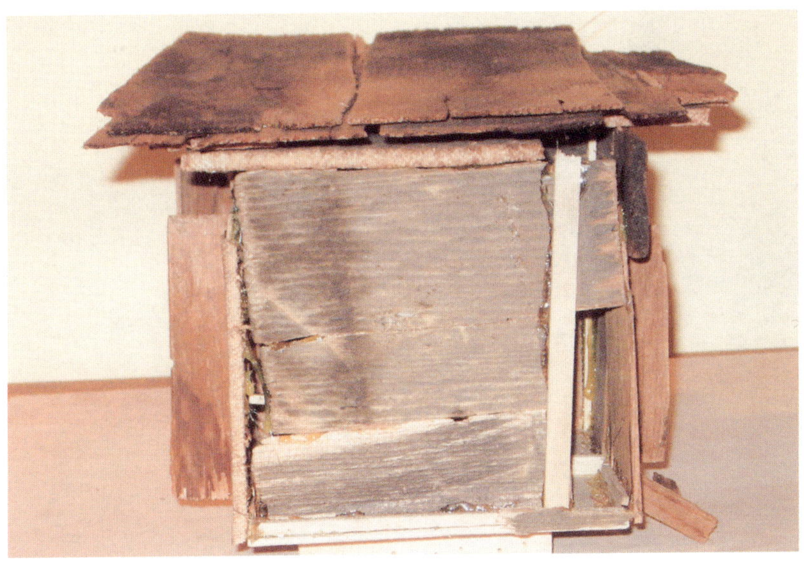

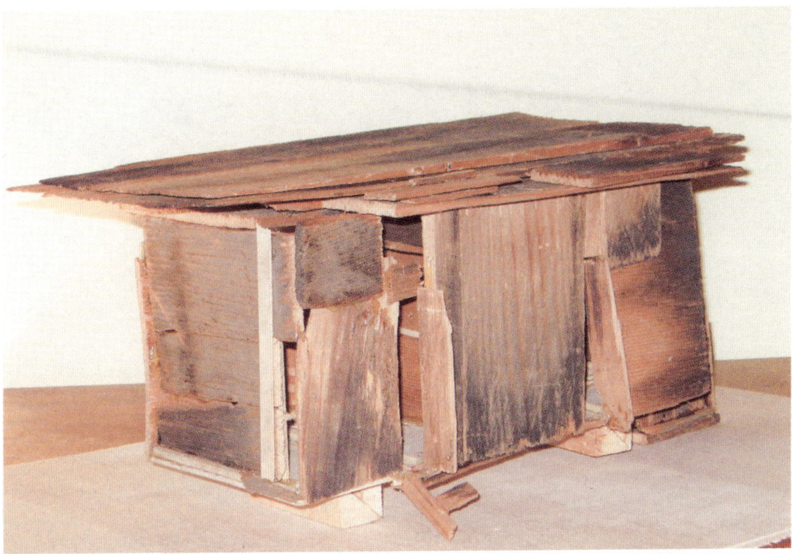

Beverly Buchanan, Documentation of *Tribute to Mary Lou Furcron*, 2009. Color photographs from photo album, 4 × 6 in. Beverly Buchanan Papers, 1912–2017, bulk 1970s–1990s, Archives of American Art, Smithsonian Institution.

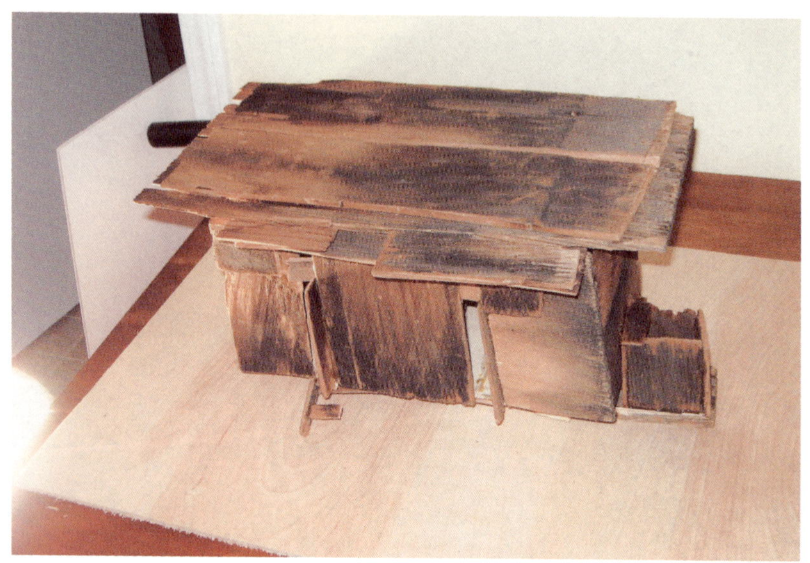

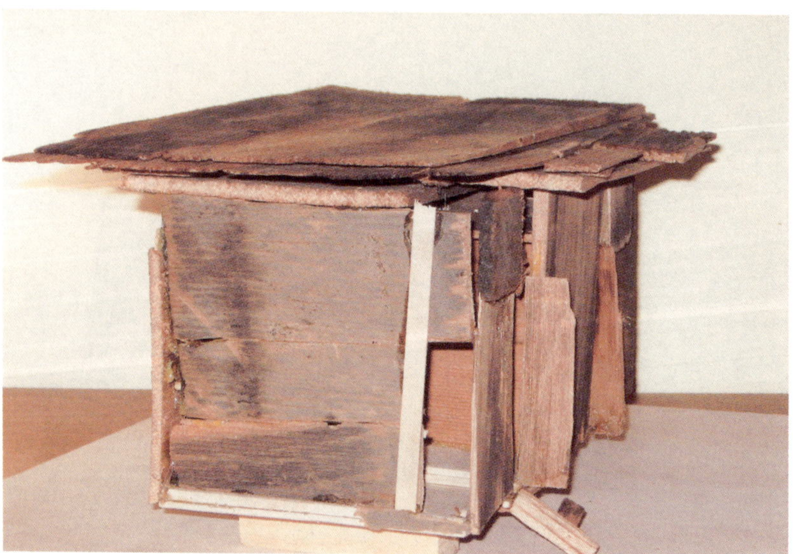

Beverly Buchanan, Documentation of *Tribute to Mary Lou Furcron*, 2009. Color photographs from photo album, 4 × 6 in. Beverly Buchanan Papers, 1912–2017, bulk 1970s–1990s, Archives of American Art, Smithsonian Institution.

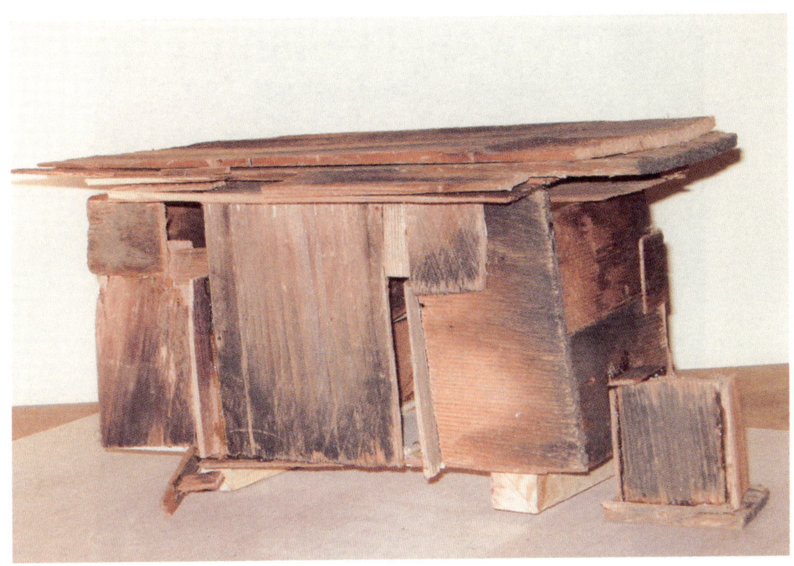

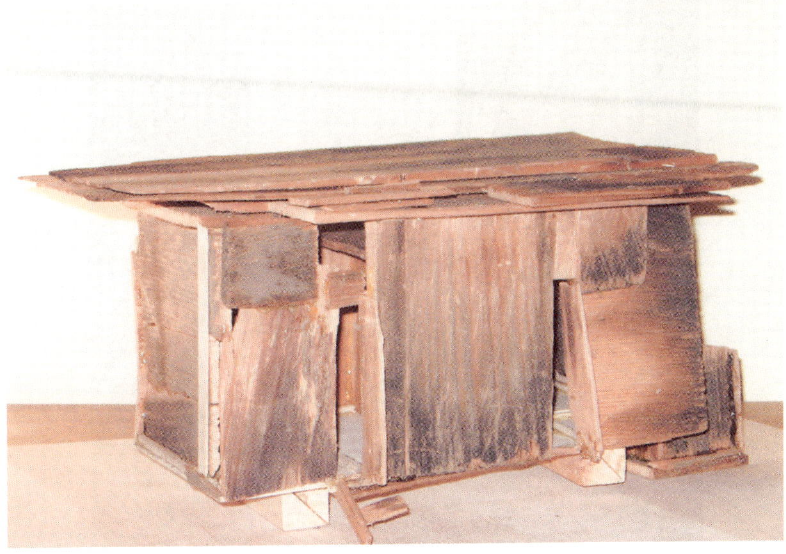

Beverly Buchanan, Documentation of *Tribute to Mary Lou Furcron*, 2009. Color photographs from photo album, 4 × 6 in. Beverly Buchanan Papers, 1912–2017, bulk 1970s–1990s, Archives of American Art, Smithsonian Institution.

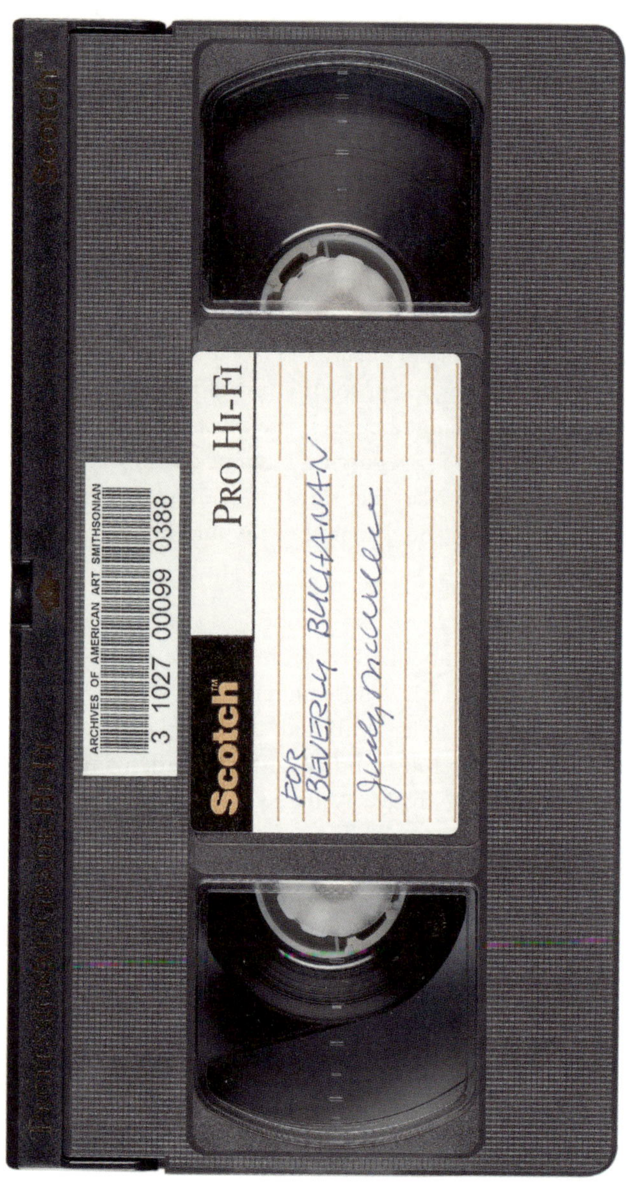

Judith McWillie, Untitled ("For Beverly Buchanan"), c. 1987–95. VHS Tape. Beverly Buchanan Papers, 1912–2017, bulk 1970s–1990s, Archives of American Art, Smithsonian Institution.

Mary Lou Furcon, Vesta GA.

A video and related materials by Judith McWillie

The archival materials presented here center Judith McWillie's seventy-nine-minute video *Mary Lou Furcron, Vesta GA.*, recorded on May 9, 1987. McWillie gifted a personally inscribed copy of this tape to Buchanan, which Buchanan kept for the rest of her life. The tape represents a form of exchange between the artists that preceded their July 8, 1995 conversation and is a recurring reference within it. In the 1995 recording, Buchanan expresses that the 1987 video "is so poetic" and that McWillie's "eye did what [Buchanan's] eye would like to do."

The following selection of stills from *Mary Lou Furcron, Vesta GA.* reflects the shifting movement of McWillie's embodied cinematography. Unfolding chronologically from the unedited recording, the selection collates specific images that Buchanan and McWillie reference in their 1995 dialogue, including Furcron's hoe, ladder, and shed; the layers of cardboard Furcron used as insulation; her carefully tended yard and garden; and the rocks that Buchanan refers to repeatedly. McWillie's video brings particular attention to the trees that encircle Furcron's "homeground," which offer a sense of abundance and refuge. In her conversation with Buchanan years later, McWillie recalled that the clearing of this forest "exposed" Furcron to the highway and precipitated her stroke. In the 1987 recording, the woods are preserved in a state of flourishing.

The video stills from 1987 are followed by selected text from a small notebook McWillie kept circa 1991. Across eleven pages of notes, she parses her unedited recording with Furcron into key movements marked with time stamps, descriptions, and selectively transcribed quotations from Furcron. The notebook reveals McWillie studying her own improvisational footage with methodical attention. Her notes register her sense of how the tape's visual and oral histories operate in relation to one another.

MARY LOU
FULCRON

VESTA GA.

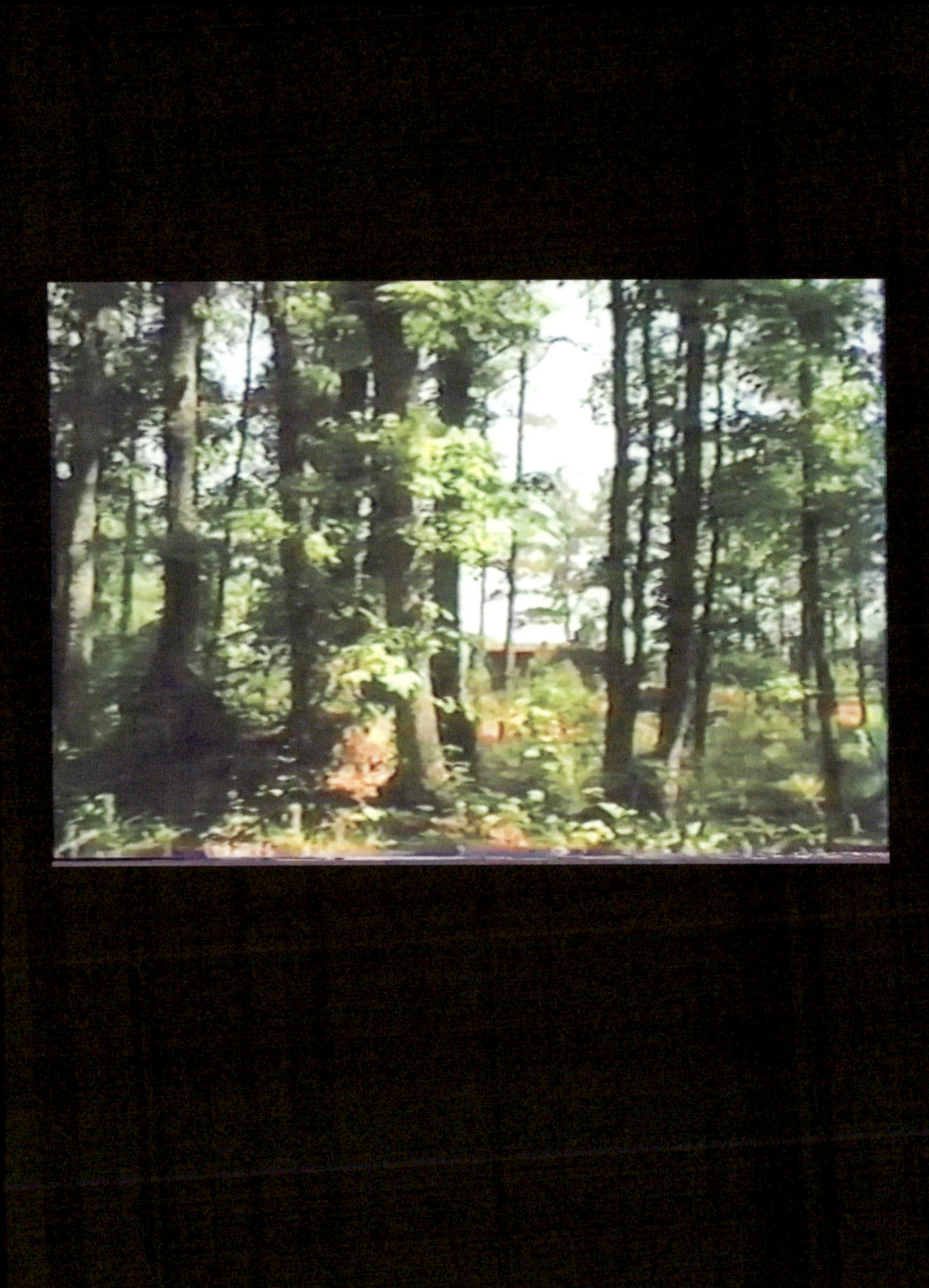

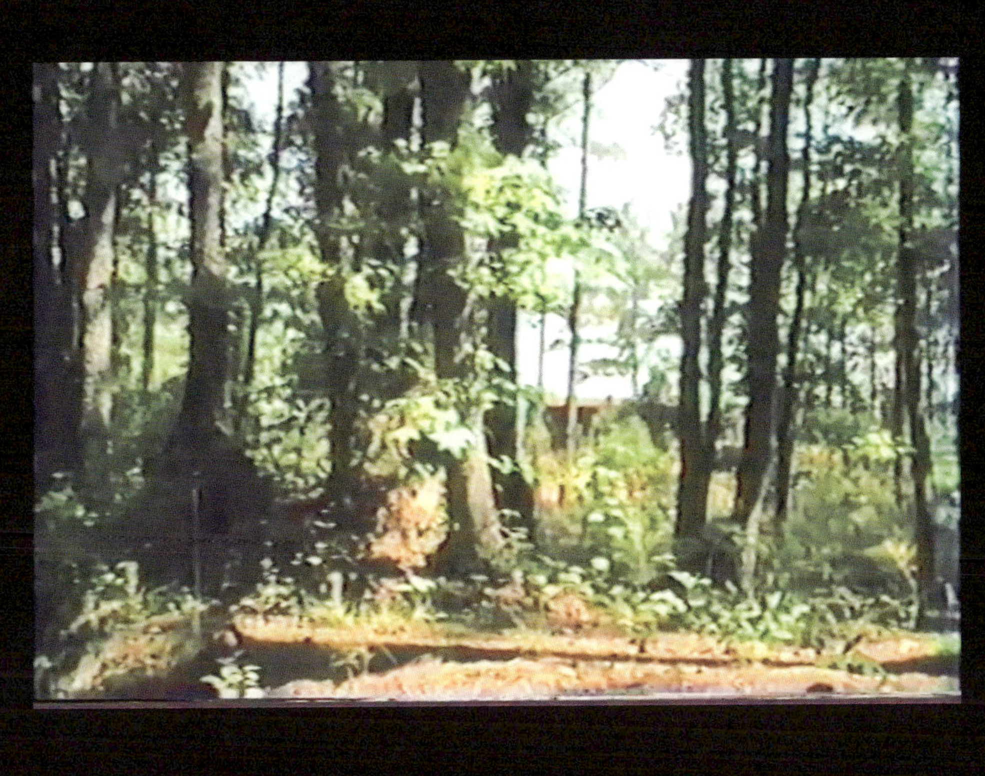

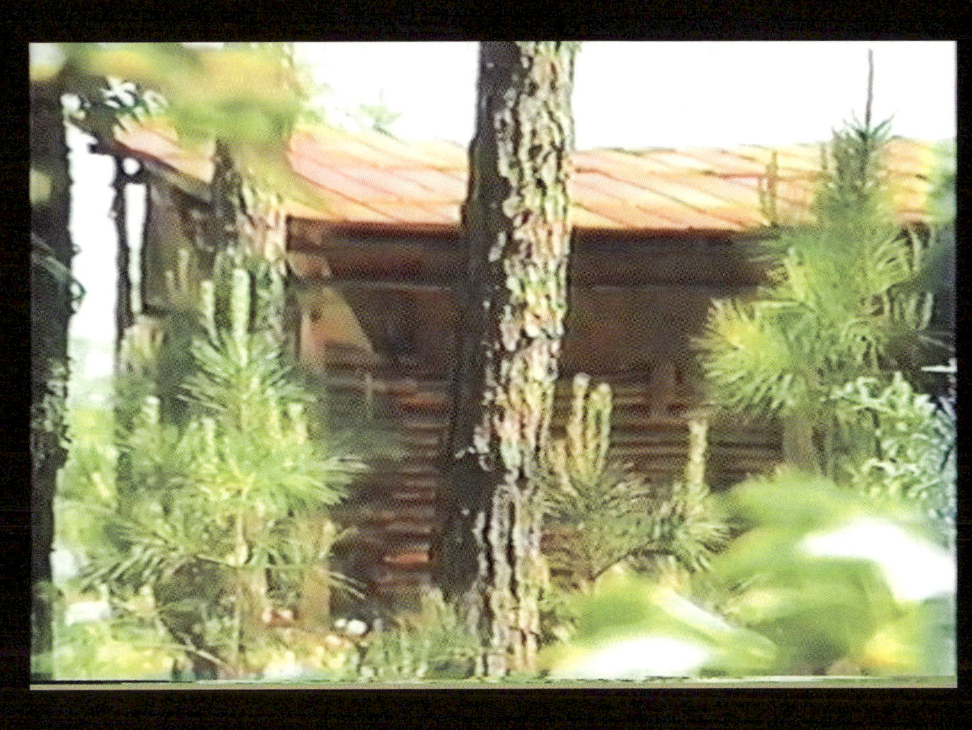

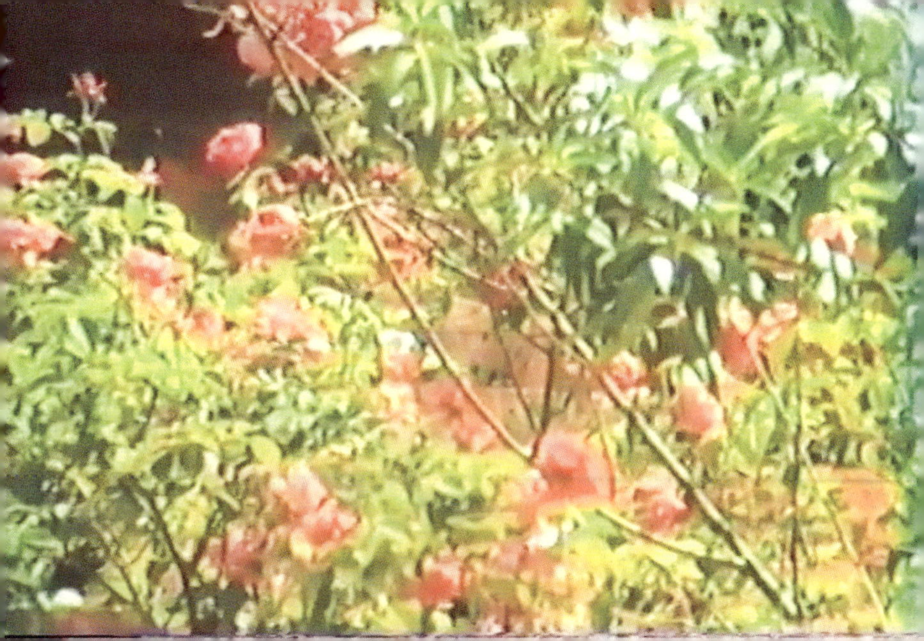

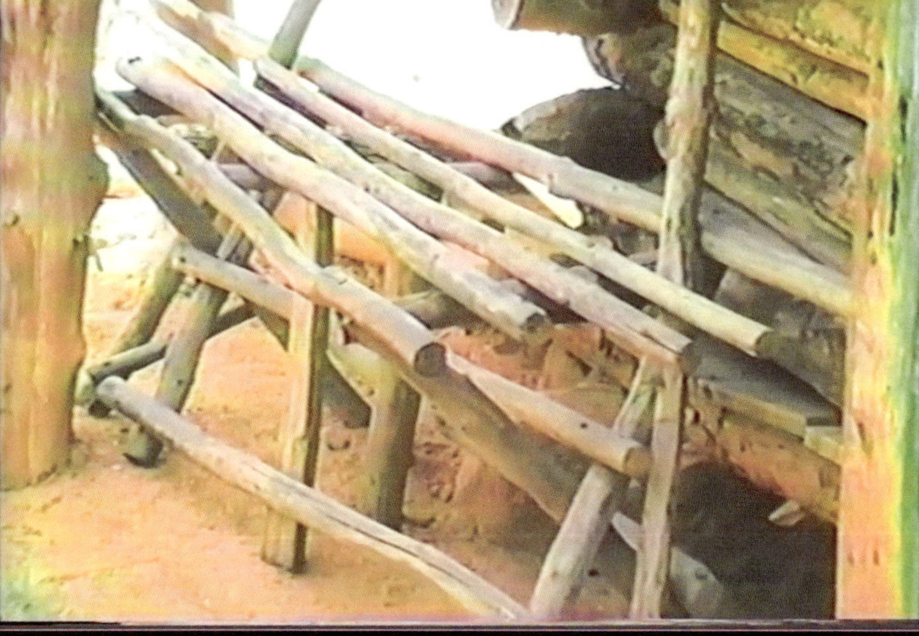

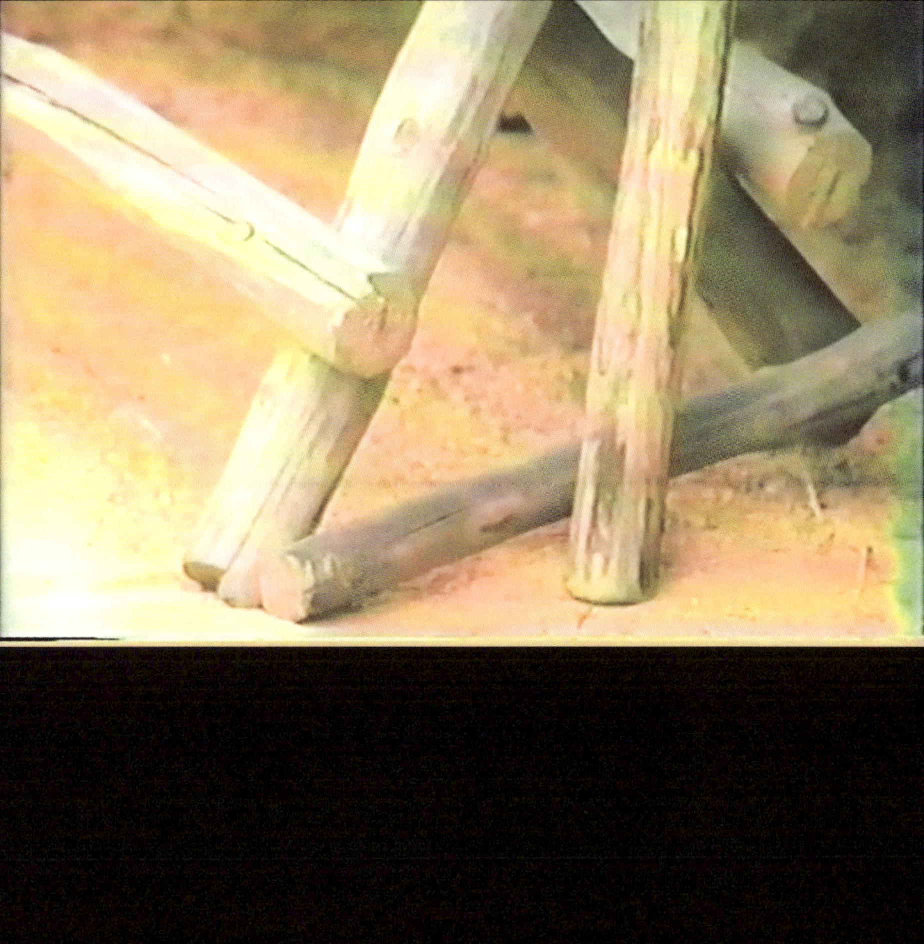

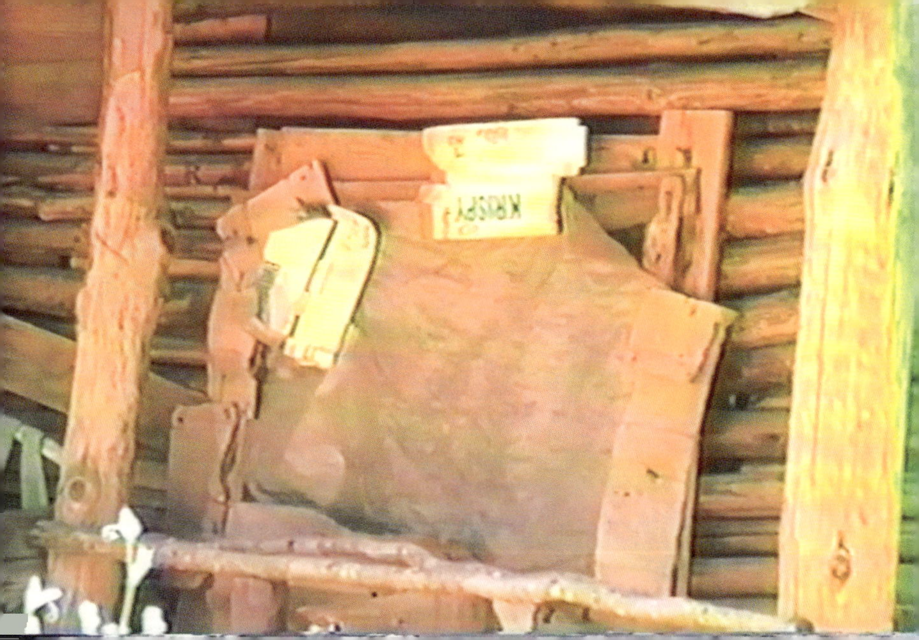
KRISPY

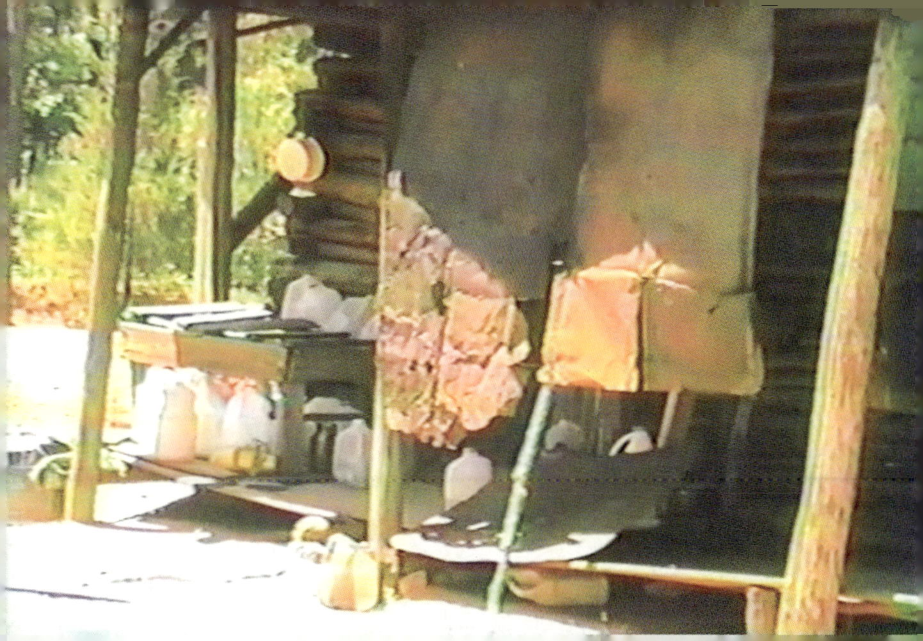

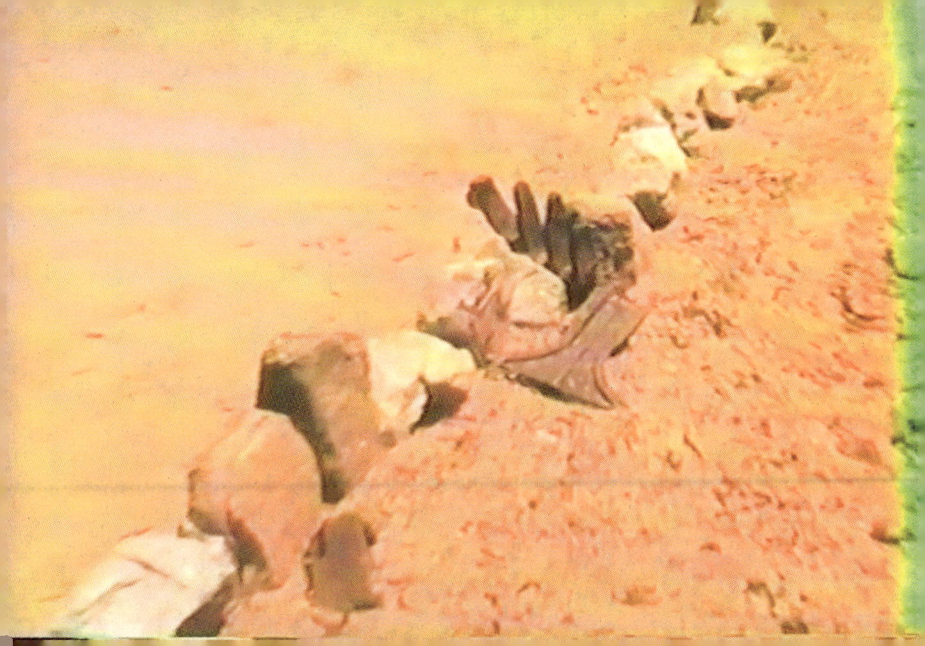

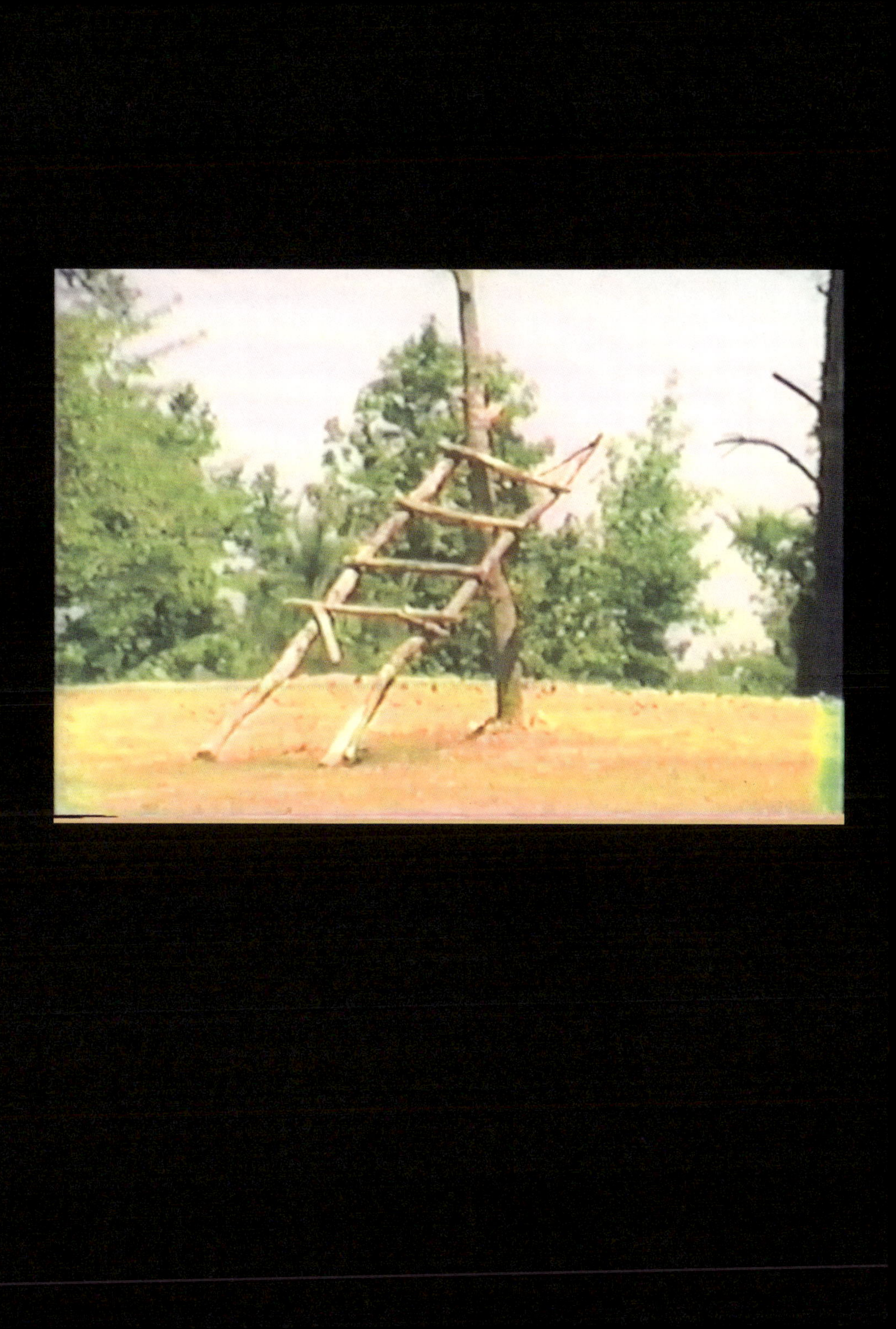

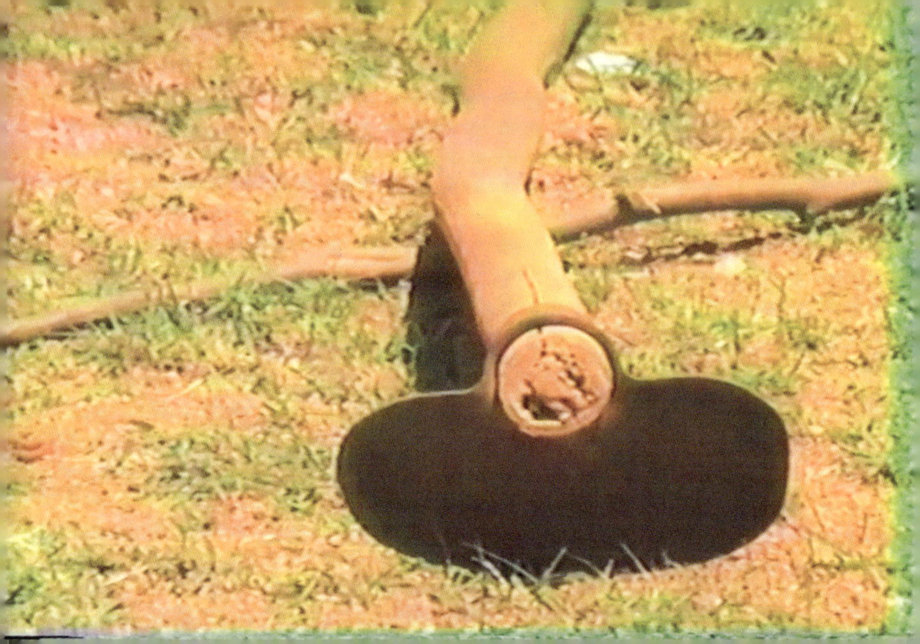

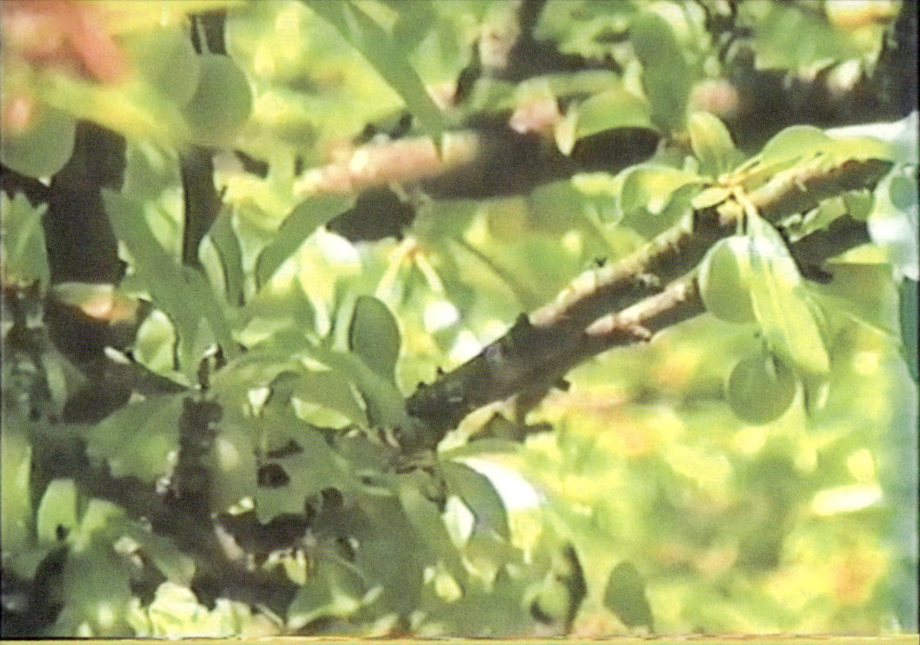

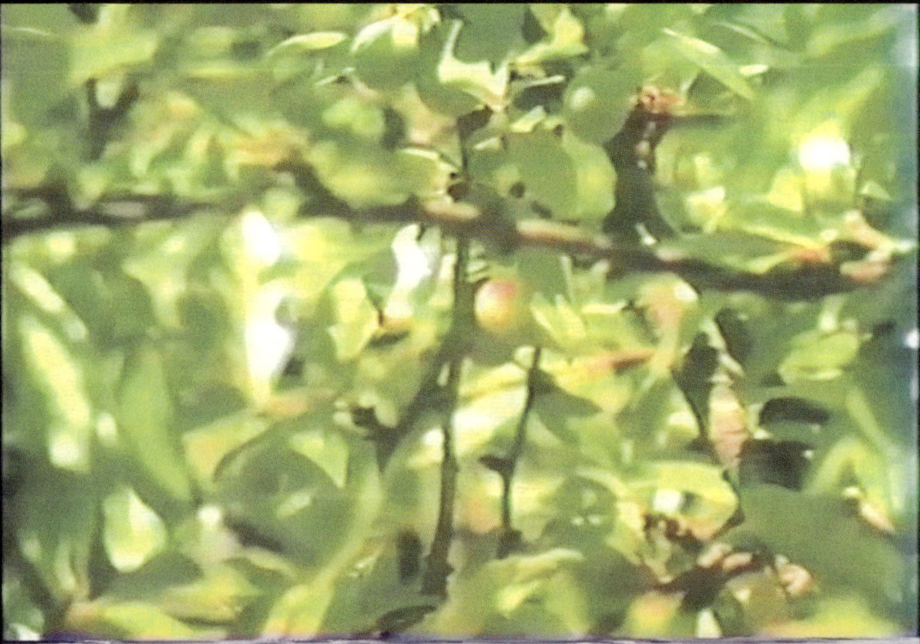

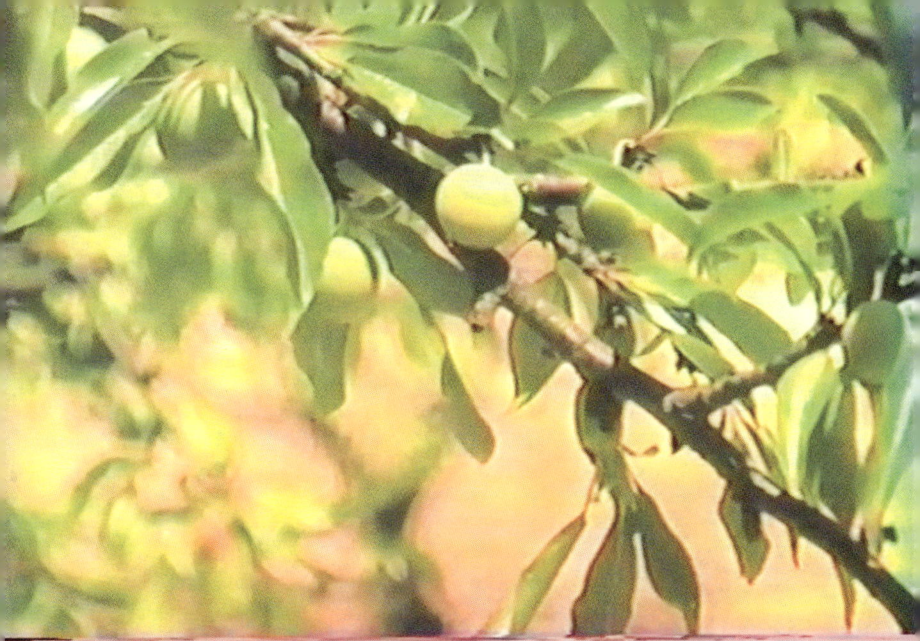

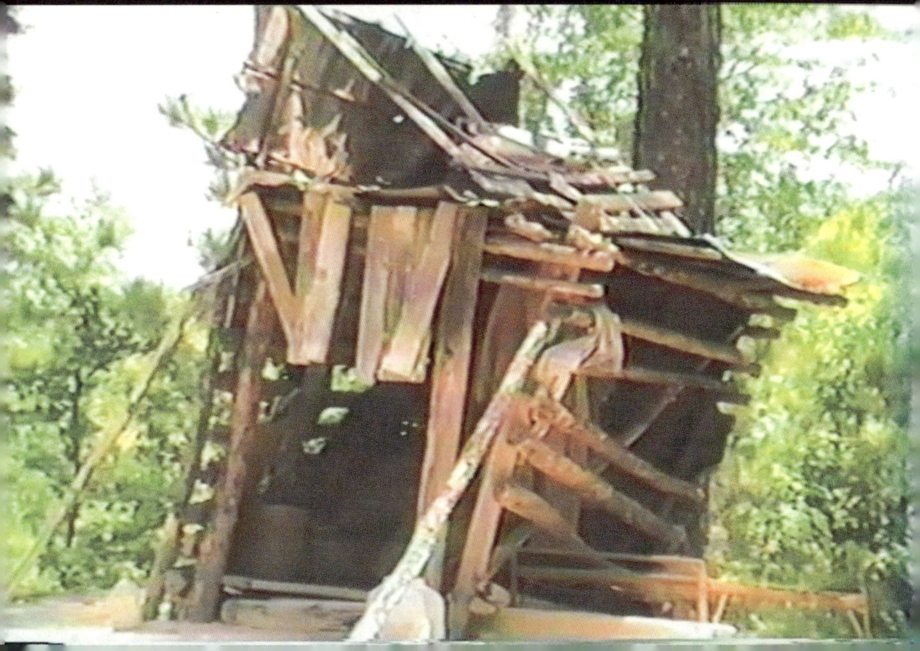

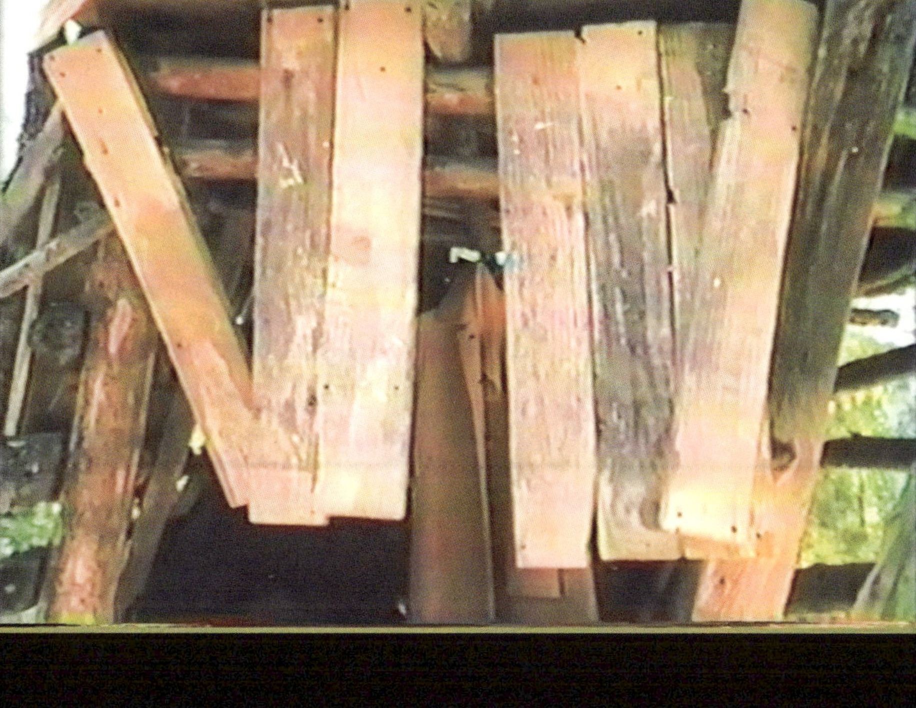

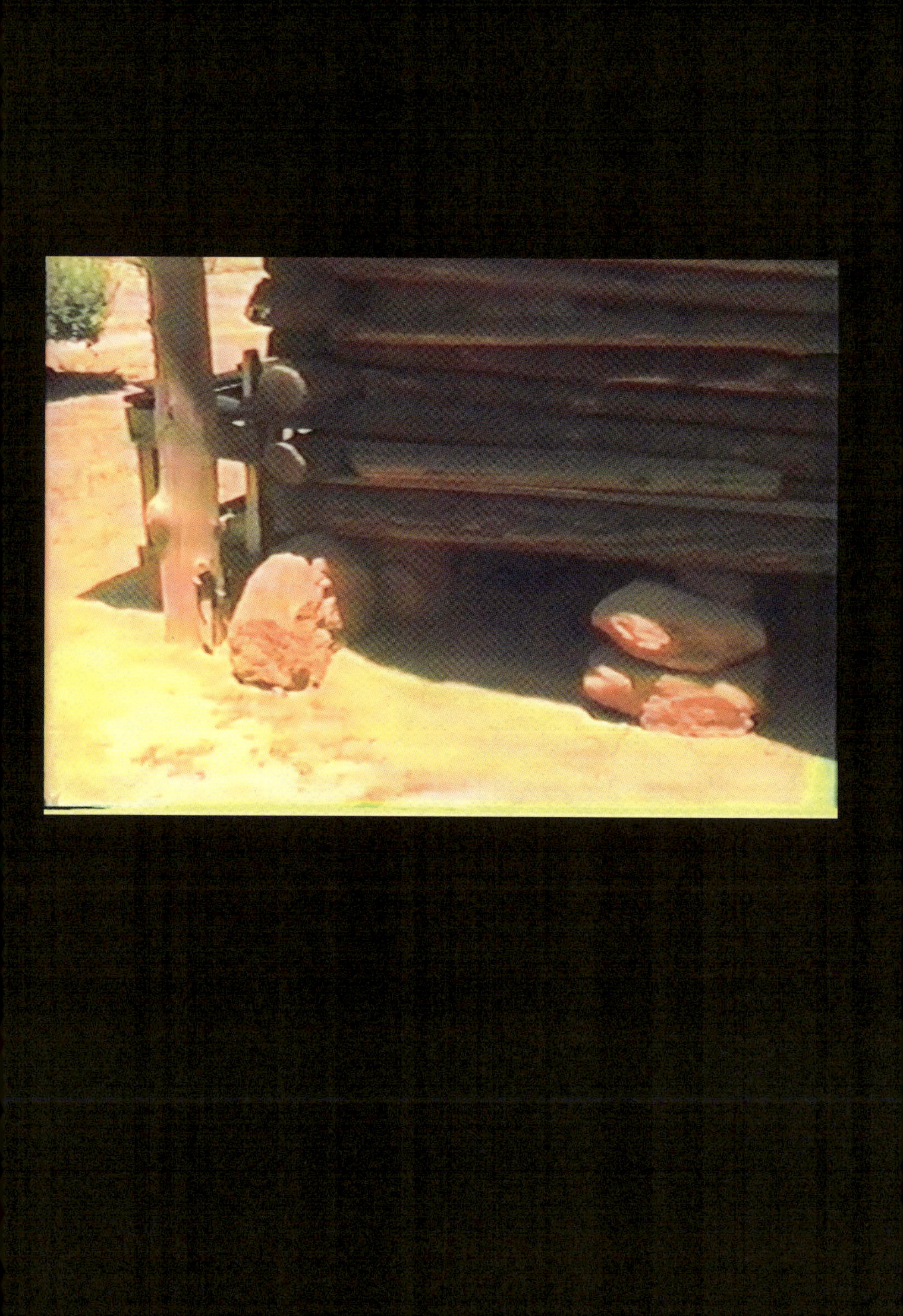

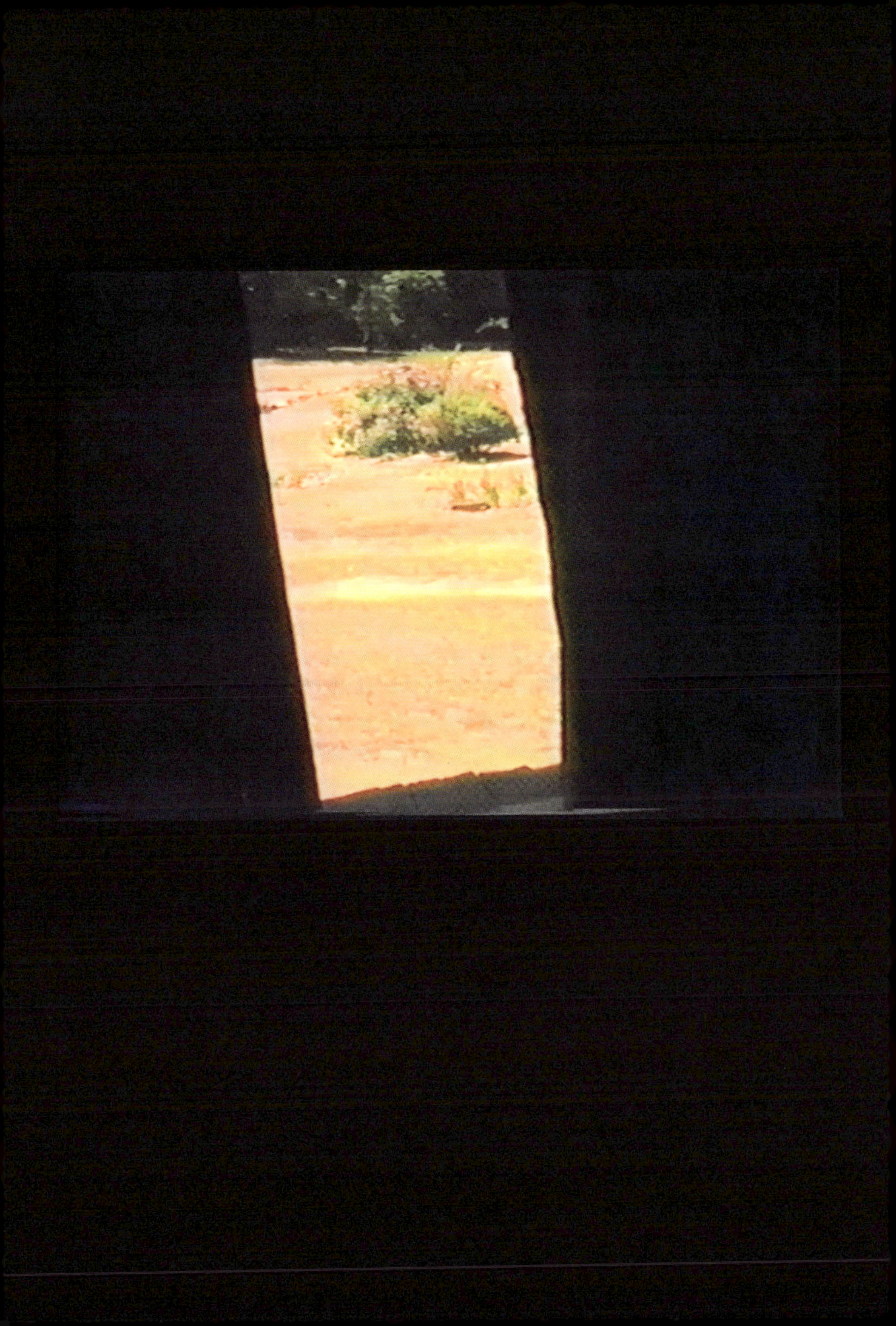

MAY 9 – 1987

opening remarks: what does it mean to be an artist? balance the world; wisdom; gentle . . .

1. Mary Lou – "we are living on the mercy of each other" 08m 59sec

2. On work: If you're working you know you have something for you . . .

3. 16:02 what food she eats, raises
bring water + wood

29:23 good stills

. . . And that's the way that is . . .

18:50 makes a bench

19:30 builds house
talks about neighbors + family

* 21:34 to 23:13 shots of house; discusses neighbors

25:35 parents houses, etc. shot of grounds, rocks stones
"but this is how I work . . . " ← not there

35:57 Roses + beans

36:21 – named for ancestors minnie +

37:20 snake appears

40:07 rootwork in shoes

46:13 snake doctor
bird hollering at person picking strawberries

49:20 pan grounds best (stones around bush)

all house details ↘

50:12 begin grounds

50:48 long shots of house

52:51 best ladder

✓ 53:25 panorama of house

54:49 out building details aesthetic fade

55:54 rocks

57:30 hoe to ladder

59:06 out bldgs

✓ 1:00:53 best of out bldg

✓ 1:01:42 " "

1:04:22 out bldg + tree (good)

1:05:05 ladder triangle fade

1:05:54 bushes, fruit plum trees

✓ 1:06:34 out

1:07:30 broom's edge / found stick stones

1:08:03 best quote

1:09:03 interior + quotes

1:11:57 single live

1:12:58 – die, live, along with bottle cleaning
<u>best</u> end
live on mercy of each other . . .
living . . .

If it's something you built and you know you have it, when folks come in to look at it if they say I'm telling a lie, I just know which way it is. As long as I've got the plum trees I'm alright.

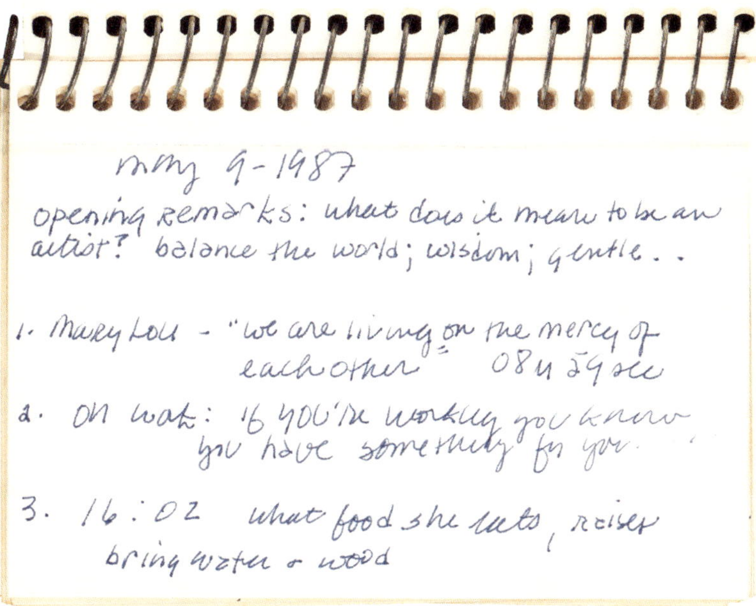

may 9-1987
opening remarks: what does it mean to be an artist? balance the world; wisdom; gentle . .

1. Mary Lou - "we are living on the mercy of each other" 08m 59 sec

2. on work: if you're working you know you have something for you.

3. 16:02 what food she eats, raises
bring water & wood

Judith McWillie, Untitled notebook, c. 1991. Page pertaining to *Mary Lou Furcron, Vesta GA.*, 11 pages total, in the Judith McWillie Videotapes 20455, Southern Folklife Collection, Wilson Special Collections Library, University of North Carolina at Chapel Hill. Used with permission of the artist.

Present Day Reflections

Judith McWillie

From 1984 to 2011, Judith McWillie recorded 150 unedited documentary videos. Collectively, these tapes comprise hundreds of hours of visual and oral history, primarily made up of informal, experimental interviews with Southern cultural producers, both formally trained and self- and community-educated, working across visual and musical forms.

The following text has been edited down from a series of conversations the editors recorded with McWillie, in person and over the phone, between March 2024 and February 2026. In their talks, McWillie shared reflections on the process, approach, and driving concerns of her videography, including the making of Beverly Buchanan, Athens, GA, 8 July, 1995 *and her experience watching it thirty years later. The editors also invited McWillie to select one of her paintings for inclusion in the book.*

If I had to look at a model for documentary filmmaking, it would be D. A. Pennebaker's Bob Dylan film *Don't Look Back*. That film introduced me to cinema verité—it's raw, it's in the field, with no setup or preplanning. I thought, "Well, when I get my camera, I can just have a camera turned on while I'm hanging out." The camera became an extension of me; it became my organ, my eyes. One of the joys in that approach was that I could engage in verbal and nonverbal languages simultaneously. I could carry on a conversation at the same time I was filming, which made it a complete, immersive, and bodily process. There's a tremendous amount of information that is conveyed in a holistic experience that doesn't come through in a formal interview. I really believed that this approach would have so many layers, conscious and unconscious, that there would be richness. I'm a big believer in the unconscious, and that there would be things in the videos that even I wasn't aware of.

People compartmentalize and have trouble recognizing that I'm also an artist. They said, "You're an ethnographer." My response was, "No

I'm not, I'm not following any kind of protocol." I'm not trained as an anthropologist—I'm a painter for heaven's sake! I'm an artist, and this is the way an artist approaches this work. The linearity of scholarly art history makes me want to bite my finger off! The videos allowed me a way to get some freedom from that. I really mean it when I say that there's a level of consciousness that isn't linear. Art has this dimension to it, far more than meets the eye. Constructing sentences, even concepts like the scientific method—rationalism, sequentialism, all that—it's not the highest state of consciousness. It just isn't.

The reason for going into art is to be in an environment where you're around other people that process the world that way, too. To me it was a matter of survival. This work created situations where I could move in a way that was super comfortable for me, spending time with artists in their studios and yards. And I brought the camera everywhere. If it was going to be some kind of religious ritual or something where it wouldn't have been appropriate, I didn't record. But I always had the camera there, even if I didn't use it—though I can't remember any incident where that happened. The people that I visited were pretty extroverted, and they loved talking.

With Beverly, everything about her was *interested* and interesting. She was so committed. And funny! I called her up and said, "Can I bring my camera and come over?" "Yeah!" She was a lot of fun, so you could have any kind of conversation with her, impromptu or whatever you call what we were doing, and there was no way it wouldn't be substantive, because of who she was and what her work is. It was Beverly's thing, and I was happy in whatever role I could play to draw her out. You draw each other out in a situation like that in a way that you can't get in a traditional interview. I just loved her as a fellow artist, and that video was two artists having a conversation, right?

And then, we're in her environment. That was in her home, over on Boulevard. And in her garden. There were so many sounds that time of year. The sound of the doves. You can really feel the impact of climate change now, compared to how the summer garden sounded thirty years ago. Inside, I remember moving in and out of different rooms, especially the back part that had a lot of glass windows in it. That particular area back there was a dream studio to me. Beverly was kind of in her prime then, if I'm not mistaken. She had just had this really successful show with

Bernice Steinbaum Gallery in New York. I talked to Bernice, and she said that she had people who came down from Harlem to see the show, who had been Southerners, and who had left maybe as recently as the 1950s. She said that when they saw those shacks, they cried. Beverly said it was one of the most gratifying shows she'd had, ever.

We were both so busy in those years that that recording was the longest conversation we'd ever had and the first time our paths crossed that deeply. But we both knew about each other. And, oh my god, just to even talk to somebody else who knew Mary Lou Furcron! Mary Lou Furcron was a massively precious and important human being. She did everything: she grew her food, made everything, washed everything. Forget that visit when it was about 3 degrees [and she wouldn't open the door]. . . But she reveled in that. She wasn't lonely. Well, I can't say that. After the trauma she experienced in Philadelphia, I don't know. I think about her all the time. It was such a blessing to meet her. I don't think there's anyone else like her. She's a monumental presence. To be gifted to meet a person who lived like that—the example of how she survived. . . She would be able to survive much better than most of us in the apocalypse.

Mary Lou is a central presence in that video. She was our common love and common experience, and that made the conversation go the way it did—because she was central. The sharing experience always yields more ridges of different kinds, as opposed to people talking at each other from their own worlds. Beverly talks about "my eye," and there were shared affinities between my videos and Beverly's photos—which begs the question of whether there is something inherent in the subject matter, in this case, Mary Lou Furcron's house-making. Like the way she stacked the stones that propped her house up. There was inherent power in details like that. They concretized her gestures, her touch. It isn't just the photographer's eye and will, it's some kind of power in the subject itself that attracts recognition.

Beverly and I talked somewhat about the fact that they had torn down the pulpwood forest right behind Mary Lou's house, and that had exposed her to the highway. When they tore down that forest, it was sacrilege. And it altered her life irrevocably. We had both known it was only a matter of time before she would be moving. And the worst part of thinking about trying to save her house, given the state of the culture in those years, is it would not have been enshrined as the beautiful tabernacle that it was. It wouldn't have been used in a way anywhere near equal to her life-force. But even at the nursing home, she had a garden. As long as she had that garden, *that* was Mary Lou.

In the video, Beverly mentioned that when the Olympics took place in Georgia, the state went around knocking down the shacks that were not occupied. And Beverly felt a sense of urgency to photograph as many of them as she could, because they were going to be knocked down. Can you imagine that? It was an erasure of culture. *Those were people's homes.* We know that the horrors of racism diffused everything. The history of the shacks was oppression and sharecropping. But not to forget—those were people's homes. I witnessed similar processes in Memphis in the 1960s. "Urban renewal" just meant Black removal. Hawkins Bolden lived in the neighborhood near my high school, and as the neighborhood was undergoing urban renewal, he refused to sell. They put up a multistory medical building next door to his house, and he had to deal with problems from their water runoff. I started visiting with him in college. He was a formative person for me. He told me about the scarecrow sculptures he made out of pots and pans, why he used reflective materials, and his homemade radio. As I got to know more yard artists, I learned that a lot of yard art had to do with saying things in code that couldn't safely be said otherwise.

Thinking more about why I did the videos, I realize the answer is something really specific: it was so the artists could speak for themselves. Beverly was a successful and distinguished professional artist, and we shared reference points in New York. But many of the artists I recorded were not aware of the workings of the art world. In that field of so-called outsider art, there was something very disturbing: the artists were mostly Black people living hand to mouth, and they were never front and center talking about their work. In those days, especially with older artists like J. B. Murray and Dilmus Hall, dealers and critics spent a lot of time describing them and interpreting their art with no input whatsoever from the artists themselves. With J.B. Murray, there was a writer who said he was a "tortured schizophrenic." This was very alarming and inaccurate. He was expressing and interpreting African American traditional religion. Video gave him a platform to speak for himself and conduct the water divination ceremony that lent context to his paintings. His point of view was essential. It's very important that somewhere in this whole process, for any artist, that the artist has the floor. The videos allow the artist to have the floor.

I know there are many subtexts to documentary and about the relationship of the camera to colonialism. To me, it was imperative to record the artists speaking for themselves, and also to make these videos publicly available. The whole purpose of going to UNC in 2011 was so all the videos could be available to stream. UNC is very distribution-oriented, and they kept their promise to digitize and host all 150 videos. There's about eighty artists and yard-workers represented in them, and probably only about ten artists made it big. Now all the videos are available free to the public, and anyone can make of them what they want. I have to say, the best thing I've gotten from that experience was when a woman wrote to me that she had found a video through a Google search looking up her grandfather. She said that finding the recording of him and watching it with her mother was very important to her family.

Presently, the world is undergoing a process of chaotic realignment. It's like the chaos of beginning a painting: we don't know where it will take us, it's all *becoming* right in front of our eyes. We can't control what all this is. We just have to live through it—but at the same time we're doing that, I know we're part of something that is way beyond it. We're going to come out of this, and it's going to be a big period of creation. Because now creation is going to be more linked to survival. Making art is an act of the future. Similar to prayer, it's creating the future on a quantum level. It ensures that we have a future.

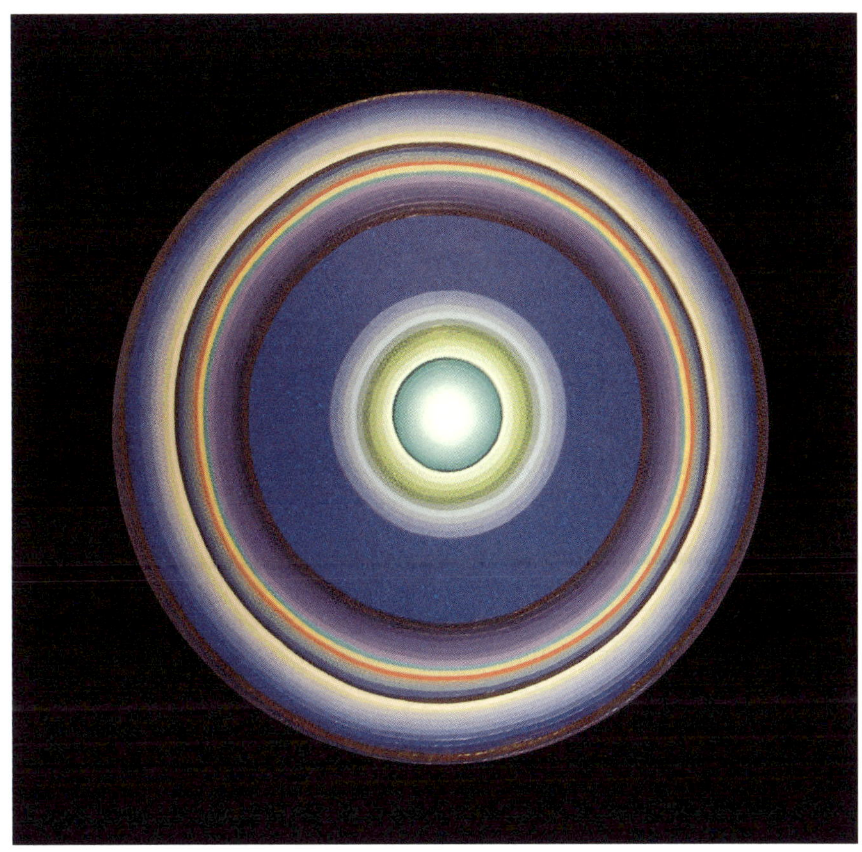

Judith McWillie, *Prodigal Star*, 2001. Acrylic on canvas, 60 in. circumference. Used with permission of Christian Brothers University, Memphis, TN.

People

Alice Walker (b. 1944) is a renowned novelist, poet, and activist from Eatonton, GA. Walker was the first African American woman to win the Pulitzer Prize for Fiction for her novel *The Color Purple* in 1982. She published the elegiac poem "Beverly Buchanan, Artist, 1940–2015" upon Buchanan's passing.

Amanda Cox (1959–2015) was an artist and gardener in Allenhurst, GA, where she worked at Seabrook Village (formerly Eddie Bowens's farm) crafting many of the costumes that actors wore for historical reenactments.

Andy Hines owned Lost N Found Antiques, which he operated alongside business partner Luke Graham in Lexington, GA. Andy and his wife, Dolores, lived in the back of the store before his passing.

Arden Scott (b. 1938) is a Long Island–based artist known for her mixed-media sculptures and the immersive installations she made from salvaged materials while living in Manhattan in the 1960s and 1970s. She met Buchanan during this period, and the two maintained their friendship through visits and regular correspondence after Buchanan moved to Georgia.

Armell Stroud (1934–2023) was an Athens-based artist, arts educator, and musician in the band Armell Stroud and the Twisters. He ran the night club Hawaiian Ha-Le Club and Event Center, and was the first Black art teacher to integrate Clark County public schools.

Art Rosenbaum (1938–2022) was an artist, painting professor, musician, and folk musicologist who moved to Athens, GA, in 1976 and lived there for the remainder of his life. In 2008, he won a Grammy award for his music collection *Art of Field Recording Volume I: Fifty Years of Traditional American Music Documented by Art Rosenbaum*. His paintings often depict the musical performances that he recorded around the country as part of the extensive fieldwork that he undertook with his wife, Margo Newmark Rosenbaum, one of McWillie's closest friends.

Aunt Lucy was a relative of Buchanan's from Harnett County, NC.

Bill Eiland (b. 1948, Dr. William Underwood Eiland) served as director of the Georgia Museum of Art at the University of Georgia from 1992 until his retirement in 2023.

Billy Evans (b. 1941) is the former attorney and Democratic Georgia congressman who served as representative of Georgia's District 8, including the city of Macon, from 1977 to 1983. Buchanan may have overlapped with him in Macon.

The Blue family is based in Glynn County, GA, where members have maintained a burial ground for multiple generations on private property owned by brothers Fred and Jim Blue. The oldest marked grave in the cemetery is that of Ellen Blue (1851–1916). The Blue family is descended from people who were enslaved on the Laurel Grove Plantation.

Bernice Steinbaum (b. 1941) operated the Bernice Steinbaum gallery in New York from 1977–2000. She represented Buchanan's work from the late 1980s through the late 1990s.

Betye Saar (b. 1926) is a pioneering assemblage and mixed-media artist and a key figure in the Black Arts and Black feminist movements. In 1975, she became the first African American woman to have a solo exhibition at the Whitney Museum of American Art. With Iverna Lockpez, McWillie curated Saar's work in the 1992 group show *The Migrations of Meaning* at INTAR Gallery in New York.

Bukka White (c. 1906–1977, Booker T. Washington White) was a Delta blues guitarist and singer from Mississippi who moved to Memphis in the early 1940s. White was celebrated for his distinct vocals and slide guitar, and he was posthumously inducted into the Blues Hall of Fame in 1990.

Carl Andre (1935–2024) was a New York–based artist known for his geometric, floor-based sculptures made from industrial materials. A central figure in the Minimalist movement, Andre was married to Buchanan's friend, the feminist artist Ana Mendieta, who died prematurely under suspicious circumstances in 1985. Her death resulted in second-degree murder charges against Andre, though he was later acquitted.

Cash was Aunt Lucy's son and a distant relative of Buchanan's in Harnett County, NC.

Cathy Fox (b. 1949, Catherine Fox) is an Atlanta-based arts writer and critic who was the art critic at the *Atlanta Journal Constitution* from 1981–2009.

Charles Radcliffe is an Athens-based artist known for his birdhouse sculptures made from found lumber. Buchanan's neighbor and friend, he occasionally assisted her with construction projects, including the renovation of her sunroom studio.

Connie Evans (Constance Evans) is a New York–based artist originally from Kentucky. Evans was on the art faculty at Southampton College of Long Island University, where McWillie was a visiting professor for a summer session in 1980.

Cyrus Bowens was a Gullah Geechee artist and preacher in Midway, GA, whose c. 1930s funerary sculptures at the Sunbury Missionary Baptist Church ranged from large-scale carved wooden abstractions to figurative assemblages and cast and incised cement grave markers incorporating mirrors and found objects.

Doc Harris (1905–1995, Washington Harris) was a renowned spiritual doctor from Mississippi, who founded the Saint Paul Spiritual Holy Temple on the outskirts of Memphis in 1957. In collaboration with his family, including children Caroline, Bert, and Washington James "Mook" Harris, he built a complex of sacred structures and sculptures in which he led a Christian congregation and performed spiritual healing for those who sought his help.

Eddie Bowens (c. 1889–1987) was born on Colonels Island, GA. A cousin of Cyrus Bowens, he was a farmer, carpenter, oysterman, root doctor, and deacon at the Sunbury Baptist Church in Midway, GA. Bowens built his own home, which has been preserved by the Seabrook Village Foundation for historical education.

Elaine de Kooning (1918–1989) was an artist, educator, and art critic who played a critical role in the Abstract Expressionist movement of the mid-twentieth century. Although she was based primarily in New York and Long Island, de Kooning served as the inaugural Lamar Dodd Visiting

Professor of Art at the University of Georgia's Lamar Dodd School of Art in Athens, GA, from 1976–78, and maintained a friendship with McWillie, who was a visiting professor at Southampton College of Long Island University in 1980.

Ella Martin (1912–1995, Annie Lou Ella Martin) was Patricia Phagan's great-aunt, who worked at a factory in Macon, GA.

Eva Mae Bowens (1917–1992) was the youngest of Cyrus Bowens's children and a member of the Sunbury Missionary Baptist Church in Midway, GA. Bowens created ornate painted signs.

Fox Fleming (c. 1916–2004, Theordies Fleming Sr.) from Crawford, GA, was known for the yard art he created with his wife, Juanita Fleming, which incorporated found objects in the garden they designed and tended.

George Kornegay (1913–2014) of Bibb County, AL, was a Methodist minister and artist who created an extensive sculptural environment in his yard, a practice that he devoted himself to full-time following his retirement in 1980. Kornegay's assemblage art included the use of found objects, electronics, paint, rocks, and various iterations of bottle trees.

Grey Gundaker (b. 1950) is an anthropologist and professor of American studies and anthropology at the College of William and Mary. Gundaker and McWillie worked together extensively collecting oral histories and documentation of yard practitioners, which culminated in their coauthored book, *No Space Hidden: The Spirit of African American Yardwork* (University of Tennessee Press, 2005).

Gus Cannon (c. 1874–1979) was a blues musician, composer, and bandleader from Mississippi. After moving to Memphis, Cannon cofounded the influential jug band Cannon's Jug Stompers and played a seminal role in the development of both jug band and early blues traditions.

Hannelore Baron (1942–1987) was a German-born American artist known for her intricate works in collage, assemblage, and mail art.

Hans Hofmann (1880–1966) was an acclaimed painter and educator who immigrated to New York from his native Germany in 1932. His approach to pictorial space and color was deeply influential to the Abstract Expressionist movement. Louise Nevelson was one of his students.

Hesikiah Allen was a reverend at the Sunbury Missionary Baptist Church in Midway, GA, and is buried in the adjoining cemetery. He served as the spiritual father to Eddie Bowens.

Irene McKay (1909–1988) was Buchanan's biological mother who lived in Fuquay, NC. Though Buchanan was raised by her relatives Walter and Marion Buchanan, whom she called mother and father, she maintained a positive relationship with Irene and visited her every summer as a child.

Jean Westmacott (b. 1947) is an artist and friend of Buchanan's based in Oglethorpe County, GA. Known for her realist sculptures, she was the gallery director at Brenau University in Gainesville, GA, from 1990 to 2006, where she organized an iteration of Buchanan's traveling *ShackWorks* exhibit in 1995. With her husband, Richard, Jean continues to be involved in historic preservation efforts in Oglethorpe County.

Jesse Owens (1913–1980) was a track and field athlete and civil rights advocate from Alabama, who became a global icon after winning four gold medals at the 1936 Berlin Olympics.

Jock Reynolds (b. 1947) is an artist, curator, and the former gallery director of Addison Gallery of American Art at Phillips Academy in Andover, MA, from 1989–98, and director of Yale University Art Gallery from 1998–2018. He curated the 1994 exhibit *House and Home: Spirits of the South*, featuring the work of Buchanan, Max Belcher, and William Christenberry.

John Whelan is a musician in Athens, GA.

Juanita Fleming (1920–2004) from Crawford, GA, was known for the yard art she created with her husband, Fox Fleming, which incorporated found objects among the vegetation in the garden they designed and tended.

Lillian was Buchanan's relative, possibly an aunt, in Harnett County, NC.

Leni Riefenstahl (1902–2003) was a German filmmaker, photographer, and actress, whose 1935 Nazi propaganda film *Triumph of the Will* was commissioned by Adolf Hitler; it is considered one of the most striking examples of propaganda cinema in history.

Leon lived with his dogs in a double-pen house, most likely in rural Georgia. Buchanan photographed Leon and his home and wrote about him.

Louise Nevelson (1899–1988) was a sculptor known for her monochromatic assemblages, which combined found objects, scrap wood, and other materials. Born in Ukraine, she immigrated to Maine in 1905 and moved to New York after high school. Her work was widely recognized with many major awards and exhibitions during her lifetime.

Lucille Sanders (1922–2010) was a farmer and gardener who, along with her husband, Willie Ed Sanders, tended to almost seven acres of land in Vesta, GA. A distant relative of Mary Lou Furcron, Lucille and Willie Ed lived near Furcron and checked in on her frequently.

Lucinda Bunnen (1930–2022) was a photographer, art collector, and arts advocate in Atlanta and Buchanan's friend and supporter. She cofounded the Nexus Gallery (now Atlanta Contemporary).

Lucy Lippard (b. 1937) is an art historian, critic, curator, and an early supporter of Buchanan's practice, which she featured in her book *Overlay: Contemporary Art and the Art of Prehistory* (1978). Buchanan and Lippard formed a long-term friendship and maintained regular correspondence.

Mallory Lopp (b. 1985) lives in Athens, GA, and was close with Buchanan as a child by way of her mother Prudence Lopp's friendship with Buchanan.

Mary Bowens was married to Eddie Bowens and lived in Midway, GA.

Mary Lou Furcron (c. 1912–2008) See extended biography on pp. 302–03.

Mary Porter (b. 1955) is an Athens-based painter and was Buchanan's next door neighbor when the 1995 video was recorded.

Max Belcher (b. 1944) is a documentary photographer from Philadelphia who spent a significant part of his childhood in Liberia, where his American-born father became a naturalized citizen. Belcher created a major body of work tracing connections between Liberian vernacular architecture and vernacular architecture in the American South. His work was featured alongside Buchanan's and William Christenberry's in the exhibition *House and Home: Spirits of the South*.

Melinda Moore Lampkin (c. 1940s) is a Detroit-based artist known for her mixed-media collages, influenced by the quilt making traditions she observed while visiting her grandmothers and aunts in Alabama as a child.

Michael Harris (1948–2022) was an art historian, artist, curator, educator, and musician, with degrees in studio art, African American studies, and art history. A member of the art collective AfriCOBRA, he taught art history at various institutions including Morehouse College, Spelman College, the University of North Carolina at Chapel Hill, and later at Emory University in Atlanta. His last book, *Art as Sanctuary: Conjuring an Africana Aesthetic*, was published posthumously in 2026 by Duke University Press.

Milton Resnick (1917–2004) was an Abstract Expressionist painter and member of the New York School. Born in Ukraine and raised in New York, he was married to fellow artist Pat Pasloff.

Mississippi John Hurt (1892–1996, John Smith Hurt) was an influential country blues singer, songwriter, and guitarist from Mississippi, who primarily worked as a sharecropper until his music achieved widespread acclaim in the early 1960s folk music revival. He spent the last years of his life recording and performing extensively.

Paige Stevens (c. 1932–2012) was an army veteran, Liberty County school bus driver, and deacon and lifelong member of the Sunbury Missionary Baptist Church in Midway, GA. He volunteered for many years with the Seabrook Village Foundation alongside his wife, Anna Stevens.

Pat Lasch (b. 1944) is an artist and former Athens, GA, resident known for her intricate sculptures depicting everyday objects. Lasch grew up in New York before relocating to Athens with her former husband, Thomas Cerbu. Lasch and Cerbu sold their home in the Boulevard neighborhood to Buchanan and Patricia Phagan in 1991.

Pat Passlof (1928–2011) was an artist from Georgia raised in New York who was known for her Abstract Expressionist paintings. She was a key member of the feminist organization, Women in Arts, and the accompanying publication, *womanart magazine*, which published a review of Buchanan's work in 1976.

Patti Phagan (b. 1995, Patricia Phagan) is an art historian and curator from Flowery Branch, GA, specializing in twentieth-century art and the history of prints and drawings. From 1987–2000 she was a curator at the Georgia Museum of Art, and from 2000–2021 she was a curator at the Frances Lehman Loeb Art Center at Vassar College. Phagan and Buchanan became housemates in the early 1980s and cohabitated in the house documented in *Beverly Buchanan, Athens, GA, 8 July 1995* from 1991–99. Phagan frequently wrote about Buchanan's work in the 1980s and supported Buchanan's practice throughout the 1990s. Phagan collaborated with Buchanan on their backyard garden, and was frequently her caregiver on work-related travel.

Precious Bryant (1942–2013) was a blues guitarist and singer from Talbot County, GA, who was known for playing Piedmont finger-style guitar and performing traditional Southern blues.

Prudence Lopp (b. 1952) is an Athens-based former real estate appraiser and friend of Buchanan's. She often accompanied Buchanan on her drives to surrounding rural counties to visit people and homes that Lopp encountered during work-related travel. In 2013, Lopp managed a living estate sale for Buchanan to support Buchanan's medical expenses while she was living in a nursing home in Ann Arbor, MI.

Rachel Bowens lived in Midway, GA, and was the wife of Cyrus Bowens and mother of Eva Mae Bowens.

Ralph David Abernathy (1926–1990) was a civil rights leader and pastor from Montgomery, AL, and a pivotal figure in the 1956–66 Montgomery Bus Boycott. He served as pastor of Montgomery's First Baptist Church until it was bombed by white terrorists in 1957; in 1961, he moved to Atlanta. Following Dr. Martin Luther King Jr.'s assassination in 1968, Abernathy led the Poor People's Campaign and served as president of the Southern Christian Leadership Conference.

Renée Stout (b. 1958) is a Washington, DC–based mixed-media artist working across sculpture and collage, whose work draws from research into African diasporic spiritual traditions and current political events. In 2018, her work was celebrated with a Women's Caucus for Art Lifetime Achievement Award.

Richard Serra (1938–2024) was a sculptor from San Francisco who moved to New York in 1966 and became renowned for his large-scale, site-specific steel installations and his role in American Postminimalism.

Richard Westmacott (b. 1941) is a landscape architect, former professor at the University of Georgia, and the author of *African-American Gardens and Yards in the Rural South* (University of Tennessee Press, 1992). Originally from England, where he studied rural English landscapes, Richard and his wife, Jean, live in Oglethorpe County, GA, where they are engaged in historic preservation efforts, specializing in rural conservation.

Robert Farris Thompson (1932–2021) was an art historian and scholar of African and Afro-diasporic art, music, and dance who taught at Yale for over fifty years. Best known for his book *Flash of the Spirit: African and Afro-American Art and Philosophy* (1983), considered a seminal text in the field, Thompson was a friend and mentor to McWillie and a fan of Buchanan's artwork.

Robert Johnson (c. 1911–1938) was an influential Delta blues musician and songwriter from Mississippi, who was first exposed to the blues in Memphis as a child. In his lifetime, Johnson worked as a traveling performer and, though he only recorded for seven months, his importance as a pivotal figure in American rock and blues music has been recognized posthumously.

Roger Manley (b. 1952) is a curator, photographer, filmmaker, and folklorist who curated the University of North Carolina–Duke iteration of *House and Home: Spirits of the South*. In 2019, his roadside photographs of Southern yard art from the 1980s were published alongside photographs by Guy Mendes and writing by Jonathan Williams in *Walks to the Paradise Garden*.

Roy Lichtenstein (1923–1997) was an American Pop artist whose work drew on comic strips and commercial printing techniques and used mass-media imagery as the basis for large-scale paintings.

Sam Chatmon (1897–1983, Vivian Chatmon) was a Delta blues guitarist and singer from Mississippi, where he grew up playing in the family string band. After working in agricultural labor for much of his adult life, his music career was resurrected during the folk-blues revival of the 1960s, and he toured and recorded throughout the 1960s and 1970s, playing in major festivals including the Smithsonian Folklife Festival in Washington, DC in 1972.

Sharon Sanderson is the former owner of Photo Express where Buchanan developed and printed her photographs while living in Athens, GA.

Tom Cerbu (b. 1955, Thomas Cerbu) is a professor of comparative literature at the University of Georgia. Tom and his former wife Pat Lasch lived at the Boulevard residence documented in *Beverly Buchanan, Athens, GA, 8 July 1995* before selling the house to Buchanan and Patricia Phagan in 1991.

Uncle Oliver was Buchanan's uncle in Harnett County, NC.

Willem de Kooning (1904–1997) was a Dutch American artist known for his pivotal role in the Abstract Expressionist movement in the New York School, and the blending of figuration and abstraction in his paintings.

William Christenberry (1936–2016) was a photographer, painter, and sculptor known for documenting the built environment in the American South, particularly his hometown of Hale County, AL, over the course of five decades. His work was featured alongside Buchanan's and Max Belcher's in the exhibition *House and Home: Spirits of the South*. McWillie studied under Christenberry as an undergraduate art student at Memphis State University.

Willie Ed Sanders (1919–1994, Willie Ed Sanders Sr.) was a farmer who, along with his wife, Lucille Sanders, tended to almost seven acres of land in Vesta, GA. A distant relative of Mary Lou Furcron, Willie Ed and Lucille lived near Furcron and checked in on her frequently.

Places

1. Arcade
2. Atlanta
3. Athens
4. Augusta
5. Brunswick
6. Eatonton
7. Elberton
8. Jekyll Island
9. Jefferson
10. Juliette
11. Lexington
12. Macon
13. Midway
14. St. Mary's
15. St. Simon's Island
16. Washington
17. Vesta

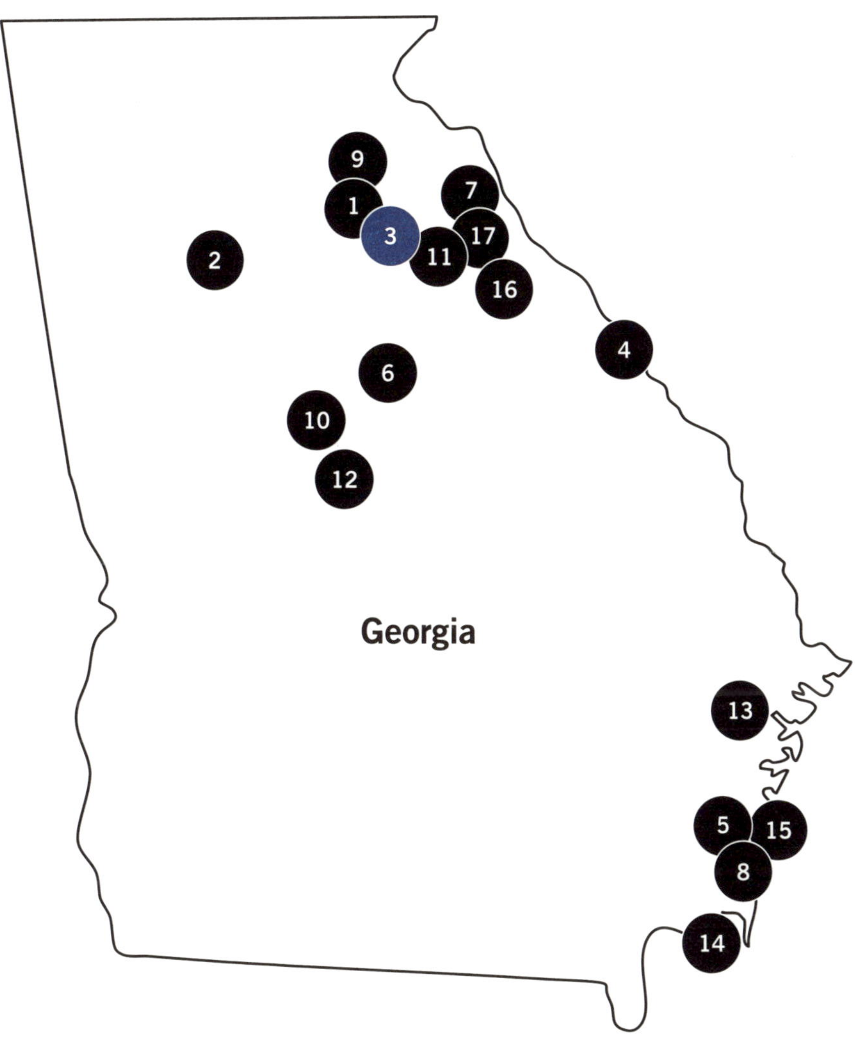
9
1
7
3
17
11
2
16
4
6
10
12
Georgia
13
5
15
8
14

Endnotes

Scene 1

Buchanan wrote extensively about gardens and yards in artist statements and in the textual "legends" that accompanied her shack sculptures. Her text *MY YARD* describes her 1990 garden. See pp. 232–33.

Scene 3

1. In the late 1980s, Buchanan installed multiple large-scale commissioned shack sculptures in Atlanta. A different metal sculpture, *Hard Day's Work Shack* (1988), still resides in Atlanta as a public sculpture in the Old Fourth Ward neighborhood.

2. The Wren's Nest is the Queen Anne Victorian House Museum and National Historic Landmark of the white author Joel Chandler Harris (b. 1848, Eatonton, GA, d. 1908, Atlanta), who is best known for writing the Uncle Remus stories in Black Southern dialect. Alice Walker criticized his work in her essay "The Dummy in the Window: Joel Chandler Harris and the Invention of Uncle Remus," found in *Living by the Word: Selected Writings, 1973–1987* (Harcourt Brace Jovanovich, 1988), 26–33.

3. *House and Home: Spirits of the South, the Work of Beverly Buchanan, Max Belcher, and William Christenberry*, was a major three-person exhibition featuring works by Buchanan, Belcher, and Christenberry that centered their interrelated interests in vernacular architecture. Curated by Jock Reynolds, the exhibition originated in 1994 at the Addison Gallery of American Art, Phillips Academy, Andover, MA, and traveled through 1996, making stops at Georgia Museum of Art, Athens; Morris Museum of Art, Augusta, GA; Duke University Museum of Art, Durham, NC; and Tampa Museum of Art, FL.

4. In a 1993 interview with curator Eleanor Flomenhaft, Buchanan locates this method in relation to Betye Saar's work, describing a feeling of "kinship" with Saar's assemblages: "I think maybe not so much the objects but I'm going to call it the collective assembly, how she puts what she does together." Beverly Buchanan Papers, 1912–2017, bulk 1970s–1990s, Archives of American Art, Smithsonian Institution.

5. In Buchanan's undated text "The Green Car," she writes: "I have always loved cars. I drew pictures of the latest models." She ends the text: "P.S. My current car collection is NOT for sale." Buchanan Papers, Archives of American Art.

6. Beginning in 1987, McWillie published numerous articles about her research and documentation of yard artists from the African diaspora working in the American South. At the time of her 1995 conversation with Buchanan, McWillie's writings appeared in the context of art catalogs as well as academic anthologies and journals, including *Visions Art Quarterly* and *Cultural Perspectives on the American South*. Notably, she partially transcribed the artists' oral histories from the videos she recorded with them and structured much of her writing around their quotations.

7. McWillie gifted Buchanan with a VHS copy of her 1987 video *Mary Lou Furcron, Vesta GA*. See pp. 240–41.

8. Sunbury refers to the cemetery adjoining the Sunbury Missionary Baptist Church, located in the old Tradehill-Seabrook area of Midway, Georgia. Founded in 1866 by formerly enslaved people and moved to its current site in 1918, the church is known for the adjoining cemetery's funerary monuments, which were created by Gullah Geechee preacher and artist Cyrus Bowens in the 1930s. A description of Bowens's grave art is featured in the "Sunbury" chapter of the book *Drums and Shadows.* First published in 1940 and reissued in 1986, this compendium of interviews with formerly enslaved people and their descendants along the Georgia coast was conducted in the 1930s by the Federal Writers' Project's Savannah Unit under the leadership of a white woman named Mary Granger. Though the methods and vantage point in *Drums and Shadows* are fraught with racialized power dynamics and lack an analysis of structural racism, the book significantly increased the visibility of Sunbury and Bowens's art. Georgia Writers' Project, *Drums and Shadows: Survival Studies Among the Georgia Coastal Negroes* (University of Georgia Press, 1986).

Scene 4

1. The Palmyra Missionary Baptist Church was established in 1874. Myers Anderson, the grandfather of Supreme Court justice Clarence Thomas and a primary subject of Thomas's autobiography, *My Grandfather's Son* (2007), was a member of the church and is buried in the adjoining cemetery. In her 1991 text *How does a legend begin and where?*, Buchanan narrates her visit to the coastal town of Pinpoint, Georgia, searching for "answers and no answers about Judge Clarence Thomas." Buchanan Papers, Archives of American Art.

2. In *No Space Hidden*, a photograph by McWillie depicts a cement slab bearing a cast handprint embedded with a mirror, created circa 1932. The book describes, "In 1987, at the age of ninety-eight, Eddie Bowens . . . recalled how his [cousin] worked on the family grave enclosure. . . . He [Cyrus] made the hand-print marker for his wife, Rachel, who was not yet deceased, and others for the rest of the family, including his father, Alec." Grey Gundaker and Judith McWillie, *No Space Hidden: The Spirit of African American Yard Work* (University of Tennessee Press, 2005).

3. McWillie recorded the 1988 event at the Sunbury Missionary Baptist Church, which included a talk by Robert Farris Thompson, alongside church services.

The tape is featured in the Southern Folklife Collection of the University of North Carolina's Wilson Special Collections Library. The digitized video is listed under the title: "Videotape 110: Robert Farris Thompson, Sunbury, Ga., 14 February 1988: Part 1."

4. In 2004, Eddie Bowens's nine-acre farm, located just down the street from the Sunbury Missionary Baptist Church, was registered with the National Register of Historic Places under the name "Eddie Bowens Farm." The register's statement of historic context notes that in 1993, the Seabrook Village Foundation acquired the property and created a cultural museum that includes a gallery space with "exhibits of 'Makin' Do' and the renowned grave art created by Bowens's cousin Cyrus Bowens." The register's Statement of Significance states that the Eddie Bowens Farm, built in 1903, is "representative of the type of African-American farmsteads developed after the Civil War" and is historically significant in the areas of architecture, agriculture, and Black ethnic heritage as "an excellent example of an early 20th-century African-American farm." United States Department of the Interior, National Park Service, "National Register of Historic Places Registration Form: Bowens, Eddie, Farm (Liberty County, Georgia)," National Register Information System ID 04001209, published October 25, 2004, https://npgallery.nps.gov/GetAsset/4d87f404-0523-4597-905e-fc6568efb596.

5. McWillie and Gundaker note that Bowens's children marked his grave site with these objects following his burial. *No Space Hidden*, 15.

6. Photographs of this structure taken circa 1935 by Orrin Sage Wightman accompany McWillie and Gundaker's account of "a metal pipe resembling a tree [which] served as an armature for bottles attached to extended limbs." *No Space Hidden*, 15–16.

7. In 1987, McWillie recorded two VHS tapes interviewing Eddie Bowens and Eva Mae Bowens. The tapes are featured in UNC's digitized archive under the titles: "Videotape 12: Eddie Bowens, Eva Mae Bowens, Sunbury, Ga., November 1987: Part 1"; "Videotape 13: Eddie Bowens, Eva Mae Bowens, tape 2. Sunbury, Ga., 15 November 1987: Part 1." Quotations by Eddie and Eva Mae Bowens, drawn from these recordings, are interwoven into *No Space Hidden*.

8. Buchanan refers to students from the University of Georgia. Founded in 1801, the state's flagship research university has its main campus in Athens and is a major structuring presence in the college town. While Buchanan did not teach at UGA, she did give a lecture in 1996 at the university's Lamar Dodd School of Art.

9. Buchanan created multiple, site-specific artworks set in the section of the Ocmulgee River that winds through Macon, where she lived from 1977–85. She staged and documented two ephemeral "happenings" at the river: *Chalk in a Box* (1980), which she photographed, and *Cherry Blossom Festival Ocmulgee River Happening* (1982), which she recorded as a silent film. Buchanan Papers,

Archives of American Art. In her multi-part 1983 sculpture *Ruins and Rituals*, she sunk a selection of cast cement works in the river, leaving this element of the installation undocumented. See Andy Campbell, "'We're Going to See Blood on Them Next': Beverly Buchanan's Georgia Ruins and Black Negativity," *Rhizomes: Cultural Studies in Emerging Knowledge*, no. 29 (2016), https://rhizomes.net/issue29/campbell/index.html.

10. In 1994, Tropical Storm Alberto brought massive rainfall to the middle Georgia region. A record amount of water in the Ocmulgee River caused it to flood over its banks. "The flooding in Middle and South Georgia killed 34 people, forced thousands of people to evacuate their homes and caused an estimated $1 billion in property damage." Ed Grisamore, "The Flood That Changed Macon, 30 Years Later," *The Macon Melody*, July 5, 2024, https://maconmelody.com/the-flood-that-changed-macon-30-years-later/.

11. While McWillie worked to archive and study overlooked funerary sites in the region, Buchanan developed an experimental sculptural practice in connection with such sites. Art historian Andy Campbell describes that in the late 1970s and early 1980s, Buchanan and her assistant "would often stop beside small, sometimes abandoned, black churches, setting out looking for slave graveyards. . . . Once [Virginia] Pickard or Buchanan found evidence of a slave graveyard (a few pieces of wood or stones placed in a particular alignment), Buchanan would retrieve a small cast concrete sculpture from her car, inscribe it with her initials, and leave it at the site." Campbell, "'We're Going to See Blood on Them Next.'" Buchanan maintained a consistent interest in searching for graves. In one photograph in her papers at the Smithsonian Archives, she is photographed in profile, holding a camera and facing a tombstone shrouded by grass in a tropical setting. The back of the photograph is captioned "Spring Island, 2003, Looking for slave graves." Buchanan Papers, Archives of American Art.

12. In her 2001 text "*What's Up?*", Buchanan writes of her photography practice: "It is about 'drawing' with my camera and documenting old, former, slave cabins, turned tenement houses instead of drawing with oil pastels." Buchanan Papers, Archives of American Art.

13. Buchanan refers to the exhibition *Shack Works*, her mid-career retrospective that originated at New Jersey's Montclair Art Museum in 1994 and traveled for two years, making stops at Museum of African American History, Detroit, MI; The Sidney Mishkin Gallery, Baruch College, New York, NY; Smith College Art Museum, Northampton, MA; Delaware Art Museum, Wilmington, DE; Columbia Museum of Art, Columbia, SC; Sharadin Art Gallery, Kutztown University, Kutztown, PA; Edison Community College Gallery of Fine Art, Fort Meyers, FL; Brenau University Galleries, Gainesville, GA; and Chattahoochee Valley Art Museum, LaGrange, GA.

14. Buchanan's 1986 work, *Blue Station Stones*, was commissioned by Miami-Dade County's Art in Public Places program and is permanently installed outside the Earlington Heights Metrorail Station in the Liberty City neighborhood of Miami. Comprised of eighteen blue-tinted cement cubic forms in two sizes, the sculptures are arranged in groupings amongst the station's oak trees and were intended to be used as seating and tables. While casting the blue-pigmented cement at the Cornell Young Concrete plant outside Macon, Buchanan repurposed the leftover cement into smaller stone works, *Blue Stones*, that she kept and later installed in her backyard. She further describes the casting process in Scene 5. A selection of the *Blue Stones* were later donated to the Oconee Cultural Arts Foundation, outside Athens, where they are installed in the outdoor sculpture garden.

15. Buchanan filled a photo album with undated, four-by-six-inch photographs documenting a single, hand-built home with two entrances, likely a double-pen house. Several images show an older Black man wearing suspenders over a striped shirt, seated with his dogs in the home's doorway. From this series, she reproduced multiple eight-by-ten inch prints and labeled them "Leon's Place." Buchanan Papers, Archives of American Art.

16. Buchanan's archive contains innumerable Photo Express envelopes of photographs from Athens' now-defunct photography store. In an undated photograph, she is seen posing at the counter inside the store, surrounded by photography supplies. Buchanan Papers, Archives of American Art.

17. In her documentary photographs of shacks, Buchanan frequently focused on the stone foundations that raise wooden structures off the ground to mediate moisture and prevent rot. Such foundations were often built from fieldstones stacked at the corners of buildings, a configuration that bears a striking resemblance to the artist's cast cement sculptures. In a 2008 typed artist statement, she reflects on her concrete sculptures, "I went later to foundations of cast concrete."

18. Park McArthur and Jennifer Burris Staton note that the majority of Buchanan's cast cement sculptures were constructed in her Macon studio (where she moved in 1977), but that their early conception began during her years living in the Bronx and East Orange, New Jersey. The artist may also be referring to exhibiting these sculptures in New York while she was living and working in Georgia. Her solo exhibition in 1978 at Truman Gallery premiered this series to a New York audience. In 1980, three of her stacked stone sculptures were included in the landmark feminist group exhibition *Dialectics of Isolation: An Exhibition of Third World Women Artists of the United States* at the women's cooperative A.I.R. Gallery in New York. Park McArthur and Jennifer Burris Staton, eds., *Beverly Buchanan: 1978–1981* (Athénée Press, 2015) 16–17.

19. McWillie contributed a catalog essay for the 1991 exhibition *Syncretism: The Art of the XXI Century* at The Alternative Museum in New York. The essay abstract reads: "Includes traditional art from Africa and North America and works of contemporary artists involved in cross cultural exchange. Defines syncretism as a

process of recombination and exchange of myths and symbols in pluri-cultural societies. Critiques cultural paradigms that produce divisions such as high/low art and folk versus fine art."

20. Buchanan's 1978, typed artist statement titled *WALL FRAGMENTS – Series Cast in Cement* begins:

    > The entire series is called—"FRUSTULUM"—or fragments. Each piece of each fragment is cast, individually, in cement using brick as molds. The newer pieces incorporate steel forms within the cement. Each fragment is then cemented to other fragments and the structure, then, becomes–FRUSTULUM.
    >
    > (An entire large wall piece could be called, FRUSTUMS or FRUSTULA. By definition, Frustum is a piece broken off; the portion of a regular solid left after cutting off the upper part by a plane parallel to the base; A portion of a fragment.)

    Reproduced in McArthur and Burris Staton, *Beverly Buchanan*, 46.

21. Buchanan's *Black Walls* series began circa 1977, following a series of paintings called *Torn Walls* and an exhibition of paintings titled *City Walls* held at the Montclair Art Museum in New Jersey in 1976. The *Black Walls* were color field paintings in the mediums of acrylic on canvas as well as ink and watercolor on paper. In her undated, circa 1977 artist statement titled *BLACK WALLS*, she writes:

    > I first visualized these walls without ever having seen a single one. They just seemed to 'come to me' and I couldn't stop painting them. I knew what they must look like, had to look like but I couldn't get a sense of how they felt until I began painting them. Then, yesterday, September eleventh, coming back from Brooklyn and turning onto a street in Soho, I saw it. The real thing. A Black wall just like the ones I had been painting. . . . I knew that that Black Wall existed though I didn't know where it was or if I'd ever for sure see one, but there it was in all its strong, soft splendor. It was not garish or frightening. It was just there. Being unnoticed.

    Buchanan Papers, Archives of American Art.

22. This refers to Buchanan's site-specific sculpture *Marsh Ruins*. In July 1981, funded by a Guggenheim Fellowship and following a thorough process of obtaining permits, Buchanan built three large cement and tabby mounds directly in the marsh off the coast of Brunswick, near the barrier islands of Jekyll and St. Simons. While in Brunswick preparing for the installation, Buchanan wrote: "July 2, 1981 Brunswick, GA. Went to Ebo Landing on St. Simons Island. Black policeman (Nathaniel) helped me find it. He'd never heard the true story of slaves chained together, walked into the water and drowned while singing, 'The water has brought us, the water will take us away.'" Buchanan Papers, Archives of American Art. There were no public markers commemorating Igbo Landing when Buchanan created *Marsh Ruins* nine miles east of the site. For more information about Igbo Landing,

see the National Museum of African American History and Culture, "The Water Spirit Will Take Us Home," Searchable Museum, accessed December 30, 2025, https://www.searchablemuseum.com/the-water-spirit-will-take-us-home.

Scene 5

1. In an artist statement from 2008, Buchanan describes witnessing storm damage in Florida and creating a body of work about "spaces, colors, visual storms between rooms and outside walls of hurricane-touched houses in Florida I have seen." She continues, "Next to an untouched home is a huge pile of rubbish and slabs and tins and steps and . . . torn walls." Buchanan Papers, Archives of American Art.

2. McArthur and Burris Staton write that Buchanan's "choice of tabby as a core material for *Marsh Ruins* embeds specific political and historical (in addition to geographic) narratives in the artwork itself: that of the relationship between settler-colonialism and slavery in the American Southeast. An amalgamation of shells, sand, and water, tabby gains its durability from the ingredient lime, which manufactures the binding component of concrete. . . . Materialized through the collective labor of slaves, tabby was used to build houses and walls on 19th century plantations in South Carolina, Georgia, and Florida." McArthur and Burris Staton, *Beverly Buchanan*, 17. Buchanan printed two artist's books with photographs documenting the labor-intensive process of making a small tabby sculpture in her backyard in Macon, circa 1982–83, including one titled *MAKING TABBY SCULPTURE IN MACON, GA*. The black-and-white images show the artist in goggles, gloves, kneepads, and an eye shield, bent over on the ground mixing concrete and oyster shells from a local restaurant. Buchanan Papers, Archives of American Art.

3. In 1987, Eva Mae Bowens recounted her father's sculpture: "The little man he had with a pipe in his mouth—he made all of them." Gundaker and McWillie, *No Space Hidden*, 18.

4. Buchanan gifted her exhibition catalogs to friends and caregivers in her extended Athens community. In 1994, she personalized a copy of the *House and Home* catalog for her pulmonologist, Dr. Stephen Lucas, with a drawing and the inscription: "For my ace Doctor, Stephen 'Miracle Grow' Lucas. To his unfailing insight (or is it eyesight) into my health and happiness. Without you, I'd be dead by now. Much love *and* respect."

5. Buchanan created a range of artist's books using different binding and reproduction methods. Many of her booklets combine photography and text, and some include drawings. In multiple texts, Buchanan references keeping booklets on hand to share with strangers. In *"What's Up?"*, she describes going on a drive to document vernacular architecture and bringing "along a small booklet of house photos to help explain when I'm asking permission to 'shoot.'" A sketchbook entry from that same year narrates an exchange Buchanan had with a man at a

gas station in town: "Gave him a 'SURVIVORS' Booklet. We talked houses, Quilts, and photographs. Coded messages in Slave Quilts. MONKEY WRENCH QUILTS MEANT → Gather Your Tools for Travel. We had read the same book." Buchanan Papers, Archives of American Art.

Scene 6

1. Buchanan created a number of life-size, figurative sculptures that combine scrap wood with found objects and other materials. In *The Doctor* (1993), she affixed medication bottles to a life-size feminine figure. In an accompanying text, she named the sculpture "Evelyn." Buchanan's candid photographs of "Evelyn" alongside the furniture in her home studio imbue the figure with the animacy of a living presence, even a companion. In her notes from July 24, 1993, the artist elucidates the slippage between sculpture and an animate person: "I was always looking for something for 'HER.' . . . This sculpture has taken almost seven months to complete. But there did come that point—as I touched the floor—when I looked up and said, 'You no longer belong to me.'" Buchanan Papers, Archives of American Art.

2. McWillie's astute observation about the role of personification in Buchanan's shack sculpture is exemplified by Buchanan's 1991 legend for the sculpture *Mr. Robert Mathis' Yellow Root House and Table*, in which the artist implies that the architecture itself has symptoms of asthma: "There is a mix of old and new in this house. Labored breathing of the old ('a little shortness of breath')."

3. The Museum of Arts and Sciences in Macon commissioned Buchanan's 1979 multipart outdoor work *Ruins and Rituals*, in which the artist combined found concrete foundation footers with her own cast cement elements. Describing the hefty blocks installed in the forest, Lucy Lippard wrote, "This is the first public part of a three-part work, the forms of which recall unburied tombs or giant reliquaries. The second part is private, hidden in the woods nearby and intended only for the searching audience. The third is still smaller, and totally personal; it was buried in a river by the artist." Lucy R. Lippard, *Overlay: Contemporary Art and the Art of Prehistory* (The New Press, 1983), 33, quoted in McArthur and Burris Staton, *Beverly Buchanan*, 16–17.

4. Complex chronic asthma played a structuring role in Buchanan's life, and she narrated her experiences of medicalization frankly in grant applications, interviews, and in her artwork. In a 1994 unspecified grant application for $25,000, she describes being a "lifelong asthmatic," noting that "over the past decade my health has dramatically deteriorated and many new allergies have cropped up as a result of many medications." Her 2001 artist's book *Historical Preservation Through Art [Between Macon and Jackson]* begins, "A Word to the Wise. This artist has multiple medical problems. A trip requires 'packing'. Along with my insulin comes potassium for 3x a day pills. Asthma, inhaler, and mobile respiratory unit, walking stick, bottled water and a pistol." Buchanan Papers, Archives of American Art.

5. Buchanan's 1994 grant application describes the medical necessity of her studio remodel: "On the medical side, my asthma requires clean, pure air. Installed in my central air and heating system is a series of electrostatic filters. My studio, which is my daily working environment, is separated from the main living area of my house and does not receive the benefit from the air conditioning and filter system. Therefore, when funds can be raised, this area must be remodeled." Buchanan Papers, Archives of American Art.

6. Buchanan's drawing practice was expansive in subject matter, including shacks as well as humorous cartoons and observational drawings of plants, animals, and self-portraits. Though they were rarely exhibited in her lifetime, she regularly made pastel drawings of flowers and flower bouquets.

7. "This book" refers to *No Space Hidden: The Spirit of African American Yard Work*, co-written with Grey Gundaker and published in 2005 by the University of Tennessee Press. A book review describes it as "an ambitious and satisfying culmination of research in which the authors have created a cogent and reliable source on African American yard workers and their material world. The volume shows how the use of material arrangements within the word yard, generally in the American South, illustrates the connection to religion, the land, and the past. In addition, this volume illustrates the connection and adaptation of similar yard ornamentation practices in Africa. Gundaker and McWillie, through many disciplines such as religion, history, and art history, attempt to chronicle the practice of African American yard adornment, but the volume really is an oral history which allows the subjects of the volume to ultimately tell their story." Patrick H. Morgan, *African Diaspora Archaeology Newsletter* 10, no. 7 (December 1, 2007).

Scene 7

1. Buchanan made many sculptures specifically for her garden, including a series of wooden and metal chicken-shaped cutouts mounted on wooden posts and staked directly into the ground. Her archive contains multiple photographs of her garden, some showing the chicken sculptures installed among the vegetation.

2. In her text *Sculpture for Ms. Mary Lou Furcron*, which has been reproduced on pp. 224–25, Buchanan writes about the "two good old Georgia white boys" who encouraged her to visit Furcron. In present-day oral histories, Buchanan's friends repeatedly speak of her ability to "talk to anyone." Patricia Phagan has specifically remarked on Buchanan's ability to carry on conversations with "good ole' boys," a term describing a specific cultural form of white masculinity in the South generally understood to be staunchly right-wing politically and committed to upholding racist and homophobic structures.

3. In her 2001 text "*What's Up?*" Buchanan describes a relational practice in which she brought copies of her photographs to the people whose homes she documented:

"I promised to bring back photos to her and I did." Buchanan Papers, Archives of American Art.

4. Due to the large quantity of granite in Elberton, the city is known for producing more granite monuments than any other city in the world, ninety percent of which are cemetery memorials and funerary headstones. The first monument company opened in Elberton in 1887, and monument companies proliferated in the area.

5. Swept yards, in which (usually clay) soil is left unplanted and maintained with a broom, is a yard practice in the American South, commonly associated with African American yards. Richard Westmacott traces resonances between the swept yards (including Furcron's) that he observed doing field work in Alabama, South Carolina, and Georgia and the swept yards in West Africa that he encountered through photographs in colonial British archives from the turn of the twentieth century. Richard Westmacott, *African American Gardens and Yards in the Rural South* (University of Tennessee Press, 1992). In *No Space Hidden*, McWillie and Gundaker pair a photo of Furcron's swept yard with the passage: "In African American yard work these surfaces are themselves as significant and potentially dynamic as what happens in and on them," 110. For a further discussion of swept yards and related practices of care toward the land, see "Architecture in Black Life: Talking Space with LaVerne Wells-Bowie," a dialogue with Wells-Bowie in bell hooks, *Art on My Mind: Visual Politics* (The New Press, 1995), 176–77.

6. Mary Lou Furcron is recorded speaking her characteristic idiom in *Mary Lou Furcron, Vesta, GA*. McWillie's subsequent notes on the video, reproduced on pp. 268–69, includes her transcription of Furcron's idiom.

7. The Westmacotts continue to care for two hand-built chairs and a bench created by Furcron and entrusted to them by the Sanders family when Furcron's home was going to be demolished in 1994.

8. Video stills corresponding to images named in Scene 7 are reproduced on pp. 242–67.

9. The one-room schoolhouse Buchanan references is located in the town of Fuquay (now called Fuquay-Varina) in the northeast central region of North Carolina. Buchanan's photographs of the schoolhouse are dated January 1994, and depict a barnlike structure surrounded by woods. In "Roots," a 2005 handwritten text written on a printout of an email with extended family, Buchanan wrote, "Carrie Buchanan McKay (pronounced McCoy) was a school principal of about 3 or 4 one-room schools. She was loved and respected by many who knew her." Buchanan Papers, Archives of American Art. The Rosenwald School project, a collaboration between Julius Rosenwald and Booker T. Washington, funded infrastructures for education in African American communities in the segregated

rural South after failures in public funding during the Reconstruction era. In 2010, Buchanan created a wooden sculpture titled *Before the Rosenwald School: For my Grandmother (A Tribute to Carrie Buchanan's School, Harnett County, NC).*

10. A 1989 photograph by Buchanan of Furcron's house, reproduced on p. 228, documents how Furcron wedged the gifted shoes between the exterior logs of her house.

11. The 1996 Atlanta Olympics spurred major redevelopment throughout the state of Georgia between 1990 to 1996, leading to the demolition of public housing and the displacement of thousands of low-income residents. Atlanta's city leaders collaborated with the Atlanta Housing Authority and Atlanta Police Department to evict over 30,000 Atlantans from their homes, and illegally arrested an estimated 9,000 unhoused people in the city. The University of Georgia in Athens was a sub-venue of the Olympics, but research on the impact of the Olympics on Athens and the surrounding counties has not been published. Seth Gustafson, "Displacement and the Racial State in Olympic Atlanta 1990–1996," *Southeastern Geographer* 53, no. 2 (2013): 198–213, https://dx.doi.org/10.1353/sgo.2013.0016.

Scene 8

1. This documentary photograph depicts the row of six shotgun houses, built around 1925, that still stand on South Rocksprings Street, between Baxter and Springdale Streets, in Athens. These one-room-wide homes, rooted in African diasporic architectural traditions, are prominent throughout the American South. While many of the buildings Buchanan documented were rapidly disappearing from the local landscape, these six were added to the National Register of Historic Places in 1996. Buchanan included an image of the Rocksprings Street shotguns in her artist's book *survivor 2*. Buchanan Papers, Archives of American Art.

Scene 9

1. Buchanan may be referring to Nevelson's steel sculpture, *Night Wall II* (1976), which was installed as a public sculpture in Miami on Florida International University's campus in the 1990s, though it was not off the Metrorail. In a 1993 interview with curator Eleanor Flomenhaft, Buchanan cited Nevelson as an artist with whom she felt "kinship." Buchanan Papers, Archives of American Art.

2. Prominent in African American yards throughout the American South, bottle trees "are a Kongo-derived tradition dating back to around the ninth century and were introduced to America as early as the seventeenth century as a consequence of the Atlantic slave trade. While the exact origin of bottle trees is unknown, the most probable beginning is in African graveyards as a funereal ritual." Susan R. Barclay, "Bottle Trees," *Mississippi Encyclopedia*, Center for Study of Southern Culture, last updated April 13, 2018, https://mississippiencyclopedia.org/entries/bottle-trees/.

3. Heath Gallery opened in Atlanta's Midtown neighborhood in 1965, and became a major regional contemporary art gallery, showcasing local and nationally renowned artists. Buchanan's first exhibition with Heath Gallery originated at New York's Kornblee Gallery and traveled to Atlanta in 1981. The paper shack sculptures she is referring to, however, are from her 1986 solo show at Heath Gallery, which did not travel. She had another solo show with the gallery the following year.

4. Alice Walker wrote about the impact of Buchanan's shacks in a commemorative poem, where she elucidates "To see the shacks/ You rescued from our shame." Alice Walker, "Beverly Buchanan, Artist, 1940–2015," 2015, https://alicewalkersgarden.com/2015/08/beverly-buchanan-artist-1940-2015/.

5. In an interview with the editors in November 2025, McWillie clarified: "I was not referring to Michael [Harris's] ideas; I was referring to the public debate taking place in the 1980s [around how to platform the work of artists beyond the Western canon]. . . . As regards 'Black folk artists,' some Black scholars were understandably suspicious of white collectors embracing artists, many, if not most of whom, were living on the edge of poverty. They wondered why whites didn't focus on college-educated Black artists who were struggling for recognition at the time. Michael Harris expressed this skepticism spontaneously (he was in the audience) during a conference on Black vernacular art that I attended in Atlanta. I agreed with him that these ironies needed to be identified and critiqued. While money politicized the issue (dealing and collecting), the debate should not be narrowed down to just collectors/dealers, etcetera. We both agreed that there needed to be a wider discussion." For a prime example of the public debates referred to by McWillie, see Thomas McEvilly's critique of MOMA's 1984–85 exhibition *"Primitivism" in 20th Century Art: Affinity of the Tribal and the Modern*, which he deemed "ultimately a demonstration of Western egotism still as unbridled as in the centuries of colonialism and souvenirism." Thomas McEvilley, "Doctor Lawyer Indian Chief," *Artforum* 23, no. 3 (November 1984), quoted in "The Controversial 'Primitivism' Exhibition," *MoMA Through Time*, Museum of Modern Art, https://www.moma.org/interactives/moma_through_time/1980/the-infamous-primitivism-exhibition/.

6. Buchanan did visit Eatonton eventually, evidenced by her undated photograph of the town signage: "Welcome to Historic Eatonton, Home of Joel Chandler Harris, Alice Walker." Buchanan Papers, Archives of American Art.

Scene 10

1. See pp. 222–23.

2. The "Blue Light Recreation Center" refers to the House of Blue Lights, a juke joint in Athens built and operated by Marion Stroud (1912–1994). The memorial published in commemoration following Stroud's passing describes: "During the

late 40s, 50s, 60s, and 70s, the House of Blue Lights, one of the very few fine night clubs in the State of Georgia, owned by a black man, was the place to be for people from all over the state. . . . Top recording artists of that time, such as Gene Allison, L. C. Cook, and Millie Jackson were brought to the House of Blue Lights, by top booking agents like 'Cutie' Marable. Local bands, like Armell and The Twisters, the Grains of Sand, The Tropics, The Imperials, and many others enjoyed regular dates at the Blue Lights. As Rev. James Kendrick, (the pastor of Friendship Baptist Church), put it, 'Marion Stroud provided us a fine place to go to when we could not go to the white places. It made us feel good and proud, like we were somebody. I remember many weddings, and other community activities.'" *Zebra Magazine* 3, no. 1 (January 1, 1995).

3. For *Spectacles* (1988–93), the High Museum of Art in Atlanta commissioned eight artists to each create a room-scaled installation designed for interactive use in their dedicated family wing.

4. In a subchapter titled "Trees" in *No Space Hidden*, McWillie and Gundaker elaborate: "The Trees that people live with are beings that they come to know and love. When a tree dies or is cut down, the loss can be devastating. When the pine forest around Mary Lou Furcron's home was cut down by a lumber company, she discovered that she did not own the land she thought of as belonging to her family. Soon after, she became too ill to live alone and had to move into a nursing home," 130.

5. See p. 230.

6. Buchanan reiterated this anecdote in multiple writings. On a sheet from a prescription notepad that she was given by her pharmacist, she wrote "Discovering a cure for asthma, she told her sister who showed her daughter, my grandmother, who cured herself. Unfortunately, no one could show me." Buchanan Papers, Archives of American Art. Other versions of this text repeat in the artist's drafts for the legend accompanying her sculpture *Lucy McLean's House*. Buchanan's great-grandmother's maiden name was Martha McClain.

7. Prednisone is a synthetic corticosteroid widely used in medicine as an anti-inflammatory and immunosuppressant medication, though it is also notorious for its side effects. In a 1990 interview with Delores Brandon on National Public Radio's *Crossroads* program, Buchanan elaborated on her experience with the medication:

    Beverly Buchanan: You don't hear much about people who are on prednisone and I'm one of them and it's very hard. And when I went up for the show, there were people who hadn't seen me in fifteen years, and you know, I look like I have the prednisone chipmunk look, and it makes you hungry and gain weight and all that stuff. . . . I'm sorry that my grandmother isn't around to tell me how she got rid of her asthma because she-she did. She used some Indian remedy and cured herself, and I didn't learn what that was. And-but I would, I would like some time to maybe get with a prednisone support group. It really is dangerous stuff. It really is.

Delores Brandon: Do you have to take this daily?

BB: Yes. And I've been taking it daily for six years now, and the side effects are beginning to take their toll. And you know, as a scientist, I know what's going on. I really do. I really know what's going on. Which you know, doesn't help much.

DB: Does everyone who has asthma take this?

BB: No, no, there are a bunch of us who, umm, are special. So I'm one of the special people.

DB: So what determines whether you take this or not?

BB: Whether it works. I had apparently made medical history in Macon in Middle Georgia by having had the worst asthma they had ever seen. And-and prednisone is what worked. I don't know what they did before prednisone. I don't think . . . I guess you didn't make it, I guess.

Transcribed from an audio file in the Buchanan Papers, Archives of American Art.

8. In an interview with the editors in September 2025, McWillie reflected on her personal connection with Doc Harris: "My healing was psychological. . . . After five years of trying, one day, for god knows why, they let me in. . . . I'm still in touch today with his grandson [Washington James "Mook" Harris], trying to save the [Saint Paul Spiritual Holy] Temple. The city gave eight acres around it, but the Trump administration got in the way of funding." McWillie is currently editing a book about Doc Harris and the Temple, and continues to work with the Harris family on conservation efforts.

Biographies

Beverly Buchanan (1940–2015) was born in Fuquay, NC, and raised in Orangeburg, SC, on the campus of South Carolina State University, where her father served as dean of the School of Agriculture. She earned a bachelor's of science from Bennett College, a master's of science and master's of public health from Columbia University, and took classes at the Art Students League before leaving the public health profession in 1977 to pursue art full-time. For much of her artistic career, Buchanan lived in Georgia—first in Macon from 1977–85, then Atlanta from 1985–87, and in Athens from 1987–2010 (split between Ann Arbor, MI and Athens from 2003–10). In her lifetime, Buchanan received major honors including a Guggenheim Fellowship, an NEA Fellowship, and the Anonymous Was a Woman Award, and her work is held in leading institutions such as the High Museum of Art, the Metropolitan Museum of Art, Studio Museum in Harlem, and the Whitney Museum of American Art. Her retrospectives include *Shack Works* (1994–96), which originated at the Montclair Art Museum, NJ; and the posthumous exhibitions *Ruins and Rituals* (2016, originated at the Brooklyn Museum) and *Weathering* (2025, Haus am Waldsee, Berlin).

Mary Lou Furcron (c. 1912–2008) was a self- and community-educated architect, furniture maker, and gardener who lived alone in rural Vesta, GA, on a plot of forested land that she cultivated as her sanctuary. Following a period in which she worked in a factory in Philadelphia, PA Furcron returned to Vesta and assembled her complex house and shed structures from salvaged materials and elements from the land, in concert with her swept yard and related landscaping practices. Black vernacular traditions like Furcron's were rapidly disappearing from the Georgia landscape when artists Beverly Buchanan and Judith McWillie made her acquaintance in the 1980s. Both Buchanan and McWillie were profoundly impacted by Furcron and created artistic work in tribute to her. These

 Beverly Buchanan, Athens, GA, 8 July 1995

forms of remembrance provide some of the only existing documentation of Furcron's work. Her home was demolished in 1994 by Oglethorpe County after she moved to assisted living, following the desecration of the forest that separated her home from the highway. Her extended relatives, the Sanders family, proudly hang her portrait in their restaurant, Sanders' Down Home Barbecue and Soul Food.

Judith McWillie (b. 1946) was born and raised in Memphis, TN, where she earned her undergraduate degree in painting at Memphis State University, followed by her MFA at Ohio State University. In 1974, she moved to Athens, GA, to teach painting at the University of Georgia's Lamar Dodd School of Art. She began recording videos with yard artists in 1984, and donated her vast videography to the Southern Folklife Collection of the University of North Carolina at Chapel Hill in 2011. The author of numerous essays in arts and culture publications including *Public Art Review*, *Visions Art Quarterly*, *Metropolis*, and *Artforum*, she is coauthor with Grey Gundaker of *No Space Hidden: The Spirit of African American Yard Work*, winner of the 2007 James Mooney Award of the Southern Anthropological Society. Her work is held in the permanent collections of the Georgia Museum of Art in Athens; the Morris Museum of Art in Augusta, GA; and Christian Brothers University in Memphis.

Mo Costello (b. 1989) is an artist, educator, and independent archivist in Athens, Georgia.

Katz Tepper (b. 1987) is an artist and writer who plays with video, text, and other materials in Chicago, Illinois.

Costello and Tepper co-curated the 2026 exhibition *Beverly's Athens: Beverly Buchanan in Athens, Georgia* at the University of Georgia's Athenaeum, with support from the Teiger Foundation. *Beverly's Athens* was featured in the *Georgia Review* Winter 2026 Issue, where Costello and Tepper's curatorial essay, "Medical Arts: Disabled Kinship as Methodology," was published alongside essays by Patricia Ekpo and Bryn Ashley Evans. A catalog for *Beverly's Athens* is forthcoming from Institute 193, with support from the Graham Foundation.

Acknowledgments

We arrived at this book through a multiyear collaborative research and curatorial project centered on Beverly Buchanan's roughly twenty-three-year period in Athens, GA, where we each lived for over a decade. Any attempt to account for everyone who made this work possible necessarily imitates this book's list of People, as narrating this undertaking traces a vast web of support and offers a glimpse at the long, immersive process that birthed this publication.

As we delved into Buchanan's history, we were introduced to the work of her extended community in Athens and the surrounding counties. Katie Geha, the former director of the University of Georgia's Athenaeum gallery, invited us to guest-curate an exhibition of Buchanan's work and suggested that Professor Emeritus Judith McWillie may have crossed paths with Buchanan during her lifetime. Prior to contacting McWillie directly, we searched through the digitized Judith McWillie Papers on the University of North Carolina's Southern Folklife online library and delighted in seeing Buchanan's name in the title of one of McWillie's 150 recorded videos. Within the first few seconds of pressing play on *Beverly Buchanan, Athens, GA, 8 July 1995*, we understood we had come upon a profound primary document.

Immediately following our first viewing of this book's titular video, we contacted McWillie. An initial phone conversation led to an invitation to attend a program at the Athens Public Library on Black artists from Athens, led by Marie Cochran. After this, our friendship with her bloomed. We spent many hours in her home and studio, in restaurants and on phone calls, not only learning about the immense scope and depth of her life's work, but also just hanging out and finding in McWillie a true kindred spirit. Early in our relationship and without hesitation, she granted us permission to use her videos, blessing us to do with them "whatever you want." Her trust, generosity, support, and friendship have anchored this process. Thank you, Judy, for your tremendous wisdom and love. The same must be said for Judy Long, close friend of both Buchanan and McWillie, who welcomed us into her home and heart and supported our process with her persistent care. We are lucky to call you both our friends.

Beverly Buchanan, whom we never met in this realm but with whom we feel an intimacy, having spent the last few years immersed in her work, in her papers, in the memories of those who knew and loved her—and centrally, in McWillie's recording. We thank you, Beverly, for your spirit of generosity, and the expansiveness of your work and way of being in the world—by turns experimental, rigorous, humorous, mournful, and reverent. Thank you for leaving such a wealth of materials preserving your radical vision. We have learned so much from you. You made us believe in angels.

Thank you to Ms. Mary Lou Furcron, whom we also never met but who changed the lives of Buchanan and McWillie, and in turn, changed ours too—the power of your work and life is at the heart of this book.

* * * * *

Thank you to each and every person who invited us into your homes, studios, businesses, phone receivers, and inboxes to share your memories and treasured collections of Buchanan's work with us: Jane Bridges, Elizabeth Bridges White, Pete Carson and the fine folks at Carson Plumbing, Brian Causey, Lori Causey, Marie Cochran, the Lopp Family, Peter Loose, Sandy Loose, Alice Lovelace and the ArtsXchange, Linda Lucas, Stephen Lucas, Lynn Marshall-Linnemeier, Mike McCain, Reid McCallister, Rebecca McCarthy, Angela Meltzer, Richard Meltzer, Annelies Mondi, Mary Porter, Lisa Tuttle, and Andy and Debbie Ullrich.

Special thanks to Prudence Lopp, in whose home we spent countless hours, who nourished us with food and stories, and who graciously gave permission to reproduce several works from her collection. Patti Phagan has been exceptionally generous in supporting our annotation process, consulting her carefully maintained family records and personal archive to assist with fact-checking. During long visits at her home, Patti offered us reassurance, affirmation, and invaluable counsel.

Thank you to Jean and Richard Westmacott for your work and for having us in your home, sharing Mary Lou Furcron's furniture, and directing us to the land she once cultivated in Vesta. Thank you to Heidi Summerall for helping us find our way around Vesta, and to the Sanders family for sharing your memories of Furcron.

Jennifer Burris, Andy Campbell, Park McArthur, Siddhartha Mitter, and Molly Superfine: thank you for your scholarship and stewardship of Buchanan's legacy, and for your generosity and support. Special appreciation to Bryn Ashley Evans and Patricia Ekpo, for nurturing and deepening our shared study of Buchanan's work through ongoing conversation over the last two years. Thank you also to Amelia Groom for your insightful scholarship. And to the artists whose expansive approach to captioning and accessibility foundationally influenced this book: Bojana Coklyat, JJJJJerome Ellis, Noa Micaela Fields, Joseph Grigely, Carolyn Lazard, Jordan Lord, Park McArthur, Finnegan Shannon, Josephine Shokrian, Christine Sun Kim, Constantina Zavitsanos, among many others who are broadening the horizons of what text can do. We are indebted to be thinking alongside you.

We would like to thank the individuals and institutions who provided materials directly for this book: Steve Weiss and Chris Dubose at the University of North Carolina Library's Southern Folklife Collection, for your kindness and responsiveness with all our requests; and Marisa Bourgoin and Lindsey Bright at the Smithsonian Archives of American Art, for being exceedingly helpful in navigating the request and reproduction process. The generous donations by Jane Bridges and Susan Welsh to the Smithsonian Archives have been an invaluable resource. Additionally, thank you to Shannon Kimbro and Chaunesti Webb-Johnson at the Spelman College Museum of Fine Art, who graciously hosted us, shared the institution's collection of Buchanan's work and archival holdings with us, and for your time and conversation. Thank you as well to Aurélie Bernard Wortsman of Andrew Edlin Gallery for your insight and generous support throughout the course of this project. Our research was also enriched by the connections we formed during visits to other institutions in Georgia and South Carolina. Thanks to Latisha Woods at the Booker T. Washington Community Center; David Jones at the Pin Point Heritage Museum; Johnathan Winbush at the Beach Institute; and Marie Gibbs and Robert Adams at the Penn Center.

We are immensely grateful to Stephanie Koch, Larissa Harris, and Andrea Escobedo at the Teiger Foundation for going above and beyond in supporting our work as independent curators and scholars. The Teiger Foundation funded multiple research trips that contributed to the scholarship in this book. Independent Curators International also offered us meaningful support and we want to particularly thank Scott Vincent Campbell and Renaud Proch for inviting us to see Lowery Stokes Sims and Lauren Haynes speak on the work of Buchanan and Benny Andrews at Ruth Arts.

Profound gratitude to Julia Klein, our publisher, editor, and friend, for being a collaborator, thinking partner, cheerleader; for believing in this book and helping us refine its shape through endless back and forth; and for many late nights and long, full hours working together over the last year. You were our dream publisher, and we are so grateful to make this book with you. Thank you for your loveliness, your rigor, and for your fierce vision for making books that bare insights into artists' processes and thinking. Thank you, also, to our friend Jordan Stein for supporting this project, inspiring us with your own books, and for introducing us to Julia.

Deep appreciation and admiration to designer Jake Brower, for your elegant vision and attention, patience, thoroughness, playful and collaborative spirit, and gentle guidance. Thank you, also, for taking care of Katz, Sparty, Delilah, Peat, and your students; and Mo, whenever she visited Chicago. To Rachel Walther, our copy editor and proofreader, thank you for sharing your expertise and thorough eye, and for your flexibility as we worked through many iterations. Thank you as well to Aaron Walker and Rita Skingle for your helpful advice on preparing the book's images for print.

We want to express gratitude to our wider community who supported us in many ways, including Nancy Brower, Alice Centamore, Patricia Ekpo, Ray Levy, Kirby Mages, Beaux Mendes, and Gabe Oladipo, who graciously provided us with critical feedback as early readers. Thank you to Maggie Taft for being a believer in artists' writing; for your long-term support, dialogue, and feedback; and for creating the haven that is Writing Space in Chicago. Much appreciation to the other members of the weekly writing group for providing community, accountability, and insights: ebere agwuncha, Alden Burke, Drue Denmon, Emily Eddy, Shir Ende, Tirtza Even, Shane Rothe, and Olive Stefanski. And we want to warmly thank the other friends, family, and caregivers who have bolstered us through this labor of love, including: Harold Batista, Sydney Benator, Liat Berdugo, Justin Boner, Patrick Bova, Aaron Brower, Andrew Bui, Amanda Burke, Luka Carter, Alex Decarli, Bill Dietz, Noa Micaela Fields, Chelsea Flowers, Adrienne Garbini, Ariel Goldberg, Becky Hall, Gordon Hall, Neil Hancock, Maia Ipp, Amy Jones, Jon Krakauer, Lauren Leving, Erin Jane Nelson, Courtney McClellan, A.J. McClenon, Jonathan McCombs, Linda Moore, Molly Colleen O'Connell, Keelan O'Sullivan, Francis Oliver, Ernesto Ornelas, Risa Pulea, Lucas Regazzi, Amy Reid, Carley Rickles, Amina Ross, Dianna Settles, Zayn Singh, Jake Stone, Arthur Weiss, agustine zegers, ever ziz; and our siblings, parents, and partners: Jake Brower, Bill Costello, Shannon Costello Düster, Kayla Edgett, Wendy Krakauer, Alex Tepper, Haim Tepper, and Sandra Tepper; all of whose conversations, hugs, hang outs, and high fives made—and make—our work possible.

The video, *Beverly Buchanan, Athens, GA, 8 July 1995*, can be viewed at the following URL:

https://dc.lib.unc.edu/cdm/singleitem/collection/sfc/id/68694/rec/1

Beverly Buchanan, Athens, GA, 8 July 1995 is one of 150 videos in the Judith McWillie Collection, 1970s-2010s, Southern Folklife Collection, Wilson Special Collections Library, University of North Carolina at Chapel Hill. Links to all of the videos can be accessed at the following URL:

https://finding-aids.lib.unc.edu/catalog/20455